The COCKTAIL CHEF

Entertaining in Style

DINAH KOO
& JANICE POON

with wine notes by JOHN SZABO

and photography by PAUL ROZARIO

DOUGLAS & McINTYRE

VANCOUVER/TORONTO

To our parents:

Art Koo, who always loved parties
Laura Koo, who can't collect enough recipes
Harry Poon, for his wisdom and stature
Star Stanley, for her intelligence and creative pursuit of beauty

Douglas & McIntyre Ltd.
2323 Quebec Street, Suite 201
Vancouver, British Columbia
Canada V5T 4S7
www.douglas-mcintyre.com

Library and Archives Canada Cataloguing in Publication

Koo, Dinah
The cocktail chef: entertaining in style / Dinah Koo and Janice Poon;
with wine notes by John Szabo.

Includes index.
ISBN-13: 978-1-55365-187-1 · ISBN-10: 1-55365-187-1
1. Cocktail parties. 2. Cocktails. 3. Appetizers. I. Poon, Janice II. Szabo, John III. Title.
TX731.K665 2006   642'.4   c2006-901738-7

Editing by Lucy Kenward
Cover and text design by Ingrid Paulson
Photos by Paul Rozario
Printed and bound in Canada by Friesens
Printed on acid-free paper

We gratefully acknowledge the financial support of the Canada Council for the Arts,
the British Columbia Arts Council, the Province of British Columbia through the
Book Publishing Tax Credit, and the Government of Canada through the Book Publishing
Industry Development Program (BPIDP) for our publishing activities.

CONTENTS

FOREWORD *by Lynda Reeves* / vi
FOREWORD *by Nina Wright* / vii

PART I **CHEF AT THE BAR** / 1
    THINKING OF DRINKING / 2
    BARTENDING: THE CRASH COURSE / 5
    THE PLEASURES OF FOOD AND WINE / 27
    THE PERFECT CHEESEBOARD / 36
    THE RAW BAR / 43

PART II CHEF AT THE STOVE / 47
    EIGHT ESSENTIAL APPETIZERS / 48

PART III **CHEF AT THE PARTY** / 61
    THE PERFECT COCKTAIL PARTY / 63
    THE MOOD RULES / 71
    THE FOOD RULES / 71

SEVEN PERFECT PARTIES / 72
    CINQ À SEPT: *Casanova's Seduction for 2* / 73
    GIRLS' POKER NIGHT: *Light Bites for 5* / 91
    SPANISH PORCH PICNIC: *All-day, All-night Tapas for 20* / 107
    FROM THE MASTER SOMMELIER: *Wine-tasting Party for 20* / 133
    NEW YEAR'S DAY RELAXER: *Condo Brunch for 30* / 149
    PAN-ASIAN BEACH PARTY: *Cocktail Supper for 40* / 171
    ENGAGEMENT CELEBRATION: *Cocktail Hour for 60* / 207

Acknowledgements / 234
Index / 235

FOREWORD

WHEN DINAH KOO's in my kitchen, I'm smiling. Of that you can be certain. I know my guests are in for a special treat, and I can relax knowing that every detail will be perfect.

Of course we've talked the party through. I may have described a summer afternoon on the lawn with tables set for a picnic, and a barbecue chef. Then Dinah will describe a menu of delights such as her Vietnamese-style Barbecued Ribs, Mango Salad Rolls and her famous Peking Duck Quesadillas, washed down with Shanghai Lily Slings and Red Sangria, and we're off to the races.

At *House & Home Magazine*, we've talked about food and entertaining, and watched the trends come and go, for over 20 years. While we once fussed and worried over elaborate meals, today, formal cocktail parties and sit-down dinners have merged into one movable feast that has become, by far, my favourite kind of entertaining. It's so much more fun to offer a kind of tapas that mixes foods from every corner of the globe and invites you to graze and taste, and enjoy.

Small plates and bowls filled with bite-sized offerings of wonderful flavours are what I love to serve. Dinah was the first to teach me the art of producing delicious tidbits that are simple to make, beautiful to look at and always memorable. I remember the first time she offered Asian Gravlax on traditional Chinese soup spoons at a cocktail party. My guests loved it. Or the time she offered noodles in tiny cardboard take-out containers with chopsticks. Another hit.

Dinah and Janice Poon set the tone. Theirs is a recipe for entertaining that produces the elegant, relaxed mix I want for all my parties. Always, there is laughter in the kitchen and nibbling long after the plates have been cleared. Entertaining should be as much fun for you as it is for your guests.

The Cocktail Chef is a collection of many of the dishes and drinks I know and love most. Make them, and smile. You're in for a treat.

Lynda Reeves
President, House & Home Media

FOREWORD

GREAT ENTERTAINING is about the little things: the temperature of the room, the ratio of guests to wait staff and the pacing of the party. Paramount also, of course, is the food and the way in which it is presented. Brilliant food deserves a brilliant environment to complete the experience.

There is no dearth of good caterers in Toronto, and I've had the good fortune of working with many of them over the past 35 years. In addition, I've organized countless cultural evenings in the United States, Canada and Europe, where art and food shared the spotlight. I learned very early on that there is no easy way of creating an evening where every guest, no matter how many of them there are, can feel special.

Dinah Koo and Janice Poon, together, have mastered this art. They work in harmony with the organizer of an event, fighting for their vision where appropriate but never so rigid in their thinking that they are unwilling to listen to a new or different approach. No situation is unworkable. Time and time again, I have seen them adapt when plans changed at the last minute because of union regulations or electrical failures, or pouring rain or sudden increases in the number of guests.

The responsibility of entertaining large groups is always stressful no matter how many years one does it, and I'm always slightly wary when I hear caterers say "no problem." But what makes working with Dinah and Janice unique is how effortlessly they work together as each challenge is answered with dispatch, each problem swiftly resolved. With Dinah and Janice, I have always been confident that the final product will be superb.

Nina Wright
Founder, Arts and Communications

Chef at the bar

THINKING OF DRINKING

The cocktail is truly an American phenomenon; on this all experts agree. In his 1820 novel *The Spy,* James Fenimore Cooper tells how the very first cocktail originated in a tavern on the American side of Niagara Falls. According to legend, the owner and barkeep, Betty Flanagan, was regaling a party of soldiers. In a creative flourish of hotel management, she made a special blend of liquors for their pleasure and stirred this seminal mix with a feather from a rooster tail. Upon tasting the drink, a French soldier shouted, "Vive le cock tail!" and distillers have never looked back.

From that moment, Americans took to cocktails with enthusiasm. Even Prohibition held no sway. On the contrary, the decree of dryness promoted the art of mixology to new lengths. Citizens would not do without drink, so illicitly produced bathtub gin poured forth. Most of this hooch was unpalatable on its own, so creative bartenders invented a myriad of concoctions to help the drink go down. This thousand-plus repertoire of recipes, and the people who made them, formed a deep well from which the culture of American cocktails continues to draw.

In spite of conventional wisdom, however, we prefer to think that the cocktail has a more exotic pedigree. Look to the Oriental outposts of the long-past British Empire and peer into the palm courts, mahogany long bars and officers' clubs. In the early 1900s, friends and gentlemen of the regiment spent afternoons and evenings raising drinks mixed by Chinos, Number One Boys and young Hindi bearers. In the Long Bar of the Shanghai Club, it was Chinese bar boys who noiselessly ferried prodigious pours of Shanghai Bucks—perfecting Bacardi with lime—at a time when Daiquiri was still just a town in Cuba. Farther down the China Sea, a Malay bartender at Raffles was making the Singapore Sling famous, and in Hong Kong, fingers of Rosy Dawn cocktails were tickling taipans' noble tonsils.

In Southeast Asia, drinks like the Rangoon Ruby, great-grandfather of the Cosmopolitan, were poured and perfected in Burma. For a non-drinking nation, India contributed much to the cocktail's history. The names alone will tell you: the word *punch* comes from *panch,* Hindi for "five," the requisite number of ingredients in the original mix of arrack (a pungent liquor made from rice), tea, lemon, sugar and water. *Sangaree* may be the etymological link between a spiced Burgundy mulled in Kashmir and *sangria,* the Spanish wine punch—they both have *sanguis* (Latin for "blood") as their root. *Julep* comes from Hindi *gulab* or Arabic *juleb,* for "rosewater." *Toddy* is the name of the palm tree from which a powerful fermentation was brewed by natives of the Molucca Islands.

Fictional cocktailers also enjoyed exotic locales. James Bond did more for the martini than any billion-dollar ad campaign. His taste was international—stirring and shaking only on the most exotic atolls. Just as far away, in Casablanca, the film star Humphrey Bogart, as Rick, suavely dispensed cocktails while the madness of pre-war French Morocco swirled around him.

Cocktails are a mixture far more potent than the sum of their parts. Flavour alone does not imbue each drink with its charm—image is as important as ingredients. Would we order martinis if they were not the mark of sophistication? A cocktail whose history is drenched by the seven seas seems far more evocative than one that has never left our shores.

American or otherwise, it's interesting to note that cocktails have held a place of conviviality in the history of very many cultures, and with every sip, you and your companions drink in the reflections of faraway places, long lost in time.

When you're in charge of making the drinks, let your inner chef shine! You wouldn't dream of using artificial flavourings or powdered mixes in your cooking, so why use them in your cocktails?

Fresh produce in season is bursting with flavour, so use it whenever you can. Try to find organically grown fruits and vegetables to juice and muddle into your drinks. You'll discover new levels of flavour intensity. Be adventurous. We encourage you to incorporate the variety of exotic fruits, herbs and vegetables that the world now brings to our local markets. Take the time to make a few of your own garnishes and flavoured syrups. All these chef's touches will reward you with cocktails that are worthy of your efforts.

UPDATING THE CLASSIC COCKTAILS

Most of the drinks recipes we're sharing with you are "signature cocktails" that we have developed for special events. These are extravagantly flavoured spectacular concoctions worthy of the party spotlight. If you are new to mixology, we recommend that you follow our recipes exactly at first. Then, once you are comfortable with our techniques, start finding your own style, adapting the recipes to your own taste.

The magic comes in creating the perfect balance. Think of music to understand how you can compose different flavours into a mix that is greater than the sum of its parts. Like musical chords, a blend of flavours is made up of many notes— all notes complementing, enhancing, counterpointing a dominant tone and all tuned to one key. So you can use "too many" flavours as long as you balance them as finely as Mozart, or a single note if it is as mesmerizing as a "One Note Samba," or a layered shot as seemingly dissonant but remarkable as the opening chord of "A Hard Day's Night." The benefit of experimenting is that you can drink your mistakes.

BARTENDING—THE CRASH COURSE

Skillful mixing is easy if you master just a few simple techniques.

TECHNIQUE: STIRRED COCKTAILS

Fill a mixing glass or pitcher two-thirds full with fresh crushed ice. Add ingredients and stir briskly but evenly with a cocktail (long-handled) spoon until the outside of the container frosts and is very cold to the touch.

When stirring, keep the bowl of the spoon close to the sides and the bottom of the mixing container so the ice swirls quickly as a mass. Keep it smooth—choppy stirring will break up the ice and result in a watery drink. And avoid thrashing, as that will promote the same tiny air bubbles and fuzzy texture that shaking creates.

You must also stir quickly to avoid excess melting of the ice. The power of a superb cocktail is in the delivery of intense layers of flavour. Just as you would not spend half the day creating a perfect dish, then toss a glass of water over it upon serving, so you want to respect the ingredients you are putting into your cocktails.

TECHNIQUE: SHAKEN COCKTAILS

At the bar, to shake is to be. This is the *sine qua non* of bartending— a couple of quick, deft shakes emulsify your concoction to a cool, velvety smoothness and evoke admiration from your guests.

Choosing a shaker for your personal bar is easy—there are only two kinds. The *cobbler* is very stylish looking, with its stainless-steel body and top with built-in strainer and little fitted cap, but it is too small for mixing larger batches quickly. The *Boston* is a bit trickier to use but chills faster and has a larger capacity. It is made of two parts—a large glass tumbler that can be used on its own for mixing, and a larger stainless-steel counterpart that inverts over the top of the glass. If you use a Boston shaker, you will need to have a Hawthorn strainer (for shaken drinks) as well as a julep strainer (for stirred).

To use the cobbler, half-fill the body with cracked ice, add ingredients, snug the top on and shake vigorously up and down, holding the little cap in place with your index finger. When beads of condensation form all over the shaker and it is almost painfully cold, remove the cap and strain the drink into glasses.

To use the Boston, half-fill the glass with cracked ice. Pour over the ingredients and fit the stainless steel half firmly over the glass. Tap the top to seal the two containers together. Pressing

SHAKEN OR STIRRED?

The answer to the eternal cocktail question is clear: stir drinks made of clear, thin liquids; shake drinks made with juices, syrups, creams and other thick ingredients.

them together with the bottom of one container in the palm of each hand, shake robustly until condensation collects and the shaker becomes very cold. Invert the shaker on the counter, glass portion on top. Hold the shaker with one hand, half on the glass part and half on the stainless part, and rap the rim of the stainless part with your other hand. This should break the seal and allow you to lift off the glass part. If the contents have not dispersed along the counter, hold a Hawthorn strainer over the stainless tumbler and pour into glasses. You are a rock star.

TECHNIQUE: MUDDLED DRINKS

If ever a bartending technique came directly from the kitchen, it is "muddling." A handy muddling tool, in fact, is the pestle half of a mortar and pestle, but a special muddling tool made of solid wood can be purchased from bartending supply shops. Alternatively, you can use a long-handled spoon or a small French rolling pin.

Ingredients such as citrus wedges and mint are dropped into the glass and crushed to release the juices and oils. Then the remaining ingredients are added to the glass to "build" the drink and mixed in with a bar spoon.

TECHNIQUE: ROLLING DRINKS

Drinks made from thick juices, such as the Bloody Mary, get a weird spumy texture when shaken but cannot be stirred effectively because they are too dense. This is where rolling is used. Simply pour back and forth from one container to another a few times until the drink is well mixed. Rolling is also used in the making of the Blue Blazer, a don't-try-this-at-home cocktail that has the experienced bartender lighting diluted Scotch and tossing the flaming liquid from tumbler to tumbler, thus creating a continuous arc of fire up to five feet long. This "extreme rolling" incorporates oxygen into the Scotch, thus feeding the ever-growing flame.

TECHNIQUE: FLOATING AND LAYERING DRINKS

For some cocktails, you want to float an ingredient on top of a mixture—sort of like a drink with its own appetizer. Gently pour the floating ingredient into the glass over the back of a bar spoon in a very thin stream and it will sit on top, not disturbing the liquid below.

The extension of this is the layered drink. Each ingredient is floated on top of the previous one, in order of density, with the heaviest on the bottom. Liquids with the highest alcoholic content are usually the lightest and can only be topped with high-fat cream.

TECHNIQUE: FROZEN COCKTAILS AND SMOOTHIES

An electric blender is essential for making frozen drinks, and you might not think you need one for your home bar, but they are really great for easygoing summer gatherings. All the ingredients can be pre-mixed in pitchers, then, when the spirit moves, just bring out the blender and whiz up drinks as the day demands.

Most frozen cocktails are made by combining ingredients in a blender with crushed ice and whirring until the mixture is thick and slushy and no ice chips remain. We like to supercharge the flavour and thicken the texture by adding frozen yogurt, sorbet or frozen chunks of fruit.

TECHNIQUE: SNOW CONES AND SLUSHIES

An ice shaver will seem like the best investment you've ever made when you're wowing your friends with show-stopping drinks like our Slushies and Snow Cones. These ice cutters work like rotary graters and are very easy to operate. You can buy them at department stores, kitchen supply stores and Japanese food stores.

To make a Snow Cone or Slushy, a strongly flavoured drink is mixed, then poured over shaved ice that has been mounded in the glasses. Large saucer-shaped Margarita glasses are fun for this kind of drink.

TECHNIQUE: MIXING WITH BUBBLES—CHAMPAGNE AND BEER COCKTAILS

Champagne literally bubbles with sumptuous luxury, adding undeniable sparkle to any occasion. For special celebrations, we like to serve Champagne cocktails to guests as they arrive. There are many excellent sparkling wines available now that are kinder to the pocketbook than true Champagne. Segura Viudas, a fine Spanish sparkler made in the Champagne method, as well as Prosecco, Freixenet and Café de Paris are excellent for mixing.

Cocktails mixed with beer have expanded beyond the classic Shandy (beer mixed with lemonade). Bartenders are now pleasing crowds with Peach-spiked Beer (beer with a splash of peach liqueur), Orange-spiked Beer (with orange liqueur) and Lager and Lime (with lime cordial). You can give your own signature to a beer cocktail like the Red Eye (equal parts tomato juice and beer) by substituting Clamato for tomato juice, adding a splash of Worcestershire sauce and garnishing with a poached shrimp.

Whether based on Champagne or beer, these cocktails should be gently built in the glass and barely stirred, if at all, so as not to lose too many bubbles. The Champagne or beer should be thoroughly chilled before mixing.

TECHNIQUE: VIRGIN COCKTAILS

Pregnant pals and designated drivers are quietly soldiering for society and, especially at a party, their needs must not be overlooked. It's nice to splash juice into sparkling water for their refreshment, but the host who takes the time to offer a special cocktail icy-cold from the Boston shaker is truly returning a kindness. When you're mixing up pitchers of our cocktail party pre-mixes, it's a good idea to keep some aside without alcohol just for shaking up into virgin cocktails. They are absolutely delicious on their own or with soda water.

TECHNIQUE: RIMMING OR EDGING THE GLASS

Salt or sugar on the lip of the glass adds an interesting layer of flavour to every sip. But it's important to keep this salt or sugar from falling into the glass and upsetting the flavour balance of the drink itself. Careless bartenders tend to dunk the inverted glass into lemon juice and then straight down into the salt or sugar, getting it on the inside of the rim where it will fall into the drink in great cloying chunks. All you want is a little hit of flavour on the lip. To that end, try to keep the "rimming" to the outside of the glass. Hold the glass at an angle while rotating the rim to dip just the outside in juice. Then, similarly, rotate the glass at an angle with the rim in the sugar or salt in a way that keeps the garnish from the inside of the glass.

TECHNIQUE: CITRUS ZEST GARNISHES

Taste is greatly enhanced by scent, and by drifting a tiny spray of citrus oil on the top of a drink, you can heighten its flavour. This can be accomplished by garnishing with a twist or with strands of citrus zest.

To make these garnishes, you can use a sharp paring knife or you can seek out a peeler, a channeller (or canaller) and a zester. These tools can be found at kitchen stores where each item is dedicated to a single purpose.

CITRUS TWIST: A small piece of citrus zest is twisted over the drink or rubbed on the lip of the glass. This squeezes out and disperses the fragrant oils that are trapped in the peel. In a more theatrical version, a piece of zest can be flamed by twisting it next to a flame held over the glass. A tiny flare will result from the expelled oils, and a pleasantly burnt note will be added to the twist. To make a basic twist, using a small paring knife or a very sharp vegetable peeler, cut away just the outer coloured skin of the citrus fruit, avoiding the bitter white pith.

LONG "HORSE NECK" GARNISH: Long strips of orange or lemon zest can be draped over the rim of a tall glass to dramatic effect. These are easily made with a channeller, a special tool that has a ⅛-inch D-shaped cutter in the metal head. By drawing the tool over and around the fruit, you can effortlessly groove out a thin long strip. To make a really long strip, work a continuous strip starting at the stem end and spiralling around the fruit until you get to the blossom end. Frugal bartenders have suggested using the nose end of a potato peeler to make these garnishes, but the savings realized by forgoing the purchase of a channeller are largely offset by the cost of finger bandages.

LONG ZEST: Delicate strips of peel can be floated on drinks so that their essence is released as the drink is sipped. A zester works like a channeller, but creates much finer strips because it has five holes. You may wish to use a plane zester, and although you will get short strips, the flavour will be imparted in the same way.

TECHNIQUE: KEEPING IT COOL

The first rule of mixing superb cocktails is to keep everything cold, cold, cold.

CHILLED GLASSES. Cold glasses are a must. But unless your signature drink is called Memories of Last Repast, do not be tempted to chill glasses for long periods in your freezer. This is because the flavour of all the food in the freezer transfers to the thin layer of frost that forms on the surface of everything. The professional technique is to fill the glasses with ice and water before you begin mixing. Once the drink has been mixed, suavely toss the water/ice out of the glasses and pour in the drink. For parties, it may be more convenient to keep a quantity of glasses chilling in a cooler with some ice.

CRUSHED ICE. To crush ice, place a layer of ice cubes on a large, clean tea towel, fold the towel over to envelop the ice and whack sharply with a hammer or a rolling pin. For large gatherings, ice can be crushed in advance and stored in plastic bags in the freezer. The chunks may stick together in the bag, but they can be unclumped by flinging the closed bag onto the counter. For parties, it's often best to buy bags of crushed ice at the last minute. You need your freezer space for more critical items. Except when used in frozen drinks, crushed ice that comes out of your refrigerator's ice dispenser may be too fine for mixing, and your efforts will melt into a watery drink.

ICE CUBES, UNFLAVOURED. For clear drinks on the rocks, it's nice to make crystal-clear ice cubes. Cloudiness is caused by air trapped in the ice as it forms, so fill your ice-cube trays with hot water, since heating forces the air out of the water and eliminates the problem. If you are pouring for the very, very particular, the best unflavoured ice for rocks is made from distilled or still spring water. Otherwise, eau du tap is just fine as long as the ice is fresh and has not spent too much time in the freezer absorbing food flavours.

ICE CUBES, FLAVOURED. Use fruit juice or herbal infusions so your drinks don't get watery as the ice melts. For punchbowls, fruit ice can be made into large pieces that stay frozen longer—formed, for example, in a bundt pan.

ICE CUBES, DECORATIVE. Fill ice-cube trays half full, freeze, then drop a berry, a blossom or a citrus twist in each compartment, fill to the top with more water and freeze.

FROZEN FRUIT. Whole fruits like grapes and strawberries can be frozen and used to garnish and chill drinks. Choose well-formed, unbruised fruits and spread them out, not touching, on small baking sheets to freeze. Once frozen, they won't lump together and can be removed from the pans and stored in bags in the freezer.

Classic Martini

The mystique of the martini is in its elegance. Made by icing two ingredients together, it epitomizes simplicity in a glass. But perfecting this drink takes a smooth, sure hand and, thank goodness, plenty of testing to find the flavour balance you seek: drier—more gin; fuller body—more vermouth; less herbal—vodka instead of gin.

This classic version is a light and dry drink—a perfect palate opener that is great with hors d'oeuvres. We like to pour a 4-oz glass. The larger 6-oz glass takes longer to consume and is rarely cold to the last drop.

> 2 oz premium vodka or gin
> 1 oz dry vermouth
> 2 to 3 lemon-vermouth olives
> GLASSWARE: one 6-oz martini glass

Fill the martini glass with crushed ice and set aside to chill. Fill a mixing tumbler two-thirds full with cracked ice. Measure in vodka (or gin) and vermouth. Stir briskly until beads of condensation form and the tumbler is very cold to the touch. Discard ice from the glass and strain in the drink. Spear olives on a toothpick and drop into the martini.

For a Dirty Martini, add a splash of the lemon-vermouth olive marinade to the mix.

Makes one 4-oz drink

LEMON-VERMOUTH OLIVES

Enormous homemade marinated olives put your signature on the classic martini. Use good-quality jumbo-sized Italian or Greek olives, preserved in brine and sold in jars. Some of them are as big as 1½ inches long.

> 2 cups jumbo brined Italian or Greek green olives
> ¼ cup freshly squeezed lemon juice
> 1 Tbsp grated lemon zest
> ¾ cup dry vermouth

In a large sterilized jar, combine olives, lemon juice, lemon zest and vermouth and shake to combine. Marinate in the refrigerator for at least 24 hours and up to 2 weeks.

Makes garnish for 20 to 30 martinis

Gibson

The Gibson was named after a clever politico who always kept his head during booze-soaked diplomatic functions by drinking water disguised as a martini. He arranged with the bartender always to put an onion in his "cocktail." In this way, he could identify his glass of water on a tray of high-octane martinis and sail through negotiations with clear-headed aplomb. To make a Gibson, garnish your martini with cocktail onions instead of olives. To become a successful politico, drink but don't swallow.

SPICED PEARL ONIONS

These are indispensable for making Gibsons, but also great for serving as a garnish with steaks or burgers.

> 10 oz pearl onions
> 1 cup white wine vinegar
> 2 Tbsp pickling spice
> ½ tsp sugar
> 1 tsp salt

Bring a medium pot of water to a boil and blanch pearl onions for 3 to 5 minutes, until onions are slightly soft. Drain and remove skins.

In another medium pot, combine vinegar, pickling spice, sugar and salt. Bring to a boil on medium-high heat. Remove from the heat and set aside.

In a large sterilized jar, combine onions and vinegar mixture and shake to combine. Marinate in the refrigerator for at least 3 days and up to 1 month.

Makes about 24 onions

Signature Martinis

The martini is an extremely adaptable cocktail. With so many alcohols and flavourings available, and endless possibilities of infusions, your imagination is the only limit to the number of different martinis that you can create. Most restaurants and nightclubs now offer a martini menu. Here are several of our signature martinis for you to enjoy at home.

LILLET MARTINI

If you've never had the opportunity to try it, Lillet is something you can look forward to. A flavourful French liquor made from a blend of brandy, wine, fruits and herbs, it gives the classic martini a fragrant lift.

> 1 oz good-quality gin
> 1 oz good-quality vodka
> 1 oz Lillet
> ½ oz Xanté (pear liqueur) or apple liqueur
> GLASSWARE: one 5- to 8-oz martini glass

Fill the martini glass with ice and set aside to chill. Half-fill a shaker with crushed ice and measure in gin, vodka, Lillet and Xanté (or apple liqueur). Shake until beads of condensation form on the sides and the shaker is very cold to the touch (about 30 seconds). Discard ice from the glass and strain in the drink. Garnish with a Brandied Cherry (page 18).

Makes one 3½-oz drink

LEMON RUM MARTINI

Lemon-scented rum makes all the difference in this classic martini.

> 3 oz lemon-flavoured rum
> 1 oz dry vermouth
> Lime zest, cut into ¼ × 2-inch strip, twisted (page 8)
> GLASSWARE: one 6- to 8-oz martini glass

Fill the martini glass with ice and set aside to chill. Half-fill a shaker with crushed ice and measure in rum and vermouth. Shake until beads of condensation form on the sides and the shaker feels very cold to the touch (about 30 seconds). Discard ice from the glass and strain in the drink. Garnish with a lime twist.

Makes one 5-oz drink

CREAMSICLE MARTINI

Forget childhood reminiscences of frozen creamsicles-on-a-stick and make new memories with classic cream and citrus flavours, accented with very grown-up vodka and Italian Galliano.

> 2 oz good-quality vodka
>
> 1 oz Galliano
>
> 2 oz frozen orange juice concentrate, thawed
>
> 2 oz whipping cream (35%)
>
> 1 slice of unpeeled orange
>
> GLASSWARE: one 8-oz martini glass or
> Champagne flute

Fill the martini glass (or flute) with ice and set aside to chill. Half-fill a shaker with crushed ice and measure in vodka, Galliano, orange juice concentrate and cream. Shake until beads of condensation form on the sides and the shaker feels very cold to the touch (about 30 seconds). Discard ice from the glass and strain in the drink. Garnish with an orange slice on the rim.

Makes one 7-oz drink

Party Pitcher Green Tea Martini

Close your eyes as you sip this fragrant cocktail and you will feel transported to a sultry tea plantation in Indochina. This recipe is proportioned for a party and will make 12 to 24 drinks. Prepare the tea and ginger ahead of time, then when guests are thirsting, shake with ice and gin and serve in cocktail glasses or porcelain Chinese teacups.

Lemon grass and cilantro (or coriander leaves) are available in most good greengrocers and large supermarkets, and all Asian food stores.

TEA MIXTURE

2 stalks lemon grass

2 cups fresh cilantro leaves and short stalks (2 to 3 bunches)

8 Japanese green tea teabags

4 cups boiling water

GINGER SYRUP

4 inches fresh ginger

2 cups sugar

1 cup water

1 bottle (750 mL/26 oz) gin

GLASSWARE: twelve 8-oz martini glasses or 24 Chinese teacups

TEA MIXTURE: Using a sharp paring knife, trim off and discard root end of lemon grass stalks, and remove and discard first outer layer. Cut stalks into 3- to 4-inch lengths and bruise slightly to release oils. Place in a large bowl and set aside.

Wash cilantro and trim off and discard roots and large stalks. Roughly chop into 2-inch lengths and add to bowl of lemon grass. Add teabags and boiling water and steep for 10 minutes. Remove teabags and leave herbs to steep and cool for 1 to 2 hours. Drain, reserving lemon grass stalks for garnish, and refrigerate.

GINGER SYRUP: Wash ginger thoroughly and slice very thinly—no need to peel. Place in a heavy saucepan, add sugar and water and melt on medium-high heat, stirring to combine. When the mixture comes to a boil, reduce the heat to low and simmer uncovered for 5 minutes without stirring. Remove from the heat, strain and cool completely.

An hour before serving, place all martini glasses in the refrigerator or a cooler of ice to chill.

To serve, make cocktails one at a time, based on measurements below, or shake in batches of 2 or 3.

2½ oz gin
2½ oz tea mixture
1½ oz ginger syrup

Chill the glasses. Fill a shaker two-thirds full with crushed ice and measure in gin, tea mixture and ginger syrup. Shake vigorously until beads of condensation form on the sides and the shaker is very cold to the touch (about 30 seconds). Strain into a chilled glass, garnish with a "swizzle stick" of reserved lemon grass and serve.

Makes twelve 6½-oz drinks

Cosmopolitan

Still the drink of choice for downtown girls, this is a wonderfully balanced cocktail that can be a base from which to create your own signature drink. Substitute raspberry-flavoured vodka or pomegranate juice, or add a splash of Champagne for sparkle. And don't feel guilty about toying with a classic. This drink has been tweaked all the way from Burma in the '20s, when it was invented by a ruby miner and dubbed Rangoon Ruby. In the '60s when cranberry juice subbed for pomegranate syrup (grenadine), it became Bog Fog and was later renamed Cape Codder. Sometime in the '80s, it slipped out of loafers into high heels, took the train to New York and, like Cher and Madonna, now just goes by one name—Cosmo.

POMEGRANATE COSMO

Infused with real pomegranate juice and garnished with pomegranate seeds, this voluptuous Cosmo is full of juicy flavour.

> 1 Tbsp each brown and white sugar to rim glasses
> 1 lime, in quarters
> 2 oz tequila
> 2 oz pomegranate juice
> ½ oz frozen lime juice concentrate, thawed
> ½ tsp fresh pomegranate seeds (if in season)
>   or a slice of lime
> GLASSWARE: one 8-oz martini glass

On a pie plate or saucer, combine sugars. Rim a well-chilled martini glass with a quarter of lime and roll in mixed sugars, pressing to adhere. Set aside. Half-fill a shaker with crushed ice and measure in tequila, pomegranate juice and lime juice. Shake until condensation forms on the sides and the shaker feels very cold to the touch (about 30 seconds). Strain into the prepared glass and garnish with a few pomegranate seeds (or a slice of lime).

Makes one 6-oz drink

CITRUS-BERRY COSMO

Fresh and tart, this Cosmo's posh flavour comes from citrus-kissed vodka.

> 3 oz mandarin-flavoured vodka
> 1 oz frozen grapefruit juice concentrate, thawed
> 1 oz frozen raspberry juice concentrate, thawed
> ¼ tsp sugar
> 1 cup canned mandarin oranges, drained
> GLASSWARE: one 6-oz martini glass

Fill the martini glass with ice and set aside to chill. Half-fill a shaker with crushed ice and measure in vodka, grapefruit and raspberry concentrates and sugar. Shake until condensation forms on the sides and the shaker feels very cold to the touch (about 30 seconds). Discard ice from the glass and strain in the drink. Garnish with mandarin segments.

Makes one 5-oz drink

PARTY PITCHER COSMO

Many happy test palates took part in the development of this Cosmopolitan. It has since become the "belle of the ball" at many of our parties. This particular recipe was developed with home entertaining in mind, as it will make about 10 cocktails. It can be prepared ahead of time as it stores well in the freezer, alcohol and all. As your guests arrive, just pour and shake.

15 oz frozen cranberry juice concentrate, thawed
5 oz freshly squeezed lime juice
1½ cups fresh cranberries (or whole frozen)
½ bottle (375 mL/13 oz) orange-flavoured vodka
½ bottle (375 mL/13 oz) lemon-flavoured vodka
7 oz Triple Sec or Cointreau
Zest of 2 lemons, 2 limes and 2 oranges, for garnish
GLASSWARE: two 1½-qt pitchers, ten 8-oz
    martini glasses

Place the cranberry juice concentrate, lime juice and cranberries in a blender and process for 1 to 2 minutes until cranberries are smooth and flecked with pretty little bits of the skin. Add flavoured vodkas and Triple Sec (or Cointreau) and mix together. Pour into 2 jugs or pitchers. The mixture can be stored in the freezer at this point until ready to serve.

To make one cocktail, pour 6 oz of the mix in a shaker over ice. Cover and shake until beads of condensation form on the sides and the tumbler is very cold to the touch (about 30 seconds). Strain into a chilled martini glass and garnish with combined zest of lemon, lime and orange.

Makes ten 6-oz drinks

MANHATTAN

The cocktail that New York named was invented as a rye drink in the late 1800s. In the mid-1900s it became wildly popular as a house favourite at the fabled Stork Club. During those heady post-Prohibition years, American café society relied on "Luscious" Lucius Beebe to dictate "le standing" of all things gastronomic, and when he wrote his *Stork Club Bar Book*, he chose the Manhattan as his opening recipe.

This version is a bourbon drink, dry to awaken the taste buds for accompanying hors d'oeuvres and garnished with our Brandied Cherries.

> 2 oz bourbon
>
> 1 oz dry vermouth
>
> 4 to 8 drops Angostura bitters
>
> 2 Brandied Cherries (right)
>
> **GLASSWARE:** one 5- to 8-oz martini glass

Fill the glass with crushed ice and set aside to chill. Fill a mixing tumbler two-thirds full with crushed ice. Measure in bourbon, vermouth and bitters. Stir quickly to blend until beads of condensation form on the sides and the tumbler is very cold to the touch. Discard ice from the glass. Drop cherries into the glass and strain in the drink.

Makes one 3½-oz cocktail

Brandied Cherries

These dark jewels must steep for at least four months to fully develop the flavour. Quick brandied cherries can be made with pitted canned cherries from Europe. Drain them, discard syrup and cover cherries with brandies and port. Marinate in the refrigerator for 3 days.

> 2 lbs dark Bing cherries, stems attached, unpitted
>
> ½ cup sugar
>
> 2 cups cherry brandy
>
> 1 cup brandy
>
> 1 cup port

Rinse cherries well. Place in a sterilized wide-mouth jar (with a lid), leaving at least 2 inches at the top, or in a 4-qt bucket. Add sugar, cherry brandy, brandy and port. The cherries should be fully immersed—if the liquid does not cover them, remove some of the fruit. Stir well. Place a clean, flat weight, such as a saucer, directly on top of the fruit to keep it immersed in the liquors. Cover tightly with a lid and store in a dark, cool place for 4 to 6 months, checking and stirring once every 2 to 3 weeks.

Makes about 2 qts cherries

THAI MOJITO

Cuba is full of Ernest Hemingway memorabilia, and every establishment that he frequented pays homage in some way. He gave off drinking Papa Dobles (double Daiquiris doused with maraschino juice and grapefruit) long enough to go down the road and write on a napkin, "My Daiquiris at Floridita, but my Mojitos at Bodeguita." Mojitos have long been a favourite of working-class Cubans and just as popular with nightclubbing northerners. Here is a Thai-influenced version.

1 sprig fresh Thai basil

1 sprig fresh mint

1 tsp honey

one 5-inch length lemon grass, in 1-inch pieces
    (optional)

2 oz amber rum

½ lime

¾ cup crushed ice

3 oz soda water

1 large Thai basil leaf, for garnish

1 stalk lemon grass or sugar cane, for garnish (optional)

GLASSWARE: one 8- to 10-oz highball glass

Into the highball glass, place basil and mint sprigs, honey, lemon grass and rum. Squeeze lime over all and drop the rind into the glass. Crush together lightly with muddler. Top up the glass with crushed ice, and stir to blend. Fill the glass with soda water and garnish with a basil leaf and lemon grass stalk (or sugar cane).

Makes one 6-oz drink

Bitter Lemon Collins

Made with old-fashioned boiled lemonade, this is the perfect tall, cool drink for steamy summer evenings.

BOILED LEMONADE (enough for 7 drinks):

4 lemons, in ⅛-inch slices

4 cups water

5 Tbsp honey

FOR ONE DRINK:

2½ oz white rum

2 to 3 oz soda water

1 sprig rosemary for garnish (optional)

GLASSWARE: seven 12-oz Collins glasses

MAKE BOILED LEMONADE PRE-MIX: Place lemons in a stainless-steel or heat-resistant glass pot. Add water and bring to a boil on high heat, then reduce the heat to low and simmer for 5 minutes. Remove from the heat and pour into a heat-resistant glass pitcher or bowl. Stir in honey and allow to cool. Refrigerate for at least 6 hours and up to 24 hours. Using a fine-mesh sieve, strain out lemon rind and seeds.

FOR EACH DRINK: Fill a glass with ice cubes and pour in 5 oz boiled lemonade pre-mix. Measure in white rum and top with soda. Garnish with a sprig of rosemary.

Makes seven 8-oz drinks

Chartreuse Margarita

For many of us, the first, best cocktail of our youth was the dizzyingly delicious frozen drink we discovered on holiday in the tropics. Here's one of our favourites. Ahhh, the smell of limes and coconut suntan lotion in the morning.

> 2 oz tequila
> ½ oz Chartreuse
> 2 oz lime juice
> ½ oz simple syrup (below)
> 1 cup ice
> Slice of lime
> Salt for rim (optional)
> **GLASSWARE:** one 12-oz Margarita coupe

Place tequila, Chartreuse, lime juice, simple syrup and ice in a blender and blend on high speed for 1 minute. To serve, rub lime around the outside rim of the glass and dip into salt. Pour the frozen mixture into the glass and serve immediately.

Makes one 12-oz drink

SIMPLE SYRUP

> 1 cup sugar
> 1 cup water

In a saucepan, bring sugar and water to a boil on high heat and boil for 2 to 3 minutes, stirring, until sugar is completely dissolved. Cool syrup before using.

Makes 1½ cups

Blue Hawaiian Snow Cone

Here is a drink that seduces on many levels. The inner child sees snowmen, snow angels and catching first snowflakes on the tongue. The inner explorer sees icebergs, adventure and polar caps. The inner hostess sees an impressive drink that's really easy to make.

> 2 oz blue Curaçao
>
> 1½ oz vodka
>
> 4 oz blueberry juice
>
> 1½ cups ice cubes, shaved
>
> **GLASSWARE:** one 12-oz Margarita coupe or martini glass

In a jug or measuring cup, mix liquors and juice. Fill the glass with shaved ice and shape into a mound. Pour drink mixture over the ice and serve immediately.

Makes one 8-oz drink

Sangria

This punch from Spain is traditionally based on red wine, brandy, soda and fresh fruit. But why set limits? Sangria can work with international cuisines. The following recipes have been weather-tested by wine connoisseurs and winos alike, to great applause.

SANGRIA RUBAIYAT

BOUQUET GARNI

6 cardamom pods, gently crushed

½ tsp fennel seeds, gently crushed

½ tsp cumin seeds, gently crushed

WINE MIXTURE

1 bottle (750 mL/26 oz) soft red wine (such as Pinot Noir)

1 tsp honey

3 oranges, zest strips and fruit, bitter white pith removed

6 dates, pitted and chopped

½ cup halved seedless green grapes

GLASSWARE: five 12-oz red wine glasses, one 2-qt pitcher

BOUQUET GARNI: On a 4-inch square of cheesecloth, bundle cardamom, fennel and cumin. Wrap cheesecloth around spices and secure with kitchen twine.

WINE MIXTURE: In a pitcher, combine red wine, honey, orange zest and fruit, dates and grapes. Add bouquet garni and stir to combine. Refrigerate for at least 24 hours.

To serve, remove bouquet garni and discard. Fill glasses ¾ full of sangria and ladle some of the macerated fruit into each glass.

Makes five 6-oz drinks

SHERRY SANGRIA

1 bottle (750 mL/26 oz) Oloroso sherry (Amontillado can be substituted)

2 oz Frangelico

1 cup canned mandarin orange segments, drained

1 cup halved seedless green grapes

1 cup sliced fresh peaches

½ bottle (375 mL/13 oz) sparkling wine

GLASSWARE: one 2-qt pitcher, five 8-oz white wine glasses

In a pitcher, combine sherry, Frangelico, oranges, grapes and peaches. Stir to combine. Allow to macerate for at least 24 hours in the refrigerator.

To serve, fill each glass ¾ full of the macerated sherry mixture, and add about 1 inch of the sparkling wine. Ladle some macerated fruit into each glass.

Makes five 7-oz drinks

SAKE SANGRIA

1 bottle (750 mL/26 oz) sake (Japanese rice wine)

3 oz Hpnotiq

2 cups peeled fresh pineapple, in ¼-inch cubes

GLASSWARE: one 2-qt pitcher, five 8-oz white wine glasses

In the pitcher, combine sake, Hpnotiq and pineapple. Allow to macerate for at least 24 hours in the refrigerator. Serve over ice with some of the macerated pineapple.

Makes five 6-oz drinks

ROSÉ SANGRIA

2 cups sliced strawberries

1 bottle (750 mL/26 oz) dry rosé wine

¼ to ½ cup simple syrup (page 20) (optional)

GLASSWARE: one 2-qt pitcher, five 8-oz white wine glasses

In the pitcher, combine strawberries, wine and simple syrup to taste. Allow to macerate for at least 24 hours in the refrigerator. Serve with some of the macerated strawberries.

Makes five 6-oz drinks

PLUM WINE SANGRIA

1 bottle (750 mL/26 oz) plum wine (such as Gekkeikan)

1 cup canned pitted cherries, drained

1 cup canned mandarin orange segments, drained

1 cup canned lychees, drained and chopped

GLASSWARE: one 2-qt pitcher, five 8-oz red wine glasses

Combine all ingredients in a large pitcher and allow to macerate for at least 24 hours in the refrigerator. Serve with some of the macerated fruit.

Makes five 6-oz drinks

Tonics and Curatives

Sailors used rum with lime against scurvy, ethno-adventurers took quinine and gin to allay jungle pip, and St. Bernards were collared with brandy and honey to rescue the snowbound. So why shouldn't you take a good tonic with a little shot of Scotch?

GINSENG VODKA

On top of its healthful properties, ginseng has a pleasant herbal flavour and is readily found in Asian markets and natural food stores. It has been linked to good health for centuries, but here's a recipe that ushers ginseng right into the New Cocktail Age. Drink this infusion straight up, on the rocks or as a martini with a splash of Scotch.

> 1 oz dried ginseng, thinly sliced
> 1 bottle (750 mL/26 oz) vodka

Add ginseng to vodka in the bottle and allow to macerate for 1 week.

Makes 1 bottle (750 mL/26 oz)

HANGOVER HELPER: THE DAY AFTER

You can't always remember to have eight glasses of water and eat plenty of protein when you're drinking deeply from the punchbowl of life, and weekend Champagne poisoning of varying degrees has for centuries resulted in Monday absenteeism. If someone you know needs to improve their productivity, or for those infrequent mornings when you are paying dearly for the alcoholic indiscretions of the night before, try these soothing concoctions.

FOR FIRST-DEGREE CHAMPAGNE POISONING
If your tummy is roiling, calm it with a big cup of strong ginger tea with honey. Crush a couple of inches of ginger root, infuse in simmering water for 20 minutes, strain and add honey to taste. Sip slowly and drink entirely. The ginger will settle your stomach, the water will rehydrate your poor, parched brain and the honey will rebalance the glucose in your system. If life does not rush back into limb, more extreme measures are called for.

FOR SECOND-DEGREE CHAMPAGNE POISONING
Have some dry wholewheat toast, take some vitamin B1 (thiamine) with lots and lots of water, put on your sunglasses and go for a walk. If you're feeling shaky, it could be because alcohol strips your body of thiamine, which is essential to your nervous system. The walk will increase your blood circulation and cleanse your system faster. Drinking lots of water hydrates the brain and buffers the pain as your short-term memory sorts through the blue bin of the previous night.

FOR THIRD-DEGREE CHAMPAGNE POISONING
Sometimes the only thing you can do is wean yourself slowly from the alcohol. That's when you need the Hair of the Dog that Bit You. A nice raw Oyster Shooter (page 156) in tomato juice and a splash of vodka should do it. The oyster gives you a bit of protein, the tomato juice rehydrates and nourishes and, most importantly, the bit of alcohol lubricates the reunion with reality. Yes, it's true: Hair of the Dog merely postpones the pain and you are going to have to face your hangover again when the Hair wears thin, but this will give you a little reprieve from your agony.

ENDNOTE
Of course, the very best cure is prevention, and drinking responsibly is the only way to go. But you already knew that.

THE PLEASURES OF FOOD AND WINE

You are planning a party. The menu is set, the music and mood established, the guests confirmed. And then, suddenly, you realize with horror that you have not considered libations beyond the cocktail hour. Wine is called for with the food, but what will you serve with the soup and the fish? Not to mention the Asian-inspired selection of appetizers? You vaguely recall some prescription for white wine with fish and red with meat, but what if the fruits of the sea are served alongside a creature of the land? And how does one classify soy sauce, tamarind and nuoc mam? There is sudden fear and apprehension that the food and wine will clash, the guests will be appalled, the evening will be an utter failure. No host should live through such anxiety. Why must it be so complicated?

A great deal of ink, and wine no doubt, has been spilled over how to match food and wine. Every approach—from the overly precise and scientific to "don't worry, anything goes"—has been examined and proclaimed as the way. The truth, as is often the case, lies somewhere in the middle. Few of us are interested in researching dry scientific principles for what is supposed to be one of life's pleasures—eating and drinking well. But though it may seem liberating just to drink what you like no matter what you are eating, that will clearly not satisfy the dedicated gourmand looking for a memorable food and wine experience. If you have purchased this book, chances are you fall into the latter category. And we won't disappoint you.

NEW FRONTIERS IN TASTE

Food and wine have changed. So has the way we taste them. Our understanding of how we perceive taste sensations is considerably deeper than it was even a short decade ago. So go ahead and throw out all of those old biology (and wine-tasting) textbooks with the tyrannical tongue map. Our amazing taste buds can indeed interpret all of the basic sensations of taste, even some tastes we didn't even know existed. Chefs have been quick to capitalize on this knowledge, and have found new ways to tantalize our taste receptors through a greater understanding of how we taste. Well-travelled people and mingling cultures have inspired new styles of cuisine and combinations of flavour, and changing lifestyles have demanded new approaches to eating and drinking. That is what this book is all about. Modern winemakers have likewise adapted their wines to meet this changing world. The majority of wines produced today are not meant for lengthy aging in perfect subterranean cellar conditions. Most of us don't have the time, the patience or the cellars to hide away wines for a generation. Full. Upfront. Fruity. Versatile. That's what people want, perhaps at the expense of the complexity that only time can forge. But it makes for friendlier wines and near foolproof food and wine pairing. Some, thankfully, dig in their heels and refuse to bend to new trends, so that today we can enjoy an unprecedented era of quality wines and embrace the diversity of both old and new worlds.

FIRST PRINCIPLES

There are certainly some basic principles that govern the chemical and physical cause-and-effect relationship between food and wines, but it is not complicated enough to cause anxiety. And the good news is that there are very few really bad food and wine matches. Most are shades of good, better and best. Only in certain cases can we say with any confidence that specific elements simply don't go well together. Tannic wines with the oils in fatty fish, for example, will cause an unpleasant metallic taste in your mouth, and very salty dishes will make the same wine even more tannic and bitter. The key is to understand the basic elements of flavour and then experiment. We could think of worse assignments!

IT'S A MATTER OF TASTE

Tasting food and wine together involves a complex interaction of aromas, flavours and textures, and often temperatures, too. The overall experience is the product of at least three different inputs: there is, of course, the contribution made by the wine and the food, but there is also the perception of the individual taster. The wine and the food both offer an external physical stimulus to our senses. But equally if not more important is the input from our brains, such as previous wine-drinking experiences, long-held prejudices, thoughts about the food, personal preferences or even our current emotional state. These internal and external factors combine seamlessly to construct the "food and wine experience" for each of us, individually,

and no single combination will be right for everyone. So put your mind at ease—there is no universally perfect match! It depends greatly on who is tasting. But you can maximize the positive reactions of your guests and guarantee a successful party by learning a few tricks of the trade.

CREATE POSITIVE ANTICIPATION

Before we even get into the physical cause-and-effect nitty-gritty, remember that the first thing to do for a successful match is to set the mood. People predisposed to like something probably will. This simple fact will take you farther than studying food and wine pairing for half a lifetime. Just think of drinking rosé on a terrace overlooking the Mediterranean, or sipping meditatively from a large goblet of heady, intense Recioto della Valpolicella Amarone by a roaring fireplace on a cold winter's night. Such environments speak so strongly to our emotional state that they can transform even an average bottle into a superlative one. Reverse the wines in the two above scenarios, and the enjoyment will surely not be the same.

This book contains many great ideas about creating a pleasant environment in which your guests can eat and drink in heightened, positive anticipation. A simple way to prepare them for enjoyment of food and wine together is to match the wine to the theme of the party. Relying on traditional, regional food and wine matches is nearly foolproof, as it is familiar and almost expected. Who wouldn't enjoy a selection of

Spanish wines served alongside the tapas for the Spanish Porch Picnic (page 107)? Also having a little anecdote or story to tell about the wine choices can tantalize your guests, building up positive anticipation and predisposing them to enjoy themselves. It will also impress them by showing the level of care and thought that went into the occasion. If you are sending out invitations, include something about the theme of the party and the drinks that will be served. Your guests will be salivating before they even arrive!

MAKING THE WHOLE GREATER THAN THE SUM OF THE PARTS

Once the general mood and theme have been set, you can look at which specific types of wine will best accompany the food that will be served. The goal of matching food and wine is to make the whole greater than the sum of the parts. When both the wine and food taste better than they did on their own and you have created a synergy of flavours, then you have a successful match. To achieve this with frequent success, you need to get a handle on the basic components of flavour (of food and wine) and learn how they interact and affect one another in positive and negative ways. Then you can match any food items with an appropriate wine without having to memorize hundreds of possible combinations and variations.

THE BUILDING BLOCKS OF FLAVOUR

In today's modern repertoire of food and wine there are six basic elements of flavour: sweet, sour, bitter, "umami," salty and spicy (hot). The first four are common to both food and wine; salty and spicy are generally confined to the food experience. When you know what sensations are provoked by each of these elements on its own and in combination with the others, you can better understand how wine will affect food and vice versa.

To taste the full effect of a food and wine combination, take a sip of the wine *before* you have swallowed the food so that they can mingle together in your mouth for a few moments. The experience is often different from that of following each bite with a taste of the wine. Together, the different elements of taste interact and enhance (or detract from) one another, creating additional layers of flavour and a new dimension to both food and wine.

SWEETNESS IN WINE

The sweet sensation in wine is caused mainly by the presence of residual sugar, the natural grape sugar that is left in the wine after fermentation ends (or has been purposely stopped).

There are three main ways to make sweet wines:

1. Use late-harvested or dried grapes that are so sugar-rich that fermentation stops naturally before all of the sugar can be transformed into alcohol. Examples include late-harvest, botrytis-affected and ice wines, and dried grape wines such as *vin de paille* or Italian *recioto*.

2. Stop the fermentation artificially before all of the sugar has been converted to alcohol. This can be done by adding alcohol, chilling the fermenting wine or adding sulphur dioxide

(all of which kill the yeasts that cause fermentation). Examples include sweet, fortified wines such as vintage and tawny port and many muscats produced around the Mediterranean.

3. Add a sweetening agent to a wine after fermentation. This is most often some form of unfermented sweet grape juice, either fresh or boiled down for concentration. Examples of this style include certain types of sherry, marsala and some German wines.

But the perception of sweetness in wines is not governed by residual sugar alone. Acidity is also an important factor. Low-acid wines often seem sweeter than they really are, and high-acid wines can seem dry because the taste of residual sugar is masked. Finally, alcohol itself has an inherently sweet taste. Dry wines produced from exceptionally ripe grapes (which make high-alcohol, low-acid wines) can also give the impression of sweetness without having any residual sugar.

Very sweet wines are often best enjoyed on their own or with similarly sweet desserts, and off-dry wines are perfect for pairing with certain foods. Many Rieslings, Gewürztraminers and late-harvest Chenin Blancs are typical off-dry wines.

Sweetness in wine has the following effects on food:
1. It takes the edge off the heat in spicy foods.
2. It balances the sweetness in condiments such as chutneys or sauces made with fresh or dried fruit.
3. It contrasts the salty flavours in many Asian cuisines (soy-based and fermented sauces) while matching some of their sweeter flavours.

Very sweet wines may be pleasantly contrasted with salty food, too. Classic examples are intensely flavoured, salty blue-veined cheeses such as Roquefort served with Sauternes, and English Stilton with port.

SWEETNESS IN FOOD

Sources of sweet flavours in food include sugar, honey, fresh or dried fruit, hoisin, chutneys and caramelized glazes.

Sweet foods have the following effects on wine:
1. They make dry wines seem even drier, bitter.
2. They emphasize tannins and the sensation of astringency.
3. They emphasize the sensation of acidity.

Sweet dishes, whether savoury with a touch of sweetness or fully sweet desserts, are thus often best matched with wines that are at least equally sweet.

SOURNESS IN WINE

The sensation of sourness is caused by high acidity in wine. Acidity is an important component in all wines, making it stable and protecting it from harmful bacteria. It is also the single most important factor to consider when matching wine with food, because it heightens flavours and cleanses the palate. There are several different types of acids in wine, of which the most important are tartaric, malic (green apples) and lactic (dairy products). Wines produced in cool climates (Germany, Austria, Alsace, the Loire Valley, Chablis, Ontario, Oregon and New Zealand, for example) are usually higher in acidity than warm-climate wines, where grapes ripen fully and acidity drops. Certain grape varieties are also naturally higher in acidity, including Chenin Blanc, Sauvignon Blanc and Riesling, as well as Nebbiolo, Gamay and Sangiovese.

Acidity causes a prickling sensation on the palate: any wine, red or white, that leaves your mouth feeling dry and crisp and that causes you to salivate is likely high in acidity. Whereas a glass of whole milk coats the mouth with a warm sweetness (low acid), unsweetened juice or tea with lemon (high acid) makes it feel fresh and clean. Some wines are so crisp that the prickling sensation is evident straightaway. In others, high acidity can be masked by high levels of residual sugar or alcohol and will become apparent shortly after you swallow—look for the telltale signs of a drying sensation and salivation on your palate. The carbon dioxide in sparkling wines also heightens the perception of acidity.

The acidity in wine affects food in the following ways:

1. It penetrates the richness of heavy sauces (butter, cream, etc.), cuts through animal fats and refreshes the palate.
2. It mirrors tart items such as vinaigrettes, citrus fruits, tomatoes and pickled foods.
3. It mitigates the oiliness in anything pan-fried or deep-fried.
4. It lightens and brightens the flavour of fish or shellfish, like a squeeze of lemon.
5. It brings out flavours in food.

Crisp, high-acid wines are often the most versatile wines to pair with food, and the least likely to clash. In fact, a wine that may seem too acidic on its own may be ideal with food. The acidity in a salad vinaigrette, for example, can make an acidic wine taste sweet and fruity. In contrast, low-acid wines can be difficult to pair with food, often coming across as clumsy or heavy.

ACIDITY IN FOOD

Sources of acidity in food include sauces or vinaigrettes cut with citrus fruits or vinegar (balsamic, rice), other acidic fruits such as cranberries or green apples, pickled foods such as beets, cabbage or pickles, and sauces made with tomatoes (another acidic fruit).

Acidity in food has the following effects on wine:

1. It increases the sensation of sweetness in wine.
2. It lowers the sensation of acidity.
3. It heightens the fruitiness.
4. It increases the sensation of astringency (tannins) in red wines.

BITTERNESS IN WINE

Sensitivity to bitterness varies greatly from individual to individual, though most people do not have an affinity for bitter flavours. We are constantly seeking to counteract bitter flavours with sweetness, such as by putting sugar in coffee and tea. We have been programmed genetically to reject bitterness, as most poisonous substances have a bitter taste. A mildly bitter flavour in wine, however, is not necessarily unattractive. Bitterness can add balance, character and appealing flavour components. Bitter tastes are also known to stimulate the digestive system, a definite advantage at the table.

Some aromatic white grape varieties naturally produce mildly bitter wines, such as dry Muscat, Pinot Gris and Gewürztraminer. The most common source of bitterness in red wine is tannin, which is naturally bitter. The presence of tannins in wine also causes the tactile sensation of astringency, a mouth-puckering, drying sensation. Tannins are extracted mainly from grape skins during the fermentation process. The higher the tannin level, the more bitter the wine. High alcohol, residual sugar and low acidity, alone or in combination, will reduce the sensation of bitterness in a tannic wine.

Mildly bitter wines work best with:
1. Foods prepared by grilling, charring and blackening.
2. Bitter vegetables such as asparagus, rapini, arugula, eggplant and bell pepper.
3. Foods with a high degree of umami (see below), such as aged cheese or sautéed mushrooms.

BITTERNESS IN FOOD

Sources of bitter flavours in food include the inherent bitterness in leafy greens and certain vegetables (collard greens, chicory, endive, dandelion, rapini), olives, fresh or dried herbs, walnuts, tea, coffee grounds and bitter chocolate. Chefs traditionally rely on sugar, salt and fat to balance bitter flavours, and highly bitter dishes are uncommon.

Bitter foods affect wine in the following ways:
1. They make astringent red wines seem even more astringent and bitter.
2. They lessen the perception of sweetness.
3. They increase the perception of bitterness.

UMAMI IN WINE

Aged red wines, those over about five years of age, develop a distinctive earthy, savoury umami flavour that intensifies with further aging. The flavour of these wines closely resembles the flavour of dried mushrooms, well-aged beef, fresh earth and decaying leaves. Such savoury, umami-rich reds are the perfect accompaniment to similarly flavoured dishes, creating a wave of concurrent flavours that reverberate and synergize. Try an old Pinot Noir with well-hung game bird, or an aged Cabernet-Merlot with wild mushroom ragout,

UMAMI (OO-MOM-MEE)

Although western science has traditionally favoured the notion of just four basic tastes (sweet, sour, salty and bitter), Asian taste scientists have long known about a fifth sensation, now called by its Japanese name, *umami*. The Japanese scientist Dr. Kikunae Ikeda first identified umami as a distinct taste in 1907, and more recently, researchers at the Miami School of Medicine have confirmed the existence of an umami taste receptor. The main substance responsible for the umami taste is an amino acid called glutamic acid, more familiar to us in the form of MSG—monosodium glutamate.

braised veal shank or Parmigiano. Umami on umami is heaven on earth.

UMAMI IN FOOD

The subtle taste of naturally occurring umami is largely responsible for the delicious savoury flavours of certain foods: ripe tomatoes; aged hard cheese such as Parmigiano; cured meats such as prosciutto; mushrooms of all kinds, especially dried; beef; pork; chicken; saltwater fish such as bonito, mackerel, tuna and cod; shellfish; oysters and squid. It also occurs naturally in carrots, potatoes, Chinese cabbage and other vegetables, and in fermented sauces such as fish sauce. Layer umami-rich foods with umami-rich wines to create intoxicating depths of flavour.

SALTINESS IN FOOD

Salt was once among the most sought-after commodities for its marvellous ability not only to preserve food, but also to bring out and intensify its flavours. Salt is used in the majority of processed foods to a greater or lesser degree, so be aware when selecting ingredients. Store-bought stocks or stock cubes, commercially prepared sauces and other flavouring ingredients such as soy sauce all usually have a high sodium content. If any such ingredients are used, their salt content needs to be taken into account when adjusting the final seasoning of your dish—trust your palate! All cheeses, but especially hard and blue-veined cheeses, are also quite salty. Although wine does contain trace amounts of salts, it rarely has a salty taste. The effects of saltiness in the accompanying food, however, can be dramatic.

Salty foods affect wine in the following ways:

1. The astringent sensation (caused by tannins) is accentuated.
2. The warming sensation of alcohol is heightened.
3. The sweet and fruity flavours are accentuated.

Looking at it the other way around, the acidity in wine often cuts the sensation of saltiness in food. Therefore, sparkling wines and other whites with higher levels of acidity generally work better with salty foods than low-acid wines (i.e., most red wines). Off-dry wines are also sound choices for mildly salty dishes, particularly those with both salty and sweet components. Very salty foods such as blue cheese are best paired with fully sweet, late harvest–style wines; the sweet-salty flavour combination brings out the best in both the food and the wine.

SPICY HEAT IN FOOD

The sensation of heat caused by spice affects both taste and touch receptors. It is an important element in matching wine and food, as its effect on a wine's flavour can be dramatic. Changing North American demographics and eating habits have brought many ethnic influences into the food culture. The once rare hot and spicy dishes of Mexico and Central America, Indian and West Indian curries, Cajun and Creole foods and spicy Asian dishes of all types are frequently encountered, and their influence on native cooking styles has been profound. Savvy winemakers have responded to these changes, and many modern-style wines have emerged to match up to this generally challenging, wine-unfriendly cuisine.

The main source of spicy heat in these dishes is one of the many families of chili peppers. Their relative heat is frequently categorized by Scoville units (su), ranging from 500–1,500 su for Anaheim, pasilla and poblano chilies at the low end, to jalapeños at 2,500–5,000 su, and habañero and Scotch Bonnet chilies clocking in at a scorching 500,000 su. When you are into the six-digit figures, reach for the *cerveza,* or beer. Even mildly spicy dishes will exaggerate the warming sensation of alcohol, turning average alcohol wines into alcoholic monsters and feeding the flames in your already burning mouth. Therefore, wines with low alcohol (or beer, which is generally low) are a good choice. The sweetness in off-dry or semi-sweet wines will also balance and lessen the burning sensation of spicy dishes. In general, however, leave the *Grand Crus* in the cellar when serving highly spiced foods. Their delicate flavours, arrived at through careful cultivation, production and aging, will be lost like a stand of trees in a raging forest fire. If the goal is mere refreshment, choose a crisp, refreshing off-dry wine like German Riesling *kabinett* or *spätlese* (late-harvested) for an enjoyable, if not memorable, match.

FINDING THE DOMINANT ELEMENT

These, then, are the basic sensations that you will encounter on your food- and wine-matching journey. Knowing the various elements and their cause and effect, we can now look at virtually any dish and select the most appropriate wine style. The key is to identify the dominant flavour element in the food to guide your wine match. Quite often the strongest flavour comes from an accompanying sauce or garnish. Pickled condiments, sweet-sour chutneys, dipping sauces,

teriyaki and high-fat sauces, for example, will often dictate the most appropriate match. Look at the recipes carefully and determine which of the ingredients will have the most impact on overall weight and flavour.

MATCHING WEIGHT AND INTENSITY OF FLAVOUR

Aside from the basic flavour interactions themselves, successful pairings are often made by matching the flavour intensity of a dish with an equally intense wine. The "weight" of a wine is closely linked to its alcohol content. Generally speaking, the higher the alcohol, the more full-bodied the wine. A low-alcohol wine (7 to 10 per cent) seems lighter in weight and texture in the mouth than a high-alcohol wine (13 to 15 per cent). Delicate scaloppine of veal, filet of sole or lobster on mini brioche (page 218), for example—would stand little chance against a big, bold, full-bodied red wine. The fine, subtle flavour of these foods will be overwhelmed by the alcohol, tannin and flavour intensity of the wine. By the same token, the spicy-sweet, intensely flavoured Vietnamese-style Barbecued Ribs (page 193) will wreak havoc with most dry, delicate whites and pale reds.

Give some thought to the richness, weight and texture of each course and select a wine with similar intensity. Although it depends a great deal on the producer, region and vintage, generally delicate white grapes include Pinot Grigio, Riesling and Sauvignon Blanc; more intense varieties include Gewürztraminer, Pinot Gris and barrel-aged Chardonnay and Semillon-

Sauvignon blends. Delicate red varieties include Cabernet Franc, Gamay and Pinot Noir; bolder grapes are Cabernet Sauvignon, Merlot, Nebbiolo and Syrah. Naturally, these are just the broad strokes. When it comes to specifics, go with the advice of someone you trust.

TEXTURE: ASTRINGENT WINES

Textural elements can frequently be a dominant factor in food and wine combinations, particularly the astringent tactile sensation caused by tannin and its synergistic partner, acidity. Match an astringent wine with high-protein foods such as rare roast beef, or foods with a high fat and umami content such as aged hard cheese. Protein lessens the sensation of astringency by binding with tannins, so a very tannic wine might be rendered gloriously round and fruity when enjoyed with rare beef. In contrast, a tannic wine (a young Cabernet Sauvignon, for instance) matched with a food high in tannins (such as walnuts) will render the wine almost undrinkably dry, astringent and bitter.

COOKING METHOD

The cooking method is often an important consideration. Poaching, searing, grilling or frying an ingredient can have a dramatically different effect on flavour intensity and therefore on the most appropriate wine match. Poaching brings out the most delicate flavours and often calls for a wine with vibrant acidity to heighten the intensity of the food. Grilling, however, adds a great deal of flavour, particularly smoky, caramelized and burnt tastes. Here the best call is often the complementary flavours of a wine aged in toasted new barrels.

EXPERIMENT AND EXPLORE

Although the food- and wine-pairing wheel has not been fully reinvented, it has definitely been modified to roll along with modern lifestyles. We hope this book will encourage you to experiment and explore on your own. Try wines that you think will work, but also those that you don't think will go at all. You may be surprised, and in any case, the not-so-good matches can be even more informative than the great ones. In the various chapters of this book you will find recommendations on wines to accompany the wonderful recipes and menus created by Janice and Dinah for each of the themed parties. Some suggestions are based as much on the mood of the party as on the food to be served. Remember that they are only guidelines. The real fun begins with you and a few friends. Specific producers and vintages have not been included, as availability varies widely from place to place. Make friends with a knowledgeable consultant at your local wine and spirits shop who will be able to suggest specific wines to match your needs.

ORDER OF SERVICE

Dry wine before sweet wine
Lower alcohol before higher alcohol
Sparkling wines before still wines
Younger wines before older wines
Light wines before full-bodied wines

THE PERFECT CHEESEBOARD

Paired with fresh fruit of the season, cheese makes a glorious end to an elegant meal. With crusty bread and fruit, it makes a balanced and soul-satisfying snack. And when accompanied by the right drink, cheese makes a treat as simple as it is decadent.

Wine and cheese are often spoken of together, but, like Lennon and McCartney, they don't always get along. Cocktails, with their strong flavours, can make a surprisingly good match, as they stand up well to the intensity of cheese. The fruit component of many cocktails can pair cleverly with cheese. For example, the acidity and high-alcohol content of a Cape Codder can cut through the richness of a triple-crème soft cheese like Brillat-Savarin; a strong, salty Parmesan-Reggiano can stand up to the bubbles of a Champagne cocktail that strip more delicate flavours from the palate; an Apple Martini is a natural with Cheddar.

It's easy to get addicted to four or five favourite cheeses, but there are hundreds of excellent varieties from which to choose and so many classic greats to enjoy. So never stop exploring the wide world of cheese. And look locally to the myriad of spectacular goat cheeses that are now being handmade by artisanal and farmstead cheesemakers all across this country.

To create a cheeseboard that will please all guests, you may wish to choose an assortment of classic favourites. For gastronomes, you may want to make more unusual picks. Choose one or two of each kind so you have a contrast of flavours, textures, shapes and colours. For after dinner, a total of 2 oz per person, augmented by fresh fruit and crackers, should satisfy.

FAVOURITE CHEESEBOARD: SOMETHING SPECIAL FOR EVERYONE

- Cashel Blue—all the colour and richness of a classic blue, but subtler in flavour and silky-soft in texture.
- Cheddar, 5-year-old—the colour and familiar sharpness make this a standard. The finest Cheddars are deeply complex in flavour with notes of caramel, hay, fruit and nuts.
- Manchego, aged—a superb Spanish hard cheese that is nutty with a crisp saltiness. It has an interesting herringbone pattern on its (inedible) dark brown wax rind.
- Vacherin Mont d'Or—buttery rich, full of complex fruity barny flavour, and so decadently supple that you have to leave it in its barkwood casing and spoon it out to eat it.
- Valençay—a pyramid-shaped ash-coated goat cheese. Creamy and smooth with a rich, tangy flavour that gets very strong with age.

Accompany cheese with colourful fruit, a plentiful cracker selection, assorted nuts and dense fruit-and-nut bread.

CHÈVRE CASSE-CROÛTE

This board is a light, casual lunch to be shared by chèvre aficionados.

Choose cheeses from traditional European regional producers or look for locally made cheeses from artisanal and farmstead producers. When selecting these products, remember that a rough, uneven appearance is often a mark of quality artisanal handmade cheese.

- Le Biquet—a herbed log of fresh chèvre. Crumble on a big salad of bitter baby greens with white balsamic vinaigrette and roasted red peppers.
- Le Chèvre Noir—Cheddar made from goat's milk is sharp and crisp in flavour. Slice and enjoy with Bosc pears and walnuts or a little tarte Tatin. Substitute goat Brie if Cheddar-style is hard to find.
- Pouligny Saint-Pierre—a pyramid-shaped cheese with a beige rind, smooth, thick texture and gently piquant flavour. Slather, rind and all, on warm, crusty baguette.

ONE-CHEESE TASTING BOARD

A whole wheel of cheese surrounded by a selection of fruits, nuts and charcuterie makes a spectacular and unusual presentation. Choose accompaniments for their ability to bring out the flavour nuances and textures of a great cheese that has been aged to perfection. Start the cheese by digging out a bit from the centre, and supply everyone with hard-cheese knives (short, stout blades designed for chipping and shaving shards out of the wheel).

Bonus for the host: If you choose a hard cheese for your one-cheese board, when all the cheese has been scraped out and enjoyed, the remaining shell of hard rind can be used as a grand bowl for serving an unforgettable Fettuccine quattro formaggio.

- Cheese—one whole wheel of aged Crotonese.
- Anjou pears—the honey fragrance and juicy softness contrast with the cheese.
- Crusty bread and water biscuits—cleanse and sweeten the palate.
- Herb and honey—organic honey sprinkled with rubbed sage for dipping or drizzling brings out the sweetness and grassiness of the cheese's complex flavour.
- Old-style mustard—the hot, bitter tang wakes up the taste buds.
- Quince compote—the fruity spiciness points to subtle characteristics of the cheese.
- Thinly sliced Bresaola—the rich, salty-sweet flavour and chewiness of this air-cured beef deepens the tones and texture.
- Walnuts—the slight bitterness fills out the sweetness of the Crotonese while underlining the nuttiness; the crunchiness accents the grainy texture.

We've listed some exceptional cheeses with the help of Ektor Stroutzas, the renowned retailer of a dizzying variety of cheeses at his Alex Farm Products stores, and Andy Shay, educator and "e-tailer" of exciting artisanal cheeses.

SOFT-RIPENED CHEESES

Bloomy rind: Brie and Camembert typify this type of cheese. Their rind is covered with a downy white bloom that yellows as the cheese ages. When ripe, the creamy, rich interior is very soft and, in a cut wedge, will bulge from the sides, threatening to run out.

Washed rind: These cheeses are scrubbed with brine, and sometimes a local liquor, during the maturation period. This makes their rinds darken to shades of gold and orange. They develop very distinct flavours and are the "smelly" cheeses. Their powerful scent often belies the subtlety of their complex character. The famously smelly Limburger and the aptly named Puant Macéré (soaked stinker) are among them.

Here are a few favourite soft-ripened cheeses:

- Brie, French—double-crème cow's milk, tender, silky and delicate, France's prince of cheese, also available in a lower-fat, single-cream version.
- Camembert—double-crème cow's milk, smooth and fragrant. The best ones come from le Pays d'Auge (Normandy), especially those produced from May to October.
- Epoisses—double-crème cow's milk, washed with herbed brine or eau-de-vie, rich, full-flavoured and tangy.
- Explorateur—a luxuriously rich and creamy cow's milk cheese, complex and piquant.
- Gratte-Paille—a triple-crème cow's milk block sometimes encased in straw matting. Super rich, slightly mushroomy flavour. Fresh and raw, yet refined. Superbly subtle.
- St. André—buttery, velvety triple-crème cow's milk with a clean, bright flavour, available in several sizes. The smaller ones are hard to get but preferable as they are usually fully ripe if eaten just before the "best before" date. The larger ones are often chalky and unripe at the core. This chalkiness can be seen as a thin white line that runs through the centre of a cut wheel.
- Taleggio—Lombardy region cow's milk, ripens from salty and fruity to almost beefy as it ages.
- Vacherin Mont d'Or—cow's milk, best November to December, very runny, super rich with fruity woodsy pungency. A superb cheese.

SEMI-SOFT AND SEMI-HARD CHEESES

Aged longer than soft-ripened cheeses, these are usually more complex and stronger in flavour but never get as pungent as the washed soft-rind cheeses. In aging, they are dried to firmness but vary in texture from soft as Gouda and crumbly as Gorgonzola to firmer cheeses such as aged Cheddar and Asiago.

- Cheddar, Canadian—semi-hard cow's milk, white or coloured bright orange. The best are aged more than 5 years and are not just sharp but fruity and complex. Cheddars aged more than 2 years are often not coloured.

- Gruyère, Swiss—semi-hard cow's milk, deeply nutty and fruity. Wonderful for cooking.
- Morbier—semi-soft cow's milk, gently piquant with a thin layer of edible ash running through the middle.
- Oka—nutty monastery semi-soft cow's milk. Like Swiss Raclette and French Comté, it is great for melting. A Canadian classic.
- Truffle Pecorino—semi-hard sheep's milk, dotted with black truffles. Fantastic grated over hot potatoes.

HARD CHEESES

Long aging has dried these cheeses to a very hard texture that is often pleasantly grainy. Grated to add richness to pastas, quiches and gratins, these cheeses are at their best thinly slivered into shards. They are utterly delicious eaten on crackers or with fruit and thinly sliced charcuterie.

- Asiago d'Allevo—cow's milk, aged for 6 months, it is called Mezzano; aged for 1 year, it is Vecchio; and the sharpest, aged for 2 years, is Stravecchio.
- Crotonese—sheep's milk, rich complexity, nutty and intense, a favourite when well aged.
- Manchego, Spanish—delicately tangy, sweet and nutty sheep's milk, fine grainy texture.
- Parmigiano-Reggiano or Parmesan-Reggiano— cow's milk, truly superior, fruity, grassy, complex in flavour and grainy in texture. Try it shaved into shards and drizzled with truffle oil.

- Peppe Pecorino, aged—sheep's milk, salty sharp creaminess, rind removed and rolled in mixed chilies. The zip of the chilies cuts through the richness of the cheese and combines in a heady mouthful.

BLUE CHEESES

Inoculated with mould-inducing *penicillium*, these cheeses have a distinct pungent flavour thanks to their distinctive blue and green veins of mould.

- Cabrales or Picón—goat's milk. The two top-rated Spanish blues have a strong, direct flavour.
- Cambozola—cow's milk, lighter in flavour than other blues, more creamy than crumbly in texture.
- Roquefort—sheep's milk, a salty, strong and creamy classic.
- Stilton—cow's milk, considered to be the best blue, smooth full flavour, rich and dense but crumbly.
- Torta Gorgonzola—cow's milk, Italian mascarpone layered with creamy, soft Gorgonzola, richly unctuous with gentle pungency.

SHEEP AND CHÈVRE

Sheep and goat cheeses are made in every style but maintain the tanginess characteristic of their milk. Most sheep cheese is aged to semi-hard and hard, thereby losing much of its tanginess and becoming sweet and nutty. Goat cheese, or chèvre, is generally lower in fat than cheese made from sheep's or cow's milk.

Goat cheese is often consumed young and unripened, when it is very white in colour and has a tender, chalky texture and a bright, tangy flavour. As goat cheeses age, they often become smoother in texture, with the very aged becoming drier and more crumbly. They lose their zingy edge and gain subtle nuttiness but can get flinty with long aging. A wonderful way to appreciate chèvre is to purchase it young and age it at home to your personal taste.

- Pecorino Siciliano—aged sheep cheese, available in several varieties such as *pepato* with black pepper and *primo sale* with salt.
- Pecorino Toscano—hard sheep cheese from Tuscany. Pecorino di Pienza is preserved in herbed olive oil or rubbed with tomato and olive oil. Another variety, di Fossa, is sometimes aged in ash or wrapped in walnut leaves and aged underground.
- Testun Capra—aged goat cheese from Piedmont, hard, creamy texture and gamey, barnyard flavour.
- Ticklemore—aged goat cheese from the south of England, firm and dome-shaped with a heavy crust. Deep flavour hints of asparagus soup.
- Valençay—aged goat cheese from France, truncated pyramid covered in ash and mould, vegetal and slightly saline with a tart finish.

BUYING CHEESE

To purchase cheese, find a reputable cheesemonger, taste lots of samples and ask lots of questions. Serious purveyors can be relied upon to handle cheese—a living thing in many ways—with care and attention. Eager to share their love of cheese, good cheese merchants will invariably offer tasting samples of anything sold by the slice or wedge.

The two most important factors affecting quality are source and age. The source is generally displayed prominently on the label, and often stamped right on the rind of the cheese. Determining the age is trickier; until you develop an experienced eye, it's best to rely on the faithful interpretations of your cheese seller. Age is a determining factor in flavour and texture, but is often a matter of personal taste.

SERVING CHEESE

One hour before serving, remove cheese from the refrigerator and allow it to warm to room temperature. Only warm the amount you are going to eat—cheese gets dry when it goes in and out of the cooler too many times—and keep it wrapped or covered with a cloche or cheese bell until serving time, to prevent surface drying.

When laying out a cheeseboard, keep the cheeses well separated, to make slicing easy and to prevent the runnier varieties from getting all over each other. Provide separate knives for each cheese. We like the knives that are sharp, serrated and have little curved picks at the point for spearing slices.

WINE NOTES

Few consumable products share as many striking similarities as wine and cheese. Both were "invented" accidentally several thousand years ago, and we have not ceased trying to perfect them since. Each is converted from a relatively simple raw material (grape juice and milk) into many marvellously complex products with a bewildering array of flavours. The region of production (*terroir*) greatly influences the final outcome, and both wine and cheese making require no small measure of *savoir-faire*. So it certainly comes as no surprise that wine and cheese are like kindred spirits, each capable of making the other greater.

But not all wine and cheese pairings are a match made in heaven. The abundant fat, protein and pungent aromas found in some cheeses can overwhelm your taste buds and ruin the subtle and delicate flavours of certain wines. Thus, when putting together your cheeseboard experience, consider not only wine style but also the variety of cheese and how it may affect the taste of wine. For example, milk may be taken from a morning or an evening milking, or from a combination of both. It may be taken during the summer months of high-mountain pasture grazing or during the winter months of farmyard feeding. The milk may be skimmed of its cream content or have cream added to it. The quality of the milk, its richness, its acid content, the degree to which it is heated, and of course the breed of cow, goat or sheep are all factors that influence the flavour. Not least, production methods vary considerably: the amount of rennet used, the way the cheese is pressed, the heating of the curds, the degree of salting, the number of times the cheese is turned from one side to another while it is maturing, the length and location of maturation, how the cheese is brushed, scraped or washed, as well as various other flavour additions—wine, beer, spirits, spices, ashes and leaves, to name but a few—will have a significant impact on the aroma, flavour and texture, and therefore, the best style of wine to match.

Such is the wonderful complexity of these products that few, if any, wines will match well with the entire selection on a cheeseboard. For a really eye-opening wine and cheese experience, serve a tasting-sized portion (about 2 oz) of a different, well-chosen wine with each cheese. Your guests will marvel at the vast and complex array of flavours found in these heavenly combinations. Try some of the recommendations below, but be sure to experiment together with different combinations.

1. **GOAT CHEESE:** The tangy acidity of goat's milk cheese calls for a wine with equally vibrant acidity.
   Cheeses: Crottin de Chavignol, St. Maure, firm or fresh
   Wines: Chenin Blanc, Grüner Veltliner, Muscadet, Pinot Grigio, Riesling, Sauvignon Blanc

2. **SOFT-RIPENED CHEESE, UNWASHED RIND:** The pungency of these cheeses depends on their age, ripeness and whether they are made of raw or pasteurized milk. The riper, more flavourful cheeses demand more intensely flavoured wines.
Cheeses: Brie, Camembert
Wines: Medium to full-bodied white wines such as Albariño, oak-aged Chardonnay, Fumé Blanc or Pinot Blanc; fruity, light- to medium-bodied reds such as Cabernet Franc, Gamay, Pinot Noir

3. **SOFT-RIPENED CHEESE, WASHED RIND:** These "I-can-smell-you-from-across-the-room" cheeses will crush any unsuspecting, delicate wines. When in doubt, switch to spirits like bourbon, malt whisky or fruit eaux-de-vie.
Cheeses: Epoisses, Livarot, Munster, Vacherin Mont d'Or
Wines: Full-bodied, full-flavoured complex whites such as Alsatian Pinot Gris, Gewürztraminer, Marsanne-Roussanne blends or Viognier; intensely flavoured, medium- to full-bodied reds such as Merlot, southern Rhône Valley blends, Shiraz, old-vines Zinfandel

4. **SEMI-HARD CHEESE:** These cheeses provide an opportunity to showcase some heavy-hitting, high-quality mature red wines.
Cheeses: aged Canadian Cheddar, Cantal, Comté, Oka, Raclette, Tomme
Wines: Cabernet Sauvignon (and blends), Pinot Noir, Sangiovese, Syrah

5. **HARD CHEESE:** The combination of moderate fat content, sharp, pungent flavour and crumbly texture calls for full-bodied, tannic reds.
Cheeses: Crotonese, Manchego, Parmesan-reggiano, Pecorino
Wines: Amarone della Valpolicella, Brunello/Sangiovese, Cabernet Sauvignon (and blends), Douro Valley reds, Nebbiolo, Tempranillo-based wines from Rioja and Ribera del Duero. Try also dry fortified wine such as Marsala Vergine or Oloroso sherry for an unusual but superb combination.

6. **BLUE-VEINED CHEESE:** The intense saltiness and pungent flavours of blue cheese make a brilliantly contrasting match with sweet wines, both red and white, fortified and late-harvest/botrytis-affected. The saltier and more intense the cheese, the sweeter the wine should be.
Cheeses: Cabrales, Gorgonzola, Roquefort, St. Agur, Stilton
Wines: Ice wine, select late-harvest wines, Banyuls, sweet Chenin Blanc (i.e., Coteaux du Layon or Vouvray Moêlleux), fortified Muscats from the south of France (Beaumes de Venise, Rivesaltes) or the raisiny Muscats of Rutherglen in Australia, port, Sauternes, Tokaji.

THE RAW BAR

Raw and racy. There's something about an icy mound of naked oysters, shivering on their silver shells, that attracts so many gastronomes. Why deny your oyster-loving friends this frisson? Offer a raw bar that all can dive into with abandon.

Build your seafood raw bar with an assortment of freshly shucked oysters and clams on the half-shell. Then add poached shrimp, cooked scallops, steamed mussels, boiled crayfish, king crab legs, cured salmon or herring rollmops for other guests who have yet to be seduced by the idea of chucking back cold, raw molluscs and swallowing them alive.

Fill a large, shallow container with cracked ice. If your raw bar is small, you can use a big copper washtub, a giant clamshell or a series of large baking dishes. For bigger parties you may want to call a party-supply place and rent clear plastic trays with drains—made especially for ice displays—or go all out and order an ice sculpture from the catering department of a large hotel (or search the Internet under "ice sculptures"). Arrange cooked, chilled seafood on top, leaving space for the oysters. Thirty minutes before serving, arrange freshly shucked oysters on top. Set out small bowls of a variety of condiments on the side: freshly grated horseradish, lemon wedges, chili sauce, warm clarified lemon butter, fried ginger salt, seasoned sea salt and balsamic vinegar, for example. Have a plastic-lined wicker basket nearby for discarding shells.

To completely thrill your guests, add a selection of Oyster Shooters (page 156) to your raw bar.

And if you want everyone to hang around the raw bar all night, round it out with servings of hot, salted deep-fried potatoes. Their texture and temperature contrast perfectly with raw oysters, and their sweet starchiness is a great counterpoint to the seafood's mineral flavours.

SHOPPING WITH CHEF: A FLASH COURSE IN OYSTERS

BUYING

Choose only the very freshest oysters from a fishmonger who specializes in shellfish. Tightly closed shells that are not chipped or cracked are good indicators of freshness. Oysters should smell clean, fresh and just like the ocean air.

STORING

Freshly harvested oysters will keep up to 1 week if kept cold and moist in a loosely covered container—ideally, wrapped in wet newspaper in a cardboard box in the refrigerator. Get some seaweed from your oyster purveyor to strew over the oysters when you store them and to decorate the raw bar or platter when you serve them. Don't store them on ice or in water, as that will kill them.

CLEANING

Wash the oysters thoroughly under running water, brushing all sand and debris from the shells until the water runs clean. Refrigerate until ready to shuck and serve.

SHUCKING

Words are inadequate in giving directions on how to perform some of the most useful human activities, and shucking is one of these activities. Get your oyster monger to give you a demonstration. He will insist you start by getting a good oyster knife. Now, try it yourself.

Run the oyster under cold water to wash off sand and broken shell. Place the oyster, flat side up, on a moistened tea towel with the small, hinged end pointing toward your knife hand. Holding the oyster firmly in place with the other hand, insert the tip of the oyster knife between the top and bottom shells at the hinge. Sometimes the roughness of the shell makes it difficult to determine where the top shell ends and the bottom begins, but just stick the knifepoint in, using your best guess, and wiggle and twist it until it finds the way and you feel it slipping in. Twist the knife back and forth until you hear a gentle *pop*. This sound signals your arrival at the top of the food chain—you have successfully severed the oyster's hinge. The rest is easy. Slide the blade of the knife along the inside top shell to cut the muscle that holds the shell closed. Discard the top and inspect your prize, carefully cleaning away any shell shards. Cut the muscle away from the bottom shell to free the oyster completely from the shell. Try not to spill too much of the oyster "liqueur," as its natural saltiness adds nicely to the flavour.

Suffice it to say, care should be taken to avoid nasty gashes in the oyster and in the cook. Practice will take care of the former, and the latter can be achieved by protecting your hand with a mesh butcher's glove or a moist wadded tea towel. Like bicycle riding, shucking is easy once you get the knack, so don't give up. Then teach someone else to do it, so you don't end up with a repetitive strain injury.

Although it's best to shuck oysters as they are being eaten, you can do some just prior to serving time. Oysters, once shucked, should be eaten within 2 hours. They will keep nicely on a bed of cracked ice.

VARIETIES

Oysters are usually named for the bays in which they are grown and are often farmed far from their ancestral beds. Although their flavour and texture are determined to some degree by species, region has the greater influence. Oysters filter huge quantities of water as they feed, so the mineral content of that water directly affects their flavour. The temperature of the water influences the speed with which they grow, and therefore their texture. Spawning—which usually occurs during the months when the waters warm—detracts from their quality, hence the old "only-eat-oysters-in-months-spelled-with-an-*R*" rule. This effect has largely been mitigated by refrigerated transport, which allows more oysters to be brought in from colder waters, and the development of non-spawning varieties.

Atlantic oysters tend to be salty and crisp. Here are a few varieties that we love:
- Bluepoint—large; creamy and pleasantly salty
- Caraquet—medium-sized; salty with a slightly bittersweet finish
- Malpeque—medium-sized to large, flat-bottomed; clean, salty flavour

Pacific varieties tend to be sweet and creamy. Except for the Olympia, all are originally Japanese species. Here are a few of our favourite varieties:

- Kumamoto—small to medium-sized; fruit-scented and mild
- Olympia—tiny; full-flavoured with a slightly coppery note
- Quilcene—medium-sized; sweet with a cucumber finish
- Skookum—medium-sized, plump and firm; fruity

European "flats," or Belon oysters, are beginning to be cultivated on both coasts of North America. The characteristically dry, intense, salty flavour of the French species is nuanced according to where the oysters are grown—stronger-flavoured in the Atlantic and milder in the Pacific.

Australian oysters are sometimes imported to the west coast in our summer months, when the southern hemisphere is experiencing its cold season.

COCKTAIL ACCOMPANIMENTS

The eponymous Pimm's Cup was invented in the 1800s by the owner of an oyster bar in England who developed six different blends—each based on a different spirit—to accompany his oysters. His Pimm's Number 1, based on gin, was the most successful and is still popular.

Currently, tastes run more to ice-cold vodka and vintage tequila, but a good Bloody Mary or Caesar makes a great flavour complement to oysters and adds the nutritional benefit of an extra food group to boot.

WINE NOTES

As with a squeeze of fresh lemon or a dash of tart mignonette, raw and cooked seafood comes to life with an electrifying jolt of acidity. Keep this in mind when selecting wines to accompany your raw bar. The classic is, of course, Champagne. Produced in the marginal climate of northern France, this wine has a fine dose of acidity that makes oysters and other creatures of the sea sing with flavour. As a bonus, it also echoes the briny mineral notes of the ocean; after all, the vines here grow in soil composed of billions of seashells. Chablis is yet another classic, made from Chardonnay grapes grown in essentially the same type of soil in a similarly cool climate.

But really, any fresh, crisp white will do the job nicely. Stick to cool growing regions and zippy white grape varieties. The tannins in most red wines clash with the salty, briny flavour of seafood and are generally less-than-ideal matches.

For something a little different (and more reasonably priced), try dry Riesling or Chenin Blanc, Pinot Grigio, Muscadet, Vinho Verde from northern Portugal, Albariño from Spain, Sauvignon Blanc from Chile, France or New Zealand, or Gavi from northern Italy. Follow your heart and the telltale, mouth-watering, prickling sensation on your tongue.

Chef at the stove

EIGHT ESSENTIAL APPETIZERS

To get the best out of life, you must celebrate the little things. After five, when you and your housemate wind down after work. In the evening, when friends curl up to watch a movie. On the weekend, when leisure triumphs over laundry. You deserve a little drink. But to complement your wonderful cocktails, you need a snack to match.

Here are eight great everyday appetizers to go with your casual cocktails and impromptu entertaining. These are the no-fail recipes that always get rave reviews. They are uncomplicated, so they are easy to make and unfussy to eat, but with flavours and textures dazzling enough to stand up to your wildest cocktail. The recipe quantities are small—enough for two or more than a few. If you master these recipes, you will need no others to ensure your reputation as a great host. Most of them can be prepared ahead, refrigerated or frozen and pulled out when you feel like having cocktails.

Cook up a batch and celebrate life, every lovely day!

Spiced Asian Walnuts

A fun recipe with surprising results. Who would have guessed that this method is based on a traditional Chinese technique? The boiling and deep-frying produce a caramelized, sweet-spicy nut, which is tender on the inside and crunchy on the outside. Eat them compulsively or sprinkle them on your favourite salad or main course. You can prepare and store these nuts, covered, at room temperature for up to 1 week.

1½ cups sugar	4 cups walnut halves
1 tsp Chinese five-spice powder	4 to 6 cups vegetable oil for deep frying

Combine sugar and five-spice powder in a medium-large bowl.

Bring a medium pot of water to a boil on medium-high heat and blanch walnuts for 2 to 3 minutes. Drain nuts very well and transfer them immediately to the bowl with the spices, and toss well to coat.

Line a baking sheet with parchment paper (do not use paper towel, as the nuts will stick to it). Heat 4 to 5 inches of oil in a large, heavy-bottomed saucepan on high heat until it reaches 375°F (or a small cube of bread browns in 30 seconds). Place ½ cup nuts in the saucepan and deep-fry until golden brown, 2 to 3 minutes. Using a metal slotted spoon, quickly transfer cooked nuts to the parchment-lined baking sheet. Spread out the nuts, separating them, and allow them to cool. Repeat with the remaining nuts, cooking ½ cup at a time.

Makes 4 cups

Pappadam Shrimp with Mango Chutney Dipping Sauce

Pappadam is paper-thin, lentil flour–based bread that originated in India. In this exotic yet easy recipe, this flavourful flatbread is used to crust tender jumbo shrimp.

MANGO CHUTNEY DIPPING SAUCE

½ cup store-bought mango chutney

½ cup water

SHRIMP

1 to 3 cups vegetable oil for frying

eight to ten 8-inch pappadams

¾ cup all-purpose flour

1 egg white, beaten until foamy

1 lb jumbo uncooked black tiger shrimp
(16 to 20 shrimp per lb), peeled, tails on

MANGO CHUTNEY DIPPING SAUCE: In a small bowl, combine mango chutney with water and stir well. Set aside.

SHRIMP: Preheat the oven to 400°F. Line a plate with paper towels. Line a baking sheet with parchment paper.

In a heavy-bottomed sauté pan, heat ½-inch oil on medium-high heat until it reaches 350°F (or until a cube of bread browns in 60 seconds). Place a pappadam in the sauté pan and fry, turning it once, until pale golden and blistered, 45 seconds to 1 minute. Using metal tongs, lift out the pappadam, hold it over the sauté pan to drain any excess oil, then transfer to the paper towel–lined plate. Repeat with the remaining pappadams, and allow to cool.

Place the cooled pappadams in a plastic bag. Using a rolling pin, crush pappadams until crumbs are the size of small flakes. Transfer crumbs to a flat dish.

Place flour in a bowl and egg white in another. One at a time, lightly coat shrimp with flour (gently shaking off excess flour), dip in egg white and roll in pappadam crumbs, gently pressing crumbs so they adhere to shrimp. Place coated shrimp on the baking sheet and bake for 8 to 10 minutes, or until shrimp are just opaque in the centre.

Serve immediately with Mango Chutney Dipping Sauce.

Makes 16 to 20 shrimp

Vegetable Pot Stickers

Pot stickers are a perennial favourite. Here is a delicious vegetarian version.

These can be made ahead and stored on the parchment-lined baking sheets, covered and uncooked, in the refrigerator for up to 2 days or in the freezer for up to 1 month. You can also cook the pot stickers the day before you plan to serve them: boiled dumplings, which should be very lightly brushed with oil so they don't stick together while being stored, can be reheated in the microwave on high power for about 2 minutes. Boiled and sautéed dumplings can be reheated in a hot oiled pan on medium-high heat until hot, 3 to 4 minutes.

SPICY SOY DIPPING SAUCE

1 cup soy sauce

½ Tbsp grated fresh ginger

1 to 2 tsp Asian chili sauce (or to taste)

POT STICKERS

30 oz (3 bags) spinach, washed, stems removed, patted or spun dry

3 Tbsp vegetable oil

1 Tbsp finely minced garlic

2 ½ lbs mushrooms, grated by hand or in a food processor

¼ tsp salt

¼ tsp pepper

cornstarch for dusting trays

45 dumpling wrappers (2 lbs/900g), 3-inch diameter, thawed if frozen

vegetable oil for sautéing dumplings (optional)

SPICY SOY DIPPING SAUCE: In a small bowl, combine soy sauce, ginger and chili sauce. Set aside.

POT STICKERS: Place spinach in a resealable food storage bag, seal and microwave on high power, shaking the bag every 30 seconds, for 1 to 2 minutes or until well wilted. Press out any excess water. Roughly chop spinach and set aside.

Heat a large sauté pan on high heat. Add 1 Tbsp of the oil and 1 tsp of the garlic and cook, softening garlic, for about 30 seconds. Add a third of the mushrooms, salt and pepper and sauté until mushroom juices are released and reabsorbed, 6 to 8 minutes. Transfer to a large bowl. Repeat twice using a third of the oil, garlic, mushrooms, salt and pepper each time, and transferring the cooked mushrooms to the large bowl. Add spinach to mushrooms, toss together and season with more salt and pepper, if necessary. Cool completely.

Line a baking sheet with parchment paper and lightly dust it with cornstarch. Place a dumpling wrapper on a clean, dry work surface (keep the remaining wrappers covered with a damp towel). Mound 1 heaping tsp of filling in the centre of the wrapper, then dip your finger or a pastry brush in water and moisten the edges of the wrapper. Fold the top half of the wrapper over the bottom half to make a half-moon shape, being careful to enclose the filling completely. Press the edges together tightly. Transfer the filled dumpling to the baking sheet. Repeat with the remaining wrappers and filling.

Lightly oil another baking sheet. Bring a large pot of water to a boil on high heat. Drop in dumplings, 10 to 12 at a time, and cook until they float to the top and the wrappers look translucent (3 to 4 minutes). Using a slotted spoon, transfer the dumplings to the oiled baking sheet. If desired, heat ⅛ inch vegetable oil in a shallow sauté pan on medium-high heat. Add boiled dumplings and sauté on both sides. Drain on paper towel. Serve immediately with spicy soy dipping sauce.

Makes about 45 dumplings

Wonton wrappers, which are square, can be substituted for round Chinese dumpling wrappers. Although they are thinner and more delicate than traditional dumpling wrappers, they will still be delicious.

Chicken Skewers in Three Ways

Skewers go global in these recipes, which infuse tender chicken with the very best flavours of Asia (satay), India (tandoori) and the Caribbean (jerk).

Almost all of the ingredients that make up these exotic mixes are available at any grocery store. Tandoori spice powder can be found in the international food section of your supermarket. Coconut cream and sesame oil can be found in Asian food stores. Don't be deterred by the long list of ingredients in this recipe—they're mostly spices that get dashed and pinched into the bowl. These marinades are quick to assemble and make it easy to escape the old flavour rut!

SATAY MARINADE

1 cup coconut cream (page 55)

1 cup peanut butter, smooth or crunchy

3 Tbsp soy sauce

1 Tbsp Asian chili sauce

1 Tbsp sesame oil

1 Tbsp rice vinegar

2 Tbsp brandy

1 Tbsp chopped garlic

½ tsp Chinese five-spice powder
(or a dash of cinnamon and ginger)

1 tsp salt

1 cup roasted peanuts, chopped,
for garnish

TANDOORI MARINADE

¾ cup Balkan-style full-fat yogurt

2 Tbsp tandoori spice powder

JERK MARINADE

2 green onions, chopped

4 jalapeño peppers, in ½-inch dice

1 Tbsp minced garlic

½ Tbsp grated fresh ginger

½ Tbsp ground allspice

½ tsp pepper

½ tsp cinnamon

¼ tsp nutmeg

½ tsp salt

2 Tbsp freshly squeezed lime juice

½ Tbsp brown sugar

1 Tbsp olive oil

CHICKEN SKEWERS

18 boneless, skinless chicken breasts (about 3 lbs), sliced diagonally in strips ¼-inch thick and 1½ inches long

72 bamboo skewers, 6 inches long, soaked in water for 2 hours

MARINADE(S): Combine ingredients for each marinade in a separate large bowl. Whisk each marinade until well mixed. Measure ¼ cup of each marinade into a separate small bowl and reserve for garnish.

CHICKEN SKEWERS: Add ⅓ of the chicken strips to each marinade in large bowls and toss well to coat all pieces evenly. Cover with plastic wrap and refrigerate for 2 to 12 hours.

Preheat the oven to broil or a barbecue to high. Thread 3 or 4 pieces of chicken onto each skewer. You should have about 24 skewers of each flavour. Broil in the oven or grill on the barbecue for 2 to 3 minutes per side. Brush chicken with reserved marinade. Sprinkle satay skewers with chopped peanuts. Arrange skewers on a serving platter and serve hot.

Makes 72 skewers

Coconut cream is available in Filipino and other Asian, Caribbean and Indian food stores. We get great results from Fiesta brand, which comes in 8½ oz (250 mL) Tetra Paks. Coconut milk is also available in cans but is often much lighter. Results with lighter types will be fine but not as rich. When buying coconut cream in cans, be sure to get the unsweetened variety.

STAR FRUIT CANAPÉS *with* MINCED PORK *and* CILANTRO

Star fruit makes a colourful star-shaped base for these Asian-inspired bites. If star fruit is not available, substitute one fresh pineapple, peeled, cored, quartered and cut in ½-inch slices.

You can make the pork mixture (leaving out the dried coconut, sesame seeds and chopped cilantro) the day before you plan to serve it, and cover and refrigerate it overnight. Just before serving, reheat the pork mixture in the microwave on high power for 2 to 4 minutes, or until hot throughout. Mix in the dried coconut, sesame seeds and cilantro and spoon onto sliced star fruit.

1 large, firm cooking apple such as Royal Gala, peeled, cored and chopped in ⅛-inch dice (about ½ cup)	1 ½ cups (10 oz) ground pork or chicken
	¼ cup coconut cream (page 55)
	2 Tbsp hoisin sauce
1 small red bell pepper, in ⅛-inch dice	2 tsp soy sauce
1 large jalapeño pepper, in ⅛-inch dice	½ cup unsweetened dried coconut flakes
½ cup sliced bamboo shoots	¼ cup sesame seeds, toasted
2 tsp vegetable oil	⅔ cup cilantro, stemmed and chopped
2 tsp sesame oil	5 to 6 whole star fruit, in ¼-inch slices
3 cloves garlic, minced	60 whole cilantro leaves, for garnish

In a food processor, combine apple, bell pepper, jalapeño and bamboo shoots, and pulse until roughly combined.

Heat vegetable and sesame oils in a large sauté pan on medium-high heat. Add garlic and sauté for 1 minute. Add minced pork (or chicken) and sauté until well browned, about 5 minutes. Add the apple–bamboo shoot mixture, coconut cream, hoisin and soy sauce and sauté for another 2 to 3 minutes until heated through. Stir in coconut flakes, sesame seeds and chopped cilantro and toss to combine.

On a serving platter, arrange sliced star fruit in a decorative manner. Spoon about 1 tsp of the hot meat mixture onto each star fruit. Garnish with cilantro leaves. Serve immediately.

Makes about 60 pieces

Stuffed Baguette

As a sandwich, this is perfect comfort food. Sliced into rounds, it also makes a delicious warm canapé that can be prepared ahead and frozen for up to 1 month. Just thaw before baking.

5 oz (½ bag) spinach, washed, stems removed and dried	½ cup grated mozzarella cheese
7 tsp olive oil	¼ cup grated Parmesan cheese
¼ cup diced onion	1 tsp chopped fresh thyme
1 Tbsp minced garlic	2 tsp chopped fresh flat-leaf parsley
½ lb lean ground beef	1 egg, beaten
one 15-inch baguette	⅛ tsp salt
2 Tbsp finely diced red bell pepper	⅛ tsp pepper

Place spinach in a resealable food storage bag, seal and microwave on high power, shaking the bag every 30 seconds, for 1 to 2 minutes or until well wilted. Press out excess water. Roughly chop spinach and set aside.

Heat 2 tsp of the olive oil in a medium sauté pan on medium-high heat. Add onion and garlic and sauté until soft, 2 to 3 minutes. Transfer onion and garlic to a small bowl. Add 3 tsp olive oil to the sauté pan and turn the heat to high. Add ground beef and brown, stirring occasionally, for 3 to 4 minutes. Season with salt and pepper and allow to cool.

Preheat the oven to 375°F. Grease a 12 × 18-inch piece of aluminum foil with nonstick spray and 1 tsp of the olive oil. Cut off the ends of the baguette and slice it open lengthwise without separating the bread into two halves. Using your fingers, hollow out each side of the baguette. In a food processor, process the soft bread until it forms coarse crumbs and set aside.

In a medium bowl, combine onion, garlic, beef, bell pepper, mozzarella and Parmesan cheeses, thyme, parsley, egg, salt and pepper, and bread crumbs. Mix until well combined.

Fill the hollowed baguette halves with the ground beef filling, packing them well. Tightly close the baguette, ensuring that no filling escapes, and drizzle with the remaining 1 tsp olive oil. Wrap baguette in aluminum foil and bake until heated through, 20 to 25 minutes.

Slice baguette into 1-inch rounds or quarters. Serve hot.

Makes 4 small plates or 12 to 15 canapés

Tortilla Crisps with Savoury Toppings

Transform plain supermarket tortillas into your own original flatbread by adding a few fresh toppings. You can make these crisps 2 days in advance and recrisp them in a 375°F oven for 5 minutes before serving.

BASIC SPREAD

2 Tbsp olive oil

½ Tbsp minced garlic

4 Tbsp finely chopped fresh oregano

4 Tbsp finely chopped fresh basil

8 flour tortillas, 7 inches in diameter

VARIATION: PESTO, ROMANO, MUSHROOM AND PINE NUT FLATBREAD

⅓ cup store-bought pesto

⅓ cup chopped pine nuts

⅓ cup sliced, sautéed mushrooms

⅓ cup freshly grated Romano cheese

⅓ cup chopped fresh basil

VARIATION: TAPENADE, CHÈVRE, PROSCIUTTO AND ROASTED PEPPER FLATBREAD

⅓ cup store-bought black olive tapenade

½ cup chopped roasted red bell peppers

16 paper-thin slices prosciutto,
    in 3-inch pieces

⅓ cup crumbled chèvre or feta

⅓ cup chopped fresh basil

BASIC SPREAD: In a small bowl, combine oil, garlic, oregano and basil. Season with salt and pepper.

FLATBREAD VARIATIONS: Preheat the oven to 375°F. Brush tortillas with the basic spread, then with pesto or tapenade. Top with nuts, vegetables, cheese, meat and fresh herbs. Cut each tortilla into 6 wedges and bake for 10 to 12 minutes, or until crisp and golden brown.

Makes 48 wedges

OLIVE BOMBES

The rustic Mediterranean flavour of good olives and great cheese make these perfect little bitefuls utterly addictive. Serve with Tomato Olive Tapenade (page 121) and garnish with prosciutto or pancetta.

1 cup Arborio rice	1 cup shredded mozzarella cheese
1½ cups water	1 tsp salt
2 eggs	2 cups panko (Japanese bread crumbs)
2 cups pitted, ½-inch diced jumbo green	or soft bread crumbs
Italian or Greek olives	vegetable oil for deep frying
1½ cups (200 g) ¼-inch diced Parmesan-	
Reggiano cheese	

In a large saucepan, combine rice and water. Cover and bring to a boil on high heat. Reduce the heat to low and simmer for 12 to 15 minutes, until rice is fluffy and grains are cooked through. Transfer to a bowl and set aside to cool.

In a medium bowl, lightly beat eggs. Add cooled rice, olives, Parmesan-Reggiano, mozzarella, salt and pepper to taste. Mix well to combine.

Place panko in a shallow pan. Scoop rounded tablespoonfuls of the rice mixture into your hand and form into 1-inch balls. Roll in panko to coat evenly.

Line a plate with paper towels. Heat a deep fryer to 375°F. Place 8 to 12 bombes in the deep fryer and fry until golden, 3 to 4 minutes. Lift up the deep fryer basket, drain bombes of any excess oil and transfer them to the paper towel–lined plate to drain. Repeat with the remaining bombes. Serve warm or at room temperature.

Makes about 4 dozen bombes

Chef at the party

What is the secret to giving truly great parties? That's the question people always ask us. After decades of catering events from the most extravagant to the most intimate, we have found successful parties come down to one thing: plan to delight each and every guest. But how can you please everyone? Simple. Have a cocktail party.

The traditional drinks party was designed for the theatre crowd, international spies and awfully active socialites. Guests were invited to visit within set hours, when the hosts would be "at Home," usually before dinner or after the opera. The Smart Set was simply too busy to sit in one spot for more than a few hours. Once again, in modern life, although no one is dashing off to meet Goldfinger, everyone has scheduling issues and the cocktail party fits perfectly with busy lifestyles.

The new cocktail party offers the same flexibility in timing but—ever more important these days—takes in stride the complicated dietary restrictions of just about everybody. Guests can graze to their heart-smart's content, picking and choosing from a variety of hors d'oeuvres and small plates according to their own whim and waistline. The cocktail supper is the new dinner party—small plates provide substantial fare while maintaining the fun and flexibility of a drinks party.

The cocktail party format has so much built-in flexibility that each guest is in control of his or her own experience. As the host, you simply provide an environment of possibilities. The menu, timing, music, decor and even the guest list should be designed with something for each one of your guests. This is not as daunting as it sounds, if you follow these five steps.

THE PERFECT COCKTAIL PARTY

STEP 1: DEFINE THE CONCEPT OF YOUR EVENT

You don't need an overblown theme, just a core concept that will keep you on track as you choose the guest list, menu, music and decor of your party. To choose the best concept, first think about the purpose of your party. Is it to introduce business associates, to catch up with old friends or to celebrate a special occasion? The answer to this question will determine the key guests. Think about the "comfort zone" of those guests and that will indicate the general mood. Take that mood and enhance it with your personal spin—elegant or sassy, cool or hot, ethnic, minimalist, cozy or retro—and remember, don't be too subtle. Special times call for special effects!

STEP 2: SELECT THE GUEST LIST, TIME AND VENUE

Be ruthless when you're making up your guest list. There must be enough "stars" to make a gathering interesting, but too many means there won't be enough listeners to go around. And there's no need to keep the male-to-female ratio equal. Change it up a bit. Invite new friends. Expand the age range. If your guests all belong to the same crowd, the conversation can devolve to "shop talk" and vicious gossip. Mix up the guest list and enjoy the surprising way people expand beyond their usual roles when they're not in a roundup with the usual suspects.

Once you have winnowed down your guest list, you have to assess whether or not your home will accommodate that number. A rough requirement is about 5 square feet per person. So for a group of fifty, you need an open area of about 250 square feet, or two average-size rooms. You can "find" space by moving bulky furniture into temporary storage, by turning closets into bars or by renting a tent and expanding into the yard. Be realistic. At a cocktail party, people arrive and depart at different times, but there will be a period of a few hours when almost everyone will be in attendance, jockeying for position at the bar, the buffet and the bathroom. If you don't have enough space and can't cut the list, then maybe you need to think about another venue. Does your best friend's condominium have a party room or a deck? Can you take your party to a park or to the beach? Maybe you can rent three adjoining motel rooms and work a campy theme around that.

NO-FAIL FORMULA: one person needs 5 square feet of standing room

STEP 3: DESIGN A MENU

Several menu ideas will spring from your concept. Also, consider the favourite foods of the season and the possible dietary requirements of your guests. So many people are vegetarian, have food allergies or are following the diet *du jour* that having a cocktail party can be much easier than hosting a full seven-course sit-down meal. Everyone is free to select what (and how much) they eat. We like to offer an equal number of vegetarian, low-fat and high-protein selections so everyone feels catered to. And, of course, close the menu with tiny irresistible desserts so everyone can flirt with temptation one last time before they head home.

We calculate food quantities based on "bites"; an hors d'oeuvre is one bite, a small plate about three bites and a nibble, such as Coconut Taro Chips, only half a bite, because nobody can eat just one. Each guest will consume about five bites per hour. The larger the party, the less food people will consume. So for forty guests, you will need about 800 bites for a four-hour cocktail party. It's not as much, or as complicated, as it sounds. Just plan a menu of items that can be prepared well in advance. At a cocktail supper, however, the food should be substantial enough to take the place of dinner, but in portions that are easy to eat while standing. As well as hors d'oeuvres, offer a few "small plates" of more substantial tapas-style selections that can be easily eaten with a fork.

NO-FAIL FORMULA: one person eats 5 "bites" per hour

Your guests will also appreciate a balance of cocktails, non-alcoholic drinks, water and wine so they can approach the dawning of their personal hangover at their own pace. One drink per guest per hour is the average, although Champagne is often consumed more quickly. An offering of freshly brewed hot coffee, regular and decaffeinated, is appreciated by departing guests who might feel they can face a breathalyzer with more vigour after a good cup of Ethiopian Harrar.

NO-FAIL FORMULA: one person has one alcoholic drink per hour

1 bottle of wine (750 mL/26 oz) will pour about 5 drinks

1 bottle of spirits (750 mL/26 oz) will pour about 12 drinks

Here are some guidelines for quantities and types of food:

EVENT	FOOD REQUIREMENT (PER PERSON)
2-hour cocktail reception	5 hors d'oeuvres, 1 small plate, 4 nibbles
3-hour cocktail brunch	8 hors d'oeuvres, 2 small plates, 4 nibbles
5-hour cocktail supper	9 hors d'oeuvres, 4 small plates, 4 nibbles, 2 sweets

Great parties just seem to flow magically, wrapping everyone up in the spirit. But it isn't magic. It's your invitations, decor, style of food service and music that create and direct the mood and, ultimately, the success of the event.

Here's how to design a great party:

A. Design the Invitations

Design your invitations in a way that reflects your concept. A casual party needs an informal-looking invitation, just as an invitation to an elegant evening should have a glamorous touch. This tells your guests what kind of event you've got in store for them. They know what to expect, what to wear and who else might be there. The invitation will have the what, where, who, when and why, but it's a good idea also to enclose a map with parking information, an RSVP card, phone number or e-mail address.

Be clear about what type of party you are giving, so people know if the equivalent of a full meal is on offer, or just cocktails and a few blotter hors d'oeuvres. Our favourite enclosure is a save-the-date reminder, which can be as simple as a card on a fridge magnet or as elaborate as a rubber bracelet stamped with the occasion and the date. You can create very personal invitations on a colour photocopier or with digital photographs, and for informal gatherings there are great e-invitation services on the Internet.

BASIC BAR REQUIREMENTS FOR 40 GUESTS

DRINK	2-HOUR RECEPTION (BOTTLES)	5-HOUR COCKTAIL SUPPER (BOTTLES)
SPIRITS:		
Cognac	0	2
Gin	1	2
Optional Bourbon	0	1
Optional Rum, dark	0	1
Optional Vermouth, sweet	0	1
Rum, light	1	1
Rye	1	1
Scotch	1	3
Tequila	1	2
Vermouth, dry	1	1
Vodka	2	4
WINE:		
Red	10	15 to 18
White	10	15 to 18
BEER:	1 dozen	2 dozen
OPTIONAL LIQUEURS:	0	2 or 3
NON-ALCOHOLIC:		
Cola and diet cola	6	12
Fruit juices	2 quarts	4 quarts
Large mineral water, sparkling and flat	6 and 6	12 and 12
Soda water	3	6
Tonic water	3	6
MISCELLANEOUS:		
Ice	½ lb per person	2 lbs per person for mixing drinks
Lemons, limes	1 dozen each	2 dozen each

B. Design the Decor

Now that you have decided on a concept, the fun can begin! Go to the library and look up your theme in the picture files, or search the Internet for images. Rent movies with the same "atmosphere," and the set designs should get your imagination going. Then, with these images in your head, walk through your party space as if you were a guest, imagining the entrance, hanging your coat, getting a drink, wandering to the various food stations, looking for the bathroom, trying to sneak a cigarette and snooping in the bedroom. This walk-through will show you where you need to place the bar and food stations and where you need to create nooks for conversation or open areas for dancing. Looking at your space through the eyes of a guest will give you an excellent perspective on where to place your decor and which doors to keep closed.

You can pull out all the stops and rent backdrops, plants and props from theatre companies and prop houses to create a complete fantasy world, dressing the wait staff to complete the illusion. Or you can simply use candles, flowers and a couple of bolts of colourful fabric for an inexpensive but transformative effect. Lighting, especially candles, twinkle lights or projected images, can define a mood. Colour works well as a theme. In the opulent '80s, the popular black-and-white theme meant diamonds, ermine and tuxedos. Now, colours of spiritual enlightenment and exoticism, such as saffron or lime, are popular.

Design the bar, food stations and serving trays with function in mind. Your bartender will need enough light and space to mix and serve drinks efficiently. The serving trays need to be easy to pass and refill with fun but unfussy decorations. A freshly cut flower on a big ti leaf is simple and beautiful and fits most themes.

C. Design the Music

Design the soundtrack of your party. If your party has a strong theme, the music can reinforce it, but never let esoterica override the spirit of a good party. The soundtrack from *Farinelli* may be in marvellous taste and suit your Baroque Italian theme perfectly, but to some guests, it will be sinus-numbing and it might not get your party started. Plan the music to build the mood as your evening progresses. For the first hour, as guests are arriving, you want to put them at ease. The music should be light and breezy as people begin to mingle. Once everyone is conversing and the air has filled with laughter and clinking crystal, the music can progress to something louder and more energetic. At the height of the party, put on the dance discs. Even if you don't have room for dancing, the rhythms add another level of ebullience. Then, before the neighbours start citing noise bylaws, put on some quiet, sentimental music. Everyone, remembering they have a home, will depart.

Music has a powerful effect on people, evoking emotion, nostalgia, excitement or calm, and great music can make or break your party. To help you manage your musical mood swings, get a music-savvy friend to compile a list of music designed for your party.

Write down your wish lists, then tweak your plans according to your ability and resources (enlist friends to help, cut the guest list, take out a loan). Be realistic. It's better to do a few things brilliantly and be a relaxed host than to have a lot of half-baked bits and a bad hairdo. Nobody will miss the empanada-twirling trapeze artist if the Margaritas are great. Most of all, you want to be able to enjoy your own party. As the host, you are the social glue that holds the guest list together and you are needed to make introductions, start conversations and smooth over rivalries.

CHECKLIST OF PARTY SUPPLIES:

Disposables to buy:
- Cocktail napkins
- Toothpicks and skewers
- Candles
- Mini hand soaps for bathroom

To rent from a party supply rental house:
- Glasses
- Punchbowl
- Plates, cutlery, cups and saucers
- Cream pitcher, milk pitcher, sugar bowl, artificial sweetener dish
- Serving trays and dishes
- Cake trays
- 25-cup coffee percolator
- Ashtrays
- Votive candle holders
- Rolling rack for coats
- Dinner napkins to dress wine bottles
- Tablecloths
- Cocktail tables and bar stools
- Folding tables for work or service

To rent from an event tent company:
- Tent for the yard
- Draping and lighting for tent
- Dance floor to cover the pool
- Outdoor heaters
- Portable toilets

To hire or commandeer:
- Wait staff (one per 20)
- Bartenders (one per 30)
- Kitchen helpers (one per 20)
- Car jockeys (two per 20)
- Disc jockey

DO THE DESIGNER WALK-THROUGH

An indispensable tool in party planning is the "walk-through." Physically go through the venue and imagine each aspect of the event through your guests' eyes. This will tell you how to design the space to enable the party to flow.

- *The party house:* Are your street number and entrance easy to see at night? Mark your home in a way that reinforces your theme. Romantic evening? Light the walkway with votive candles. Film-shoot theme? Mark your driveway with location pylons. Cheerful ribbons tied to the doorknob of your condominium can put guests at ease even before they step inside.
- *The entrance:* Everybody feels great when they get a big welcome from the host. But they also need to have their coats taken and will benefit greatly from a welcome drink. These needs will become increasingly difficult for the solo host to meet as more guests arrive. So it's a good idea to get a bit of help here. Several designated co-hosts, hired on the buddy plan (pro bono), can make a big difference in the crucial first moments when a party-goer's fight-or-flight instincts are on orange alert.
- *The party room:* This is usually the living room. It needs to be invitingly open with just a few seating areas. That means moving out as much furniture as possible. The main pleasure of a cocktail party is mixing and meeting many people. Movement is the medium. If there is too much seating, guests will park themselves in comfy chairs next to their friends and stay there all evening. Think about putting a punch-and-wine bar at the far end of the room and a food station midway, to tempt your guests to cross the floor. The farther they are from the front door, the deeper they are, psychologically, into your party.
- *The kitchen:* Everyone is drawn to the kitchen, but unless you need more party space, close off the kitchen as a work area. You don't want to accidentally drop a pan of hot tarts on a guest as he gropes for his Manhattan. Closing off the area is not an option in the open floor plan featured in most condominiums, where, happily, the open kitchen works beautifully as a bar. Of course, you need kitchen space to heat food and fill platters, so keep guests out of the inner work area with a well-placed tea cart or machete.
- *Secondary rooms:* More food stations can go in the dining room and, if you can put the dining table and chairs in storage, you will gain valuable floor space for impromptu dancing. You may want the music louder here, but keep it below conversation level. Close off all the other rooms or floors you want to keep private.
- *The bathroom:* Most guests will eventually find themselves looking in your powder room mirror. If possible, dim the lighting. Or put in pink light bulbs to make the light in the powder room as flattering as possible. When people feel beautiful, they have a better time.

Flowers, small soaps, fingertip towels and guest hand lotion are nice touches. Necessary touches: an extra roll of toilet paper and a wastepaper basket.

- *The balcony, deck or yard:* Except in the very coldest months of winter, any outdoor space can be used as a barbecue station. And even during an ice storm, smokers will brave the outdoors, so you may want to rent an outdoor gas heater and, with a few chairs and side tables, create an outdoor extension to your party space. We know a very gracious New Year's party hostess who draped several of her vintage fur coats and Hudson's Bay blankets over chairs on the balcony for the comfort of her smoking guests.

If you are using your yard and covering the pool or tennis court to create the main party space, you will want to rent a tent, no matter what Ms. Meteorology says. Rental tents are now available with clear plastic roofs that give the illusion of open sky and, when decorated with swags of fabric and twinkle lights, create a magical and weatherproof atmosphere.

To get that South Beach chic, rent sleek white loveseats and side tables and place them in the tent under swags of white organza. It's a perversion of style that indoor things, like sofas and sheers, look fabulous outside and outdoor things, like trees and fountains, look cool inside.

BAR SET-UP PER 25 GUESTS

1 bartender
one 6 to 8-foot table or counter for service
one 3-foot shelf or cart for bottles, glasses
1 or 2 shakers and strainers
1 cocktail mixing spoon
2 large pitchers for mixing large batches
1 small pitcher for water
Measures for 1-oz and 1½-oz shots
1 ice bucket and tongs
1 paring knife and small cutting board
1 muddler (optional)
1 bottle opener and corkscrew
1 lemon juicer or reamer
4 bar towels
1 sink or "slop" tub for discarded ice, peels, etc.
1 blender (if required)
1 electrical outlet for blender
2 tubs for 5 to 10 bags of ice
Bowls for lemon wedges, lime wedges, olives, twists and other garnishes
Plates of rimming sugar and salt (if required)
Fridge space for chilling wine, beer, soda and fruit juices or insulated coolers with ice
Task lighting if party room is to be dark

GLASS REQUIREMENTS PER 25 GUESTS

GLASS	2-HOUR RECEPTION	5-HOUR COCKTAIL SUPPER PARTY
Martini glasses	24	60
Double old-fashioned	12	48
Highball/water/beer	24	60
Wine	48	60

Optional: Special menus may require Champagne flutes, Pilsner glasses, punch glasses, shooter glasses, sling glasses or Margarita glasses

DISASTER RELIEF

Some common problems and how to fix them:

- Too little food? Get takeout pizza, dim sum and/or sushi delivered to the back door.
- Too little drink? Make an unusual punch.
- Toilet backed up? Immediately shut off the water supply to the tank using the little knob on the pipe that comes out of the floor right next to the toilet bowl. (If you can't remember which way to turn the knob, the universal rule is righty tighty; lefty loosey.) Stay calm and pretend your house is not falling apart, while you quietly seek out a guest with plumbing acumen.
- Hoisin on your silk tie? Scrape off as much as possible, then lick off the rest (honestly—the enzymes in saliva will break down proteins and release stains without shrinking sensitive fabric).
- Candle wax on the sofa? Soften chunks of wax with a hair dryer, scrape off as much as possible with a credit card, cover with paper towel and heat with an iron, changing the paper towel as it wicks off the melting wax.
- Sangria on your suit? Using a clean absorbent cloth, dab on hydrogen peroxide mixed with equal parts of Woolite.
- Red wine on the Flokati rug? Cover the area thickly with salt or baking soda to soak out the wine, leave to dry and vacuum in the morning. Rinse out any remaining stains by blotting with soda water.
- Broken glass on the floor? Sweep up the large pieces, then blot up any splinters and shards with a wet paper towel.
- Stove malfunctioning? Fire up the barbecue, a crockpot or your George Foreman grill, or call a party-rental company for a portable.
- Fridge too full? Cool bottles in an ice-filled bathtub or washing machine or in a nearby snowbank. Slip each wine bottle into a plastic bag first, so the label doesn't soak off.
- Fire on the range? Douse the area with baking soda or salt.
- Drunken guests want to drive home? Have cards printed with taxi numbers and your address and stick them by the phone.

THE MOOD RULES

1. Place the bar and food stations well apart (and far away from the entrance) to minimize crowding and encourage circulation.
2. Minimize seating. Cocktail parties are about mingling and mixing. Provide places for your guests to perch, lean, slouch and generally show off their outfits, but don't make the seating too cozy. Once a guest sinks into a comfy chair, he or she is out of circulation.
3. Decorate above eye level. Lighting, flowers or fabric overhead can be enjoyed by everyone, even in a standing-room-only crowd.
4. Do a sound check. Select the music, the volume and the placement of your speakers with respect to the mood you want to create throughout the evening. Levels of conversation change as the party energy grows, and well-chosen music will guide and enhance the progress of the evening.
5. Test the party lighting. Next to music, lighting is the most influential aspect of creating mood. Do a pre-party "light check" at a parallel time to be sure you're creating the right sparkle and glow.
6. Keep your guests' safety in mind. Obviously, fabric with candles can be a peril, but there are even trickier combinations to be mindful of—anyone who wants to put bubble machines on the dance floor has never got a concussion from doing the samba on soap-bubble film.
7. Provide conversation pieces. Food and drink are often conversation starters and closers. You can help conversation flow even more by providing a few interesting props such as disposable cameras for playing paparazzi.

THE FOOD RULES

1. Plan a menu that's within your comfort range. No ice cream parties in Tongatapu if you don't have a freezer and a jet.
2. Choose menu items that are seasonal. Produce in season is better and often less expensive.
3. Balance menu items. But remember it is a party, so vegetarian and high-protein selections need to be balanced by super-rich, artery-choking treats.
4. Calculate quantities generously. Running out of food and drink can have you panicking in the last hour of your event, when you should be partying. Most leftover food can be frozen, and unopened liquor can usually be returned to the store as long as the label is pristine.
5. Flavour-match your drinks. Serve cocktails and wine whose flavours complement those of the food. And offer lots of iced water garnished with fresh mint or citrus twists.
6. Get ahead. You can make most things ahead of time, since many items hold well in the refrigerator or freezer. But consider your storage space. Bags of ice can be picked up at the last minute, leaving the freezer clear for your homemade goodies.
7. Get help. Either hired or conscripted, extra help will make all the difference to everyone's enjoyment. You don't have to hire professionals: a neighbour's daughter or a helpful nephew won't cost you much.

CINQ À SEPT

Casanova's Seduction for 2

In the affairs and the art of the heart, a lot can be learned from history. For example, one might leap to the conclusion that it would be easy to seduce a man as debauched as Casanova. But any girl who has fought through a busload of cheerleaders to kiss the quarterback knows better, and might take this page from the past.

In the eighteenth century, Casanova was famously seduced by a nun who invited him to meet her, masked and alone, at her private apartment in Venice. More skilled in seduction than her status as a vestal might suggest, she served a light but extravagant meal: light, to lessen demands on the blood, and extravagant, to encourage an atmosphere of excess. Each course was held on warming trays so as not to press the timing of dinner against the timing of desire. The drinks were chosen for their gentle effect and for the sensuousness involved in their preparation and presentation. She decorated the apartment with richly textured fabrics and flattering candlelight and scented the air with roses. The effect on Casanova lasted all his life. We have much to learn from nuns.

MENU FOR AN EVENING OF
SMALL PLATES AND COCKTAILS

OYSTERS GRATINÉES *with* CREAMY LEMON SAUCE

PROSCIUTTO *and* CHÈVRE-STUFFED FIGS *with* WALNUTS *and* BALSAMIC HONEY DRIZZLE

ROMEO *and* JULIENNE RADICCHIO

CHOCOLATE FONDUE *for* TWO

MIDNIGHT SNACK

GRILLED LOBSTER *and* CHEESE SANDWICHES

MORNING AFTER

BRIE STRATA *with* MAPLE-CINNAMON SAUSAGES

COCKTAILS

BLACK VELVET

MARTINI BAR

FRENCH KISS MARTINI

FRESH FIG MARTINI

SETTING THE SCENE

DECOR IDEAS

For seduction, candlelight is essential, but be mindful of fire hazards. Absolutely do not leave lit candles unattended. Blowing out candles can be very sexy anyway. Hold your hand with the flat of your palm facing you and directly behind the flame. Then you don't have to blow as hard to extinguish the flame and you won't splash hot wax on your date…unless you want to.

Even if your look is minimalist, offer comfort and sensuality by draping chenille throws on your chairs and big, soft cushions on the sofa. Cover your table for two with a richly textured cloth and keep the Champagne bottle in a standing bucket so you can take it from table to sofa as the evening progresses.

Flowers add not only their great visual beauty, but their subtle perfume as well. Be wary of some lilies, which can smell like onions because they come from the same family. Hyacinth, as well, can be overpowering. The scent of lavender has an aphrodisiac effect but is cloying and, if used, should be mixed with roses, carnations and such herbs as sage and lemon balm.

SMELLS LIKE TEEN SPIRIT

Some important aromas for seduction are sage, cinnamon, vanilla and licorice. Serious aromaphiles will also recommend ambergris, vetiver, ylang ylang, bergamot, sandalwood and that old hippie favourite, patchouli. Others, like Napoleon, swear by sweat alone, saying that perfumes mask the powerfully attractive pheromones that we all emit naturally.

CANDLE TIPS

A little water in the bottom of votive holders makes them easy to clean when the votive has burned away.

CINQ À SEPT SEDUCTION

Parisians have always conducted their affairs with enviable élan. The proof of their love is in their language. Because men habitually visited their mistresses after work and before going home, the romantic interlude was referred to as *cinq à sept*. Now, perhaps due to spouse-busting reality TV detectives, long office hours and a general decline in quality of life, the term *cinq à sept* is used to describe the cocktail hour, where the fun centres on slipping into bars, not beds.

MUSIC PICKS

CBC TV's George Stroumboulopoulos started his career of cool in rock radio, moved quickly to talk radio, then to Citytv. There, at MuchMusic, he created a unique style of news delivery and was wooed away by CBC Newsworld. Now, he's in bedrooms across the nation every night—albeit on the television—with his program on current events, *The Hour*. Knowing a thing or two about music and mates, he has made these music suggestions:

"Seduction music used to be Sade and Barry White records," he says. "While the intention today is the same, the music has definitely changed. To get it right, you have to measure the depth of your intentions with the time of day and the one you are with. Happy and light, or dark and moody."

Here are his annotated picks for seductive albums:

- Massive Attack, *Mezzanine* (Virgin): This one starts so quickly and so seriously that you almost need to skip foreplay just to keep up.
- Otis Redding, *Otis Blue: Otis Redding Sings Soul* (Atco): It sounds like he wrote this for the person you are hoping to seduce.
- The Doves, *The Last Broadcast* (Heavenly): This is the record for very moody seductive moments.
- Air, *The Virgin Suicides Soundtrack* (Astralwerks): Another very moody seduction disc.
- Nick Drake, *Five Leaves Left* (Hannibal): God almighty! This is great for late, late night or late afternoon in the fall.
- Spiritualized, *Royal Albert Hall Live* (Arista): A double album, so be prepared.

SZABO'S WINE ALTERNATIVES

COUNTLESS LEGENDS of great love have been inspired by the elixirs of Bacchus and Dionysus. Your wine choice tonight will be the ultimate symbol of your intentions, and the menu here lends itself perfectly to all the most seductive of wines. If you serve them in the right succession, and in moderation, the overall effect will be irresistible.

Champagne, of course, is *de rigueur*. But not just any Champagne. This occasion calls for rosé; glittering, shimmering in the candlelight, it is a reflection of love itself. Have the bottle chilling in a bucket of ice water, with a fresh white linen towel draped over top. Sensually towel off the bottle before serving to show your caring, sensitive side, and serve alongside the gratinéed oysters for a decadent and perfectly seductive match. The aromas of freshly toasted bread and biscuits found in fine vintage rosé are also known to have an aphrodisiac effect, appealing perhaps to our yearning for bread itself, the symbol of life. Be sure to have at least a couple of bottles of Champagne at the ready. It makes for an ideal thirst quencher with the midnight lobster snack and is also perfect for toasting *le grand amour* at breakfast.

Speaking of love, if time is of the essence, waste none and pull out the Saint Amour from France's Beaujolais region. Slightly chilled, this soft, fruity red has an unmistakable come-hither appeal and versatility with food, not to mention a clear message.

As the soirée progresses, it is time for a direct assault on the most primeval senses. Select a wine that appeals to our basic instincts: smooth, lusty, well-aged reds whose aromas have evolved from the frivolous fruitiness of youth into the deep, sensual and meaningful scents of Mother Earth: mushroom, truffle, forest floor, incense, roasted meat, dried violets and roses. Aged wine from most classic regions will do, but Casanova's choice is undoubtedly red Burgundy, and in particular the silky wines of Chambolle-Musigny, which are considered the most seductive in the region. These are pricey wines, but the occasion, you hope, is worth it. The names of the vineyards in this village are also the most romantic in the world. Look for 5-plus year-old examples from the premier cru Les Charmes, or more evocative yet, *Les Amoureuses* ("the lovers") for a master stroke of seduction. The wine will surrender softly into the folds of the tangy-sweet chèvre-fig combination, while mirroring the complex earthy-resinous flavour of the balsamic drizzle.

Note the names of Burgundian wines: pass on the vineyard called Clos de Tart to avoid any misunderstanding, as well as Chapelle-Chambertin, unless you are hoping for more than a mere *cinq à sept*.

If the deal is not yet sealed, you have a last resort: the stickies. The chocolate fondue for two yearns for a sweet companion, at least as intense and bittersweet as the chocolate itself. Wines made from grapes raised in the hot Mediterranean sun yield the right amount of mouth-filling richness, such as the exotic Muscats of Samos or Patras in Greece, or a nutty sweet Pedro Jimenez sherry from southern Spain. An excellent alternative would be the legendary late-harvest, "nobly rotten" *tokaji aszú* wine of Hungary, with a history as romantic as the one you are creating tonight. It is filled with orange marmalade, dried apricot and crème brûlée flavours intimately linked with refreshing acidity sure to perk up the senses.

GET AHEAD SCHEDULE

2 MONTHS BEFORE

- Have three dates with the person to make sure you want to go to all this trouble.

3 DAYS BEFORE

- Infuse vodka for FRESH FIG MARTINIS.

2 DAYS BEFORE

- Organize the decor, get fresh flowers to arrange in vases and rose petals to drift in the bath or around the candles.
- Check the time and lighting. The sun sets late on midsummer nights and you don't want candles blazing if it's light outside.

1 DAY BEFORE

- Prepare CHOCOLATE FONDUE, cover and store in a cool place.
- Prepare BRIE STRATA WITH MAPLE-CINNAMON SAUSAGES, cover and refrigerate.
- Make PINK PEPPERCORN SHERRY DRESSING for ROMEO AND JULIENNE RADICCHIO.

THE MORNING OF

- Make ROMEO AND JULIENNE RADICCHIO, wrap and refrigerate.
- Poach lobster for GRILLED LOBSTER AND CHEESE SANDWICHES.
- Prepare the spinach and CREAMY LEMON SAUCE for OYSTERS GRATINÉES.
- Make PROSCIUTTO AND CHÈVRE-STUFFED FIGS, wrap and refrigerate.
- Make BALSAMIC HONEY DRIZZLE for CHÈVRE-STUFFED FIGS.
- Put CHOCOLATE FONDUE and strawberries in serving dishes, cover and set aside in a cool place.
- Chill Champagne and beer.

2 HOURS BEFORE

- Assemble GRILLED LOBSTER AND CHEESE SANDWICHES but do not grill. Wrap and refrigerate.
- Prepare pineapple purée for FRENCH KISS.
- Set up the bar with ingredients, glassware and equipment for cocktails.
- Set the table with small plates, cutlery, napkins. Place the platters for OYSTERS GRATINÉES and CHÈVRE-STUFFED FIGS.

1 HOUR BEFORE

- Arrange CHÈVRE-STUFFED FIGS on a serving platter, drizzle and place on the table.
- Have a little disco nap; you're going to be up all night.

JUST BEFORE

- Assemble OYSTERS GRATINÉES on a broiling pan.
- Turn off your telephones, turn down the lights and turn on the music.

Oysters Gratinées with Creamy Lemon Sauce

Be careful not to shuck the oysters any more than 2 hours before serving. (For more on oysters, see pages 43–45.) The reserved oyster liquor lends a hint of brine to sautéed spinach, which makes a buttery bed for oysters blanketed in lemon sauce. Serve these oysters in a bed of rock salt placed on a platter.

CREAMY LEMON SAUCE

½ cup butter

3 egg yolks, room temperature

2 Tbsp lemon juice

pinch of cayenne pepper

OYSTERS GRATINÉES

1 cup rock salt for platter (optional)

12 meaty oysters, shucked, ¼ cup oyster liquor reserved

2 Tbsp butter

3 shallots, diced

one 10-oz package spinach, stems removed, washed and dried

⅛ tsp nutmeg

CREAMY LEMON SAUCE: In a small saucepan on medium-high heat, melt butter until hot and bubbling. Place egg yolks, lemon juice and cayenne in a blender or food processor and blend for 3 seconds. Remove the lid, scrape down the sides and blend for another 3 seconds. With the motor on high, pour hot butter over the egg mixture in a steady stream (takes about 30 seconds). The sauce should be smooth and well combined. If it is not, blend for another 5 seconds on high.

OYSTERS GRATINÉES: Preheat the oven broiler. Line a baking sheet with crinkled aluminum foil. Spread a serving platter with rock salt to a depth of ½ inch.

Remove oysters from their shells (page 44), reserving the shells and any additional oyster liquor. Discard any shell fragments remaining on the oysters, then transfer oysters to a bowl. Arrange the bottom (cupped) halves of the oyster shells on the baking sheet.

In a large sauté pan on medium heat, melt butter until foaming subsides. Add shallots and cook until soft and translucent, 2 to 3 minutes. Add spinach and cover pan, allowing spinach to wilt for about 2 minutes. Stir nutmeg and ¼ cup of the reserved oyster liquor into the spinach-shallot mixture. Cook spinach, uncovered, stirring gently, until liquid is absorbed, 3 to 4 minutes.

Divide the spinach mixture evenly among the oyster shells and top each with an oyster. Spread ½ Tbsp of creamy lemon sauce over each oyster. Broil oysters 6 inches from the heat for 5 to 7 minutes, or until brown and bubbling. Transfer oysters on their half shells to the platter, arranging them in the salt. Serve immediately or while warm.

Makes 12 oysters

APHRODISIACS

Volumes have been written on the aphrodisiac effects of certain foods. Oysters, shad roe and asparagus are perennially cited, but the only positive effect we have noticed from "known aphrodisiacs" is that we can wash the dinner dishes faster after eating chocolates. Scent tends to have a greater effect on the libido than taste, and it has been clinically proven that, on average, the smell of lavender combined with pumpkin pie will increase penile blood flow by about 40 per cent. The smell of donuts combined with cola has also been shown to be very sexually compelling to men, as is the aroma of grilling meat. Draw your own conclusions.

French Kiss Martini

Vanilla vodka gives this martini its heady lushness. It's readily available, but you can make your own by infusing 2 whole vanilla beans, split lengthwise, in 8 oz of vodka in a glass jar with a tight-fitting lid. After a week, strain out the vanilla beans. The vodka is ready to mix into martinis.

PINEAPPLE PRE-MIX
¼ large ripe pineapple, peeled, cored, in 1-inch chunks
½ cup frozen pineapple concentrate, thawed

MARTINI
8 ice cubes or 1 cup crushed ice
4 to 8 oz vanilla vodka
1 to 2 oz Chambord
GLASSWARE: two 10-oz martini glasses

PINEAPPLE PRE-MIX: Place pineapple chunks and concentrate in a blender, and blend until smooth. There will be enough purée to make 4 drinks.

TO SERVE: For 2 drinks, fill glasses with ice and set aside to chill. Place ice cubes (or crushed ice), 4 oz pineapple pre-mix and 4 oz vanilla vodka in a blender, and process just until thick and smooth. Discard ice from glasses and pour in blended mixture. Place Chambord into a shot glass with a spout, and, using ½ oz for each drink, slowly drizzle a heart shape on top of the blended mixture. Serve immediately.

Makes two to four 10-oz drinks

Fresh Fig Martini

The fig-infused vodka can be made up to a week in advance and kept in the freezer until you are ready to mix it into this velvety drink.

FIG-INFUSED VODKA
4 fresh black figs, washed and quartered
½ bottle (375 mL/13 oz) vodka

FIG MARTINI
½ oz plum wine
2 sprigs of fresh mint, for garnish
4 port-preserved cherries, for garnish (optional) (page 18)
GLASSWARE: two 8-oz martini glasses

FIG-INFUSED VODKA: Place figs in a large glass jar with a lid. Add vodka, then seal tightly. Refrigerate for 3 days, stirring occasionally. The vodka will turn a lovely mauve colour. Strain the vodka through a fine-mesh sieve. Discard the figs. Refrigerate or freeze fig-infused vodka until ready to use. There will be enough to make 4 drinks.

FIG MARTINI: For 2 drinks, fill two glasses with crushed ice and set aside to chill. Half-fill a shaker with crushed ice. Measure in 5 oz fig-infused vodka and ½ oz plum wine. Cover and shake vigorously until the shaker is very cold to the touch and beads of condensation form on the sides. Discard ice from the glasses, strain in the mixture and garnish with sprigs of mint or cherries preserved in port.

Makes two to four 5½-oz drinks

PROSCIUTTO *and* CHÈVRE-STUFFED FIGS *with* WALNUTS AND BALSAMIC HONEY DRIZZLE

Use a soft, white unripened goat cheese for the stuffing, or be more daring and use a chèvre that is slightly more aged and whose fragrance hints at fecundity.

BALSAMIC HONEY DRIZZLE

4 Tbsp honey	2 Tbsp balsamic vinegar

STUFFED FIGS

2 Tbsp chèvre	8 to 12 paper-thin slices prosciutto
2 tsp whipping cream (35%)	2 Tbsp crumbled walnuts, toasted, or
4 large fresh figs	Spiced Asian Walnuts (page 49)

BALSAMIC HONEY DRIZZLE: Using a whisk, mix together honey and balsamic vinegar in a small bowl until smooth. Set aside.

STUFFED FIGS: Using a fork, mix chèvre with whipping cream in a small bowl until smooth. Using a sharp knife, cut an × into the top of each fig, cutting about two-thirds down into the fruit. Spoon one-quarter of the chèvre mixture into each fig opening, allowing some to spill over the top. Fold prosciutto slices in half lengthwise. Using 2 or 3 folded slices of prosciutto for each fig, wind them loosely around the bottom half of each fig. Arrange prosciutto-wrapped figs on a platter. Sprinkle with walnuts. Figs can be made ahead to this point, covered in plastic wrap and refrigerated.

An hour before serving, allow figs to come to room temperature. Serve, with balsamic honey drizzle in a small bowl on the side. Using a small spoon, drizzle figs suggestively when serving.

Serves 2

ROMEO *and* JULIENNE RADICCHIO

Cupped in individual edible bowls, this colourful salad of julienned vegetables is a perfectly charming palate opener.

PINK PEPPERCORN SHERRY DRESSING

½ cup olive oil

¼ cup sherry vinegar

½ tsp grated orange zest

¼ tsp cinnamon

1 tsp pink peppercorns, slightly bruised

½ tsp salt

RADICCHIO SALAD

1 head radicchio (with deeply cupped outer leaves)

1 cup mixed baby greens

6 snow peas, in 1⁄16 × 2-inch julienne

¼ red bell pepper, in 1⁄16 × 2-inch julienne

½ small carrot, in 1⁄16 × 2-inch julienne

12 sprigs chervil or cilantro, washed, stems removed

PINK PEPPERCORN SHERRY DRESSING: Place oil, vinegar, orange zest, cinnamon, peppercorns and salt in a small glass jar with a lid. Tightly seal the lid and shake well. Allow to rest for 6 to 24 hours before serving.

Makes 3/4 cup

RADICCHIO SALAD: Carefully remove outer leaves from radicchio. Select 2 leaves that are unblemished and bowl-shaped. Wash and pat dry with paper towels, then arrange the 2 leaves on a serving platter and set aside.

Shred radicchio leaves into strips ⅛ inch by 2 inches until you have ½ cup, and place in a medium bowl. Toss in mixed baby greens, then divide evenly between the radicchio "bowls" on the serving platter.

In a small bowl, combine snow peas, bell pepper and carrot. Divide evenly between radicchio bowls.

Just before serving, drizzle salad with dressing, making sure to spoon pink peppercorns over each. Garnish with chervil (or cilantro).

Serves 2

Chocolate Fondue for Two

Use the best-quality chocolate, such as Valrhona or Callebaut, and the biggest, sweetest berries. Make the chocolate mixture up to 1 day ahead and store it in a cool place. Reheat on medium power in microwave until warm and runny.

8 oz semi-sweet chocolate, chopped

½ cup honey

1 cup whipping cream (35%)

1 tsp vanilla extract

12 large strawberries with stems, washed but unhulled

Place a fondue pot or a pretty heatproof bowl on a large round platter.

In a heatproof bowl set over a pan of simmering water, melt together chocolate and honey. Remove from the heat and stir in cream and vanilla.

Transfer warm chocolate sauce to the fondue pot (or bowl). Arrange strawberries around the pot, ready to dip in the warm sauce. Serve immediately.

Makes 2 cups of chocolate fondue

BLACK VELVET

The perfect sexy after-sex beverage—Champagne for her and beer for him, all bubbled together.

8 oz well-chilled stout (such as Guinness)

8 oz well-chilled Champagne

GLASSWARE: two Champagne flutes

Half-fill each flute with stout. When the head subsides, gently top up with Champagne. Serve immediately.

Makes two 8-oz drinks

Grilled Lobster and Cheese Sandwiches

When midnight cravings move to the munchies, this is just the right blend of comfort food and luxury. Make these sandwiches ahead and store them, covered in plastic wrap, for up to 6 hours.

6 slices soft white bread (such as challah, French or Italian), ¾ inch thick	1½ lbs cooked lobster meat, thinly sliced (page 88)
3 to 4 Tbsp butter, softened, for spreading	6 oz medium Cheddar cheese, in ¼-inch slices

Preheat a grill pan, heavy-bottomed sauté pan or sandwich maker to medium heat. Place bread slices on a clean, dry work surface and butter both sides. Divide lobster meat into three equal portions and mound on three of the buttered bread slices. Season to taste with salt and pepper and top with the Cheddar. Top each sandwich with another slice of buttered bread. Press gently on each sandwich.

If using a grill pan or a sauté pan, place a sandwich on the hot pan and grill, covered with a tightly fitting pot lid or pressing gently with a spatula, for 2 to 3 minutes. Turn over the sandwich and cook for another 2 to 3 minutes, or until cheese melts, ingredients adhere and both sides are golden. If using a sandwich maker, toast sandwich until cheese is melted and bread is golden, about 5 minutes.

Makes 3 sandwiches

THE DELICATE ART OF LOBSTERCIDE

THE ADVICE FROM OUR Haligonian lobster man is unequivocal: the lobster must be killed quickly, without struggle and just before cooking, so the meat remains tender. His method is to sever the spinal cord by firmly inserting the point of a knife into the lobster in the joint where the shell of the head ends and that of the thorax begins. Even describing this makes us tense, so he had to oblige us with another method. For better or for wusses, here it is:

Bring a big pot of water to a full boil. Grasp the victim from the back, holding the tail curled under the body. This will keep her—we hope you got female lobsters because they are sweeter and fatter—from flexing her tail up, thus tensing and toughening the muscle. Plunge the creature head first into the roiling waters. This head-first business ensures instant death. Slap on the lid and mutter apologies for being at the top of the food chain. Reduce the heat to low and simmer. A 1½-lb lobster will take about 10 minutes to cook fully.

You can also try lobster-lulling. This is a magical Vulcan pinch-like technique that you can use if you are at all squeamish about life-death struggles with crustaceans. Simply rub the lobster on the back of the head, hard and quickly, with your index finger. Use a back-and-forth movement— as if you were trying to remove a stubborn spot—until the lobster goes completely limp. This should take only 5 to 10 seconds. Toss the lobster into a waiting pot of boiling water before she wakes up. Cover the pot and simmer until cooked:

10 minutes for a 1½-pounder and 15 minutes for a 2-pounder. Remove lobster and cool.

Allow cooked lobster to rest and cool so the juices are reabsorbed into the flesh. Twist the front claws, including the knuckles, to remove them from the body. Set aside. Twist the tail and pull it away from the upper body. Set aside. The entire upper body can be discarded, although many connoisseurs love the green tomalley, or liver, which can be scooped out and incorporated into sauces or bisques. To locate this delicacy, pull the upper shell away from the lower carapace and legs to reveal the pale green mass behind the head sac.

To remove the meat from the tail, firmly hold the tail—with the underside up—on a cutting board and, using the point of a sharp chef's knife, slice through the thin whitish shell on both sides where it is joined to the red upper shell. Using your fingers, wriggle the meat out in one piece. There may be a thin black vein in the tail, which should be removed and discarded. A thick red vein is delicious roe and can be eaten.

To remove the meat from the claws and knuckles, use a nutcracker to crack them in several places. Pry off the shell and gently work the meat out with your fingers. Smaller bits of meat in the knuckles can be removed with a nut pick or an oyster fork.

One 1½-lb lobster will yield about 1 cup of lobster meat, if you don't eat too many of the juicy bits while you are picking out the shells.

BRIE STRATA *with*
MAPLE-CINNAMON SAUSAGES

From ancient times, cinnamon has held sway as the spice of resurrection. The mythical phoenix burned, then rose again from cinnamon ashes. Pharaohs and saints were embalmed in cinnamon oil to ensure a second coming. It is in this spirit that we offer you this spice-laced breakfast—more as a wish than as a recipe.

6 slices panettone (or challah or brioche), ½-inch thick	2 Tbsp maple syrup
	1 tsp cinnamon
2 breakfast sausages, cooked, in 1-inch chunks	¼ cup milk
	¼ cup whipping cream (35%)
1 baking apple, peeled, cored and sliced	2 eggs
6 oz Brie, in 1-inch chunks	¼ tsp salt
½ cup pecans, roughly chopped	

Lightly butter the bottom and sides of two 1-cup soufflé dishes. Place one slice of panettone (or challah or brioche) in the bottom of each dish. Divide sausage between the dishes, then top with apple. Cover each strata with a second slice of panettone (or challah or brioche), then top with Brie and pecans. Drizzle strata with syrup and sprinkle with cinnamon, then top with the last slices of panettone (or challah or brioche).

In a small mixing bowl, combine milk, cream, eggs and salt and whisk together until well blended. Carefully pour half of the egg mixture into each dish. The liquid should fill the dish to ¼ inch from the lip. Refrigerate overnight.

Forty-five minutes before you wish to eat, preheat the oven to 325°F. Bake the strata for 20 minutes, or until puffy and golden. Allow strata to rest for 15 to 20 minutes before serving.

Makes 2 strata

GIRLS' POKER NIGHT

light bites for 5

Who's cheating? You're bluffing. She's out! And that's just the gossip—the card playing is even more deadly. Gambling and girl talk is a dangerous mix, no doubt. That's why it's so much fun.

You won't want to stop the game when chips and quips are flying. Not even for a snack. That same reluctance to leave the gambling table was what inspired the Earl of Sandwich to invent his eponymous handheld lunch. That was more than three centuries ago and the sandwich is still the best snack to serve on Poker Night.

We've designed a menu of finger foods that won't mark the cards and is easy to munch on while you count your chips. For the dining comfort of your card sharkettes, we suggest portioning food onto personal trays and pre-mixing cocktails in pitchers, ready to pour. The menu includes a tray of mini-jello shots to keep on hand to celebrate frequent victories and a box full of easy homemade candies to serve for dessert.

MENU FOR AN EVENING OF GIRL DRINKS, GREAT HANDS AND FINGER FOODS

POKER MIX SANDWICHES

SHRIMP-STUFFED EGGS

SKINNY DIP *with* CRUDITÉS

PESTO PARMESAN PALMIERS

CANDY BOX: CARAMEL NUT CLUSTERS, ESPRESSO FUDGE,
FLUFFY HOMEMADE MARSHMALLOWS

COFFEE *and* TEA

COCKTAILS

PINK PUSSYCATS

GRASSHOPPER SHOTS *in* CHOCOLATE CUPS

COCONUT MARGARITAS

SETTING THE SCENE

DECOR IDEAS

Here's an excellent reason to call Auntie Macassar and borrow her folding TV tables. They're perfect for placing beside each card player's chair to hold food, drink and those extra aces. Crisply starched, oversized linen napkins make neat "tablecloths" for each little table.

TRAY CHIC

Portions of sandwiches, crudités and crisps can be arranged in shallow Lucite boxes or in Japanese bento boxes so each guest can nosh from her own tray as the card playing allows. Place a little stack of paper cocktail napkins next to each tray for sticky fingers.

MUSIC PICKS

Holly Cole sang with Aaron Davis for the launch of *Dinah's Cupboard Cookbook*, and their trio (with David Piltch) has gone on to global fame. When thinking about Girls' Poker Night, Holly was reminded of the lines, "Let me fall out of the window with confetti in my hair, deal out jacks and better from a blanket by the stair." It's from one of their albums, *Temptation*, which consisted entirely of Tom Waits tunes. She recommends these music picks:

- Holly Cole Trio, *Temptation* (Blue Note)
- The Bee Gees, *Saturday Night Fever* (Polydor)
- Shirley Bassey, *Live at Carnegie Hall* (United Artists)

SZABO'S WINE ALTERNATIVES

BE WARY OF THE wine drinkers at the card table. They may be carefully gauging their alcohol consumption and counting on the clouded judgement that accompanies serious cocktailing in the late innings of the game. Level the playing field by serving serious bad-girl wines with their own measure of potency: youthful, fruity Australian Shiraz or California Zinfandel both have the right measure of smooth drinkability without excessive, distracting tannins, and sweet, succulent ripe fruit that keeps you coming back for more. If dark and swarthy is more your type, bring along Zin's Italian cousin, a Primitivo di Manduria from Apulia in southern Italy.

This evening without the boys may also have a celebratory feel to it. If that's the case, then be sure to serve plenty of vivacious bubbly to toast the freedom to trash talk and wash down the sandwiches. Spanish Cava and Italian Prosecco are two excellent and inexpensive alternatives to Champagne. These are sure to keep the betting lively until the wee hours. Their vibrant acidity and fruitiness also contrast beautifully

with the crispy, salty and nutty pesto Parmesan palmiers, and the sweet briny-rich flavour of the shrimp-stuffed eggs.

When it comes time to pass the candy box, take a cue from the old boys' club and pass around the port, the ideal match for the intense sweetness of fudge and caramelized nuts. Tradition has it that the port—vintage port is most decadent but a late-bottled vintage will do nicely—must be served from a decanter. If any men are present in the room at this time, they should be asked to withdraw until the ritual is finished. It is the responsibility of the host to taste first and begin passing with her left hand, clockwise around the table. Thus the decanter must pass from your left hand to the right hand of the person on your left. Each guest must serve herself. The decanter must never touch or cross the table, or be touched by the hand of a man. The left hand is used for historic reasons: it corresponds to the side of the heart, symbolic of the longing for a heart so often lacking in a man, and it also leaves your right hand free to wield a sword if necessary, or to ante up without missing a hand.

GET AHEAD SCHEDULE

EARLY MORNING

- Wake up with the idea of having the girls over tonight.

MID-MORNING

- Make shopping list and head out to the store.

BEFORE NOON

- Make GRASSHOPPER SHOTS IN CHOCOLATE CUPS.
- Chill sparking wine for PINK PUSSYCATS.
- Pre-mix COCONUT MARGARITAS.
- Make CARAMEL NUT CLUSTERS, ESPRESSO FUDGE, HOMEMADE MARSHMALLOWS.

AFTER LUNCH

- Make PESTO PARMESAN PALMIERS.
- Make SHRIMP-STUFFED EGGS.
- Make SKINNY DIP WITH CRUDITÉS.

2 HOURS AHEAD

- Make POKER MIX SANDWICHES.
- Arrange sweets in candy boxes.

1 HOUR AHEAD

- Set up card table, chairs, TV tables and music.
- Set up bar with blender, ice bucket, glasses, melon baller or sherbet scoop, garnishes and water.

WHEN THE GIRLS ARRIVE

- Pour everyone a COCONUT MARGARITA and arrange POKER MIX SANDWICHES, SHRIMP-STUFFED EGGS, PESTO PARMESAN PALMIERS and SKINNY DIP WITH CRUDITÉS in individual trays.

HALF-TIME STRETCH

- Pour everyone a PINK PUSSYCAT and replenish trays, if necessary.

BEFORE THE LAST GAME

- Pass the GRASSHOPPER SHOTS IN CHOCOLATE CUPS.
- Make coffee and tea.
- Remove sandwich trays and replace with candy boxes.

Poker Mix Sandwiches

Make three each of three different kinds of sandwiches. Cut each sandwich in half and place a half of each variety on each person's tray. Keep the remaining sandwiches on the side for seconds.

When deciding on your sandwich selection, remember that the filling may be thrilling, but love is in the loaf. For really superb sandwiches, you must use handmade-quality breads, such as herb-scented focaccia, chewy wholegrain and sourdough, delicate ficelle or fruit and nut–studded pumpernickel. You can't go wrong with combinations like these:

- **BRIE AND ASPARAGUS:** Grill the asparagus with a drizzle of olive oil and rosemary, then layer on focaccia with Brie.
- **CHICKEN WALDORF SALAD:** Add cubes of raw apple to chicken salad and heap open-faced on slices of multigrain bread.
- **CRAB CROISSANT:** Stuff crab or shrimp salad into a croissant with strips of spicy pancetta bacon.
- **FIGS AND MASCARPONE:** Spread mascarpone or St. André cheese thickly on slices of walnut-raisin bread and top with slices of fresh fig.
- **GRILLED RED BELL PEPPERS AND HUMMUS IN CHAPATTI:** You can make these from all store-bought ingredients. Freshen pre-made hummus by adding toasted pine nuts and a splash of fresh lemon juice.
- **SMOKED SALMON AND CAVIAR CLUB:** Alternate three slices of dense white bread with one layer of smoked salmon and one layer of black caviar. Trim into three fingers and you have a clubhouse sandwich colour-coordinated to the cards.
- **TUNA MUFFULETTA:** Give tuna salad a New Orleans twist by adding chopped olives and mixed pickled vegetables and spoon generously onto a split sesame roll.

CATERER'S TRICK OF THE TRADE

To keep sandwiches fresh and moist, cover them with a paper towel, then spritz with water until the towel is damp but not wet. Cover tightly with plastic wrap and refrigerate until ready to serve.

SHRIMP-STUFFED EGGS

Blessed with shrimp, devilled eggs become divine. And once you try your own homemade mayonnaise, you won't believe what a difference fresh, quality ingredients can make. Be sure to bring your ingredients to room temperature so they emulsify more easily, and for this recipe, you can blend them with a whisk or a hand mixer.

If you add the oil too quickly, your mayonnaise may separate instead of becoming the smooth sauce you were anticipating. If this happens, simply crack one more room-temperature egg yolk into a separate bowl and whip it until frothy. Very slowly add the separated mayonnaise to the whipped yolk until all is incorporated.

HOMEMADE MAYONNAISE

4 large egg yolks	1¾ cups vegetable oil
1 tsp salt	1¾ cups olive oil
white pepper to taste	3 Tbsp white wine vinegar
1 tsp dry mustard	1 to 2 Tbsp lemon juice

STUFFED EGGS

12 large eggs	½ lb frozen baby shrimp, thawed (at least 250 count per lb)
4 Tbsp mayonnaise	
1 tsp chopped fresh dill	12 small sprigs dill weed, for garnish (optional)

HOMEMADE MAYONNAISE: In a medium bowl, whisk egg yolks until frothy. Add salt, pepper and dry mustard and whisk to combine. Add oils, a drop at a time, until the mixture begins to thicken. Add the remaining oil in a steady stream, thinning it occasionally by adding a little of the vinegar. Continue until all oil and vinegar have been incorporated. If mayonnaise is too thick, dilute with a little tepid water. Adjust the seasonings and add lemon juice to taste. Transfer mayonnaise to a sealed jar and refrigerate until needed. Will keep for up to 2 weeks.

STUFFED EGGS: Place eggs in a large pot and cover with cold water. Bring to a boil on medium heat, then turn off the heat and allow eggs to rest in water for 8 minutes. Drain and rinse eggs with cold water.

In a medium bowl, combine mayonnaise and chopped dill. Season with salt and pepper to taste. Set aside 2 Tbsp of this dressing in a small bowl. Add shrimp to the remaining dressing and toss to coat shrimp evenly.

When eggs are completely cool, peel them carefully and discard the shells. (Peeling eggs under running water helps loosen the skins.) Using a paring knife, slice ½ inch off the thicker end of the egg to expose the yolk. Slice ¼ inch off the opposite end, allowing the egg to stand upright, thick end up. Using a small spoon, gently scoop out the cooked yolk, leaving a hollowed white.

Spoon ½ tsp of the reserved dressing into each egg cavity. Top up with dressed shrimp, ensuring there are 12 to 14 baby shrimp per egg. Place any broken shrimp into the bottom of the egg and cover with whole shrimp. Garnish each egg with a sprig of dill weed. Transfer to a serving platter and refrigerate, covered in plastic wrap, until serving time.

Makes 12 stuffed eggs

SKINNY DIP
with CRUDITÉS

Sliced into elegant fingers and served in a large martini or V-shaped glass, raw vegetables become a sophisticated treat.

SKINNY DIP

1 cup plain yogurt	2 Tbsp chopped chives
2 Tbsp chopped flat-leaf parsley	1 clove garlic, minced
2 Tbsp chopped fresh basil leaves	½ tsp Hungarian paprika
2 Tbsp chopped fresh dill	1½ tsp salt
2 Tbsp chopped fresh thyme	¼ tsp cayenne pepper

CRUDITÉS

10 skewers, 6 to 8 inches long	5 stalks asparagus, trimmed to 5-inch lengths, blanched
20 grape cherry tomatoes	
20 baby bocconcini or 5 large bocconcini, quartered	5 broccolini stalks, blanched
	5 celery sticks, each ½ × 5 inches
1 cup Skinny Dip (above) or favourite store-bought dip	10 carrots sticks, each ½ × 5 inches

SKINNY DIP: Combine all ingredients in a small bowl, mixing well. Cover with plastic wrap and refrigerate for at least 2 hours.

Makes 1 cup

CRUDITÉS: On each skewer, thread 2 tomatoes and 2 bocconcini, alternating the red and white.

Place about 2 Tbsp of dip in the bottom of each of 5 martini glasses. Arrange an assortment of vegetables and tomato-cheese skewers over the dip, ensuring that one end of each crudité or skewer is immersed in the dip.

Makes 5 servings

Pesto Parmesan Palmiers

These light and buttery canapés are sure to impress with their complementary basil, Parmesan and pine nut flavours baked into pretty shapes.

1 egg, lightly beaten

1 tsp cold water

2 sheets frozen puff pastry (1 lb), thawed, chilled

¼ cup store-bought pesto

¼ cup pine nuts, toasted and roughly chopped

3 Tbsp freshly grated Parmesan-Reggiano cheese

Line a baking sheet with parchment paper.

Using a fork, beat egg with cold water in a small bowl. Set aside this egg wash.

On a lightly floured board, roll both sheets of puff pastry to ⅛-inch thickness. Spread 2 Tbsp pesto evenly over each sheet, then sprinkle each with 2 Tbsp pine nuts and 1 Tbsp Parmesan.

Starting at the bottom edge, tightly roll the pastry halfway, to the centre of the sheet. Starting at the top edge, tightly roll the other half of the pastry toward the centre of the sheet until the puff pastry looks like two logs lying side by side but connected underneath. Repeat with the second sheet of puff pastry. Brush off any excess flour.

Brush egg wash on the seam between the rolled dough halves. Repeat with the second rolled sheet of puff pastry. Reserve the remaining egg wash. Refrigerate rolls for 30 minutes.

Using a sharp knife, cut the rolled dough crosswise into ½-inch slices. Place palmiers flat on the baking sheet, leaving 1 inch around each slice. Lightly press down on the pastry with your fingers to an even ¼-inch thickness. Refrigerate for at least 1 hour and up to 24 hours.

Preheat the oven to 400°F. Bake palmiers for 10 minutes. Turn over, glaze with the remaining egg wash and sprinkle with the remaining 1 Tbsp cheese. Bake another 8 to 10 minutes, until palmiers are golden and crisp. Remove from the oven and serve warm or at room temperature.

Makes about 25 palmiers

Candy Box Selection
CARAMEL NUT CLUSTERS

These sweets have the buttery richness of caramel and the crunch of nuts in a golden, glossy bite.

2 cups walnuts, toasted and roughly chopped	⅓ cup water
½ cup butter, cubed	1 Tbsp lemon juice
1½ cups sugar	1 tsp pure maple or vanilla extract
	pinch of salt

Generously coat 1 mini-muffin tin (for 24 mini-muffins) with nonstick spray. Half-fill each muffin cup with walnuts.

Place butter, sugar, water, lemon juice, maple (or vanilla) extract and salt in a heavy-bottomed or copper pan and stir to combine. Bring to a boil on medium-high heat, swirling the mixture once to combine, and cook without stirring until the mixture is golden brown, 5 to 7 minutes. Be sure to keep an eye on the pan while cooking to ensure the sugar does not burn (the mixture turns from golden to burned very quickly). Remove caramel from the heat and transfer to a heat-resistant glass measuring cup.

Pour enough hot caramel into each muffin cup to just cover nuts. If caramel starts to thicken, briefly return to the heat to thin it. Cool completely before removing nut clusters from muffin cups.

Makes 24 clusters

ESPRESSO FUDGE

This sweet indulgence has all the makings of a girls' night hit—chocolate, to satisfy cravings, and real brewed espresso, to keep everyone alert into the wee hours of the morning.

3 cups brown sugar, lightly packed

1 cup butter, cubed

¾ cup strong brewed coffee or espresso

1 cup cocoa, sifted

3 cups icing sugar, sifted

1 cup chopped semi-sweet chocolate
    or chocolate chips

Line an 8-inch square cake pan with plastic wrap and coat generously with nonstick spray.

Place brown sugar, butter, coffee (or espresso) and cocoa in a heavy-bottomed or copper pot on medium heat. Slowly bring to a boil and cook, uncovered, for 5 minutes, stirring occasionally. Pour into a large mixing bowl and add icing sugar, 1 cup at a time, stirring until smooth and lump-free, about 2 minutes. Cool for 10 minutes. The mixture should be warm but not hot enough to melt the chocolate. Fold in chopped chocolate until well combined. Spread fudge into the lined pan, smoothing the top with a spatula. Cool, then cut into 1-inch squares.

Makes forty-nine 1-inch squares

FLUFFY HOMEMADE
MARSHMALLOWS

Fun and yummy, homemade marshmallows are delicious and low in fat. To make a lemon-coconut variation, add 1 tsp grated lemon zest to the white sugar and vanilla before beating, then roll the marshmallows—once they have set—in 1½ cups of toasted coconut, omitting the dusting of cornstarch and icing sugar.

2 Tbsp unflavoured gelatin powder

4 Tbsp cold water

½ cup boiling water

1½ cups white sugar

½ tsp vanilla extract

½ cup icing sugar

1 Tbsp cornstarch

Line an 8-inch square baking dish with plastic wrap and coat generously with nonstick spray. Place in the freezer to chill.

Soften gelatin in a medium bowl by adding the cold water and stirring to combine. Add boiling water and stir until gelatin has dissolved. Add white sugar and vanilla and continue to stir until sugar crystals disappear.

Using a hand mixer, beat the gelatin mixture on medium speed until thick, foamy and sticky, about 10 minutes. Pour into the chilled baking dish and smooth out with greased fingers so that marshmallow is evenly distributed in the pan. Allow to set.

Sift icing sugar and cornstarch into a small bowl. Cut marshmallow in 1-inch squares and roll in the sugar-cornstarch mixture.

Makes about 35 marshmallows

Pink Pussycat

A great girl's drink, this whimsical concoction is sparkling, fruity and refreshing. This recipe will make 2 rounds.

> ½ bottle (375 mL/13 oz) Alize Red Passion (passion fruit–cognac blend)
> 2 bottles (each 750 mL/26 oz) sparkling wine, chilled
> 2 pts strawberry sorbet
> **GLASSWARE:** 5 to 10 Champagne flutes

For the first round, line up 5 Champagne flutes on a tray. Into each flute, pour 1 oz Alize. Top with 4 to 5 oz sparkling wine, leaving enough room for the foam that forms when sorbet is added. Using a small melon baller, scoop 3 to 4 balls of sorbet on top of the wine. Serve immediately with a straw.

Makes five to ten 8-oz drinks

GRASSHOPPER SHOTS *in* CHOCOLATE CUPS

The Grasshopper has always been a creamy, sweet, after-dinner favourite, but as a jello shot encased by a crunchy, chocolate shell, it's a party in your mouth.

1 tsp unflavoured gelatin

2¼ oz vodka

2¼ oz green Crème de Menthe

1½ oz white Crème de Cacao

twenty ½-oz chocolate cups

1 cup whipping cream (35%), whipped
        with 2 tsp sugar

¼ cup chocolate shavings (optional)

In a small glass bowl, sprinkle gelatin over ¼ oz of the vodka. When gelatin has absorbed the liquid and is softened, about 1 minute, stir in another 1 oz vodka. Heat for 5 seconds in a microwave oven, or just long enough to melt the gelatin.

Fill a large bowl with cold water. In a medium bowl, mix together the remaining vodka, Crème de Menthe and Crème de Cacao. Stir in the melted gelatin-vodka mixture until well combined, then transfer to a glass measuring cup. Place the measuring cup in the bowl of cold water to cool it.

Place 20 chocolate cups on a platter. Fill each cup ¾ full with the gelatin mixture. Refrigerate until set. When set, top with whipped cream and sprinkle with chocolate shavings. Refrigerate until ready to serve.

Makes twenty ½-oz cups

COCONUT MARGARITA

Totally girl-on-the-beach, this frozen Margarita is pre-mixed in pitchers, then simply whirred up with ice to serve. Players who fold early can man the blender. For variety, serve this drink as a martini.

12 oz tequila

6 oz Amaretto

36 oz coconut cream (page 55)

24 oz frozen pineapple juice concentrate, thawed

12 oz freshly squeezed lime juice

1½ to 2 cups toasted flaked coconut, for garnish

GLASSWARE: one 3-qt pitcher; five 12-oz
        Margarita coupes or 6-oz martini glasses

Combine tequila, Amaretto, coconut cream, pineapple juice concentrate and lime juice. Mix well and refrigerate in pitchers until ready to serve.

TO SERVE AS A FROZEN MARGARITA: For each drink, combine 6 oz of pre-mix with ½ cup of ice in a blender, and process until thick and smooth. Pour into a Margarita coupe, garnish with a sprinkle of coconut and serve with a straw.

TO SERVE AS A MARTINI: Rim chilled martini glasses with toasted coconut. Fill a shaker two-thirds full of cracked ice and add, for each drink, 6 oz of pre-mix. Cover and shake until condensation forms on the sides and the shaker is very cold to the touch. Strain into a glass.

Makes fifteen 6- to 12-oz drinks

SPANISH PORCH PICNIC

all-day, all-night tapas for 20

When summer's sultry days seem to stretch forever and the mood is sweet and unhurried, why not indulge in a little bit of Spain? Go where life is measured by a slower sun and the pleasures of the table are taken at a civilized pace: have an all-day, all-night Spanish porch picnic.

This is a lazy, informal event, perfect for a family birthday or a reunion of close friends. You can graze on tapas in the afternoon, dip into paella at dusk, then barbecue into the night. Take your vintage record player onto the verandah, drop the needle on some old LPs and salsa until the stars disappear. With gypsy music in your ears and sangria on your lips, it's hard to imagine winter was ever a possibility.

The food on this rustic menu is hearty, yet gently seasoned. Oddly, for a country whose history is deeply entangled in the spice trade, Spain is not characterized by a highly spiced cuisine. With the exception of the hotness of chilies that Columbus brought back from the New World, the flavours of Spanish cooking are not aggressive. Dishes are pungent with saffron, olive oil, garlic and onions—relying on the natural robustness of tomato, ham, lemon and wine, and redolent of the sea air itself. The goodness comes not only from the balanced Mediterranean diet, but from the relaxed way in which it is consumed.

MENU FOR A LAZY SUMMER AFTERNOON
AND A SULTRY SPANISH EVENING

AFTERNOON TAPAS

SUN-DRIED TOMATO GARBANZO DIP

ARTICHOKE, ASIAGO *and* ROASTED HAZELNUT DIP

COCONUT CAYENNE ALMONDS

ORANGE *and* FENNEL SPICED OLIVES

SPICY LEMON EDAMAME

SWISS CHARD, MUSHROOM *and* EMMENTAL HAND PIES

GRILLED SHRIMP IN SMOKED PAPRIKA *with* CITRUS PEEL DIP

FETA-STUFFED LAMB MEATBALLS *with* TOMATO OLIVE TAPENADE

SMALL PLATES DINNER

PAELLA SALAD *with* LEMON-HERB AIOLI

HANGER STEAKS GRILLED *with* DIJON-BBQ SAUCE

DESSERT

ORANGE AND ALMOND SHORTCAKE *with* BERRIES AND CREAM

COCKTAILS

SPARKLING WHITE SANGRIA

BRANDIED RED SANGRIA

GAZPACHO SLING *with a* CAPRESE SKEWER

SETTING THE SCENE

DECOR IDEAS

For this small, casual, all-day party, the food is best served from one buffet table, and the drinks from a bar that has been set up at a smaller table.

Everything terra cotta—from candles in clay flowerpots to Mexican pottery platters—will enhance the mood without being contrived or clichéd. Bottles of wine or Mexican beer can be cooled in an oversized clay flowerpot full of ice. Use new yellow and red cotton tea towels as napkins and stuff big yellow sunflowers and white daisies into graniteware jugs or big glass canning jars and dot them everywhere. Hand-blown Mexican glasses and bowls will add rustic elegance.

On a porch or backyard patio, the lighting can always go a little retro and romantic, so bring out a couple of table lamps and drape vintage Spanish scarves over the lampshades.

MUSIC PICKS

When Citytv first hit the airwaves to reinvent urban television, Jojo Chintoh was there, broadcasting the news in a street-savvy way. The station's slogan was "Citytv: EVERYWHERE," and Jojo was—everywhere in the news, the streets and always in the clubs. A long-time proponent of the local jazz and blues scene, Jojo's fancy has lately led him to Latin-inspired beats. He's given us this list of great CDs *en espagnol*.

- Francisco Céspedes, *Autorretrato, okán eyo* (Warner Music Latina)
- Gilberto Santa Rosa, *Auténtico* (Sony Discos)
- Marco Antonio Solís, *Razón de sobra* (Fonovisa/Univision Music Group)
- Negros, *Sin fecha de vencimiento* (Sony Discos)

SZABO'S WINE ALTERNATIVES

THIS ALL-DAY affair in the Spanish style calls for leisurely eating and sipping. Logically, your selection of wines should reflect the theme, and fortunately the Spanish wine scene has much to offer: it is among the most exciting in the world today. World-class wines at reasonable prices are every host's delight.

For the early afternoon, begin with what the Spaniards themselves would choose: a pale, light and ocean-air-scented manzanilla sherry from the coastal town of Sanlúcar de Barrameda, or its equivalent from just farther inland, around the town of Jerez de la Frontera itself, fino sherry. These, the driest and most elegant of all sherries, are uniquely aged under a layer of *flor*, a naturally occurring yeast that confers a remarkable fresh-almond, yeasty and white flower-tinged bouquet. Their intensity of flavour is more than sufficient to match the Orange and Fennel Spiced Olives and Coconut Cayenne Almonds.

Spain has a few regions contending for the title of best Spanish white wine. The Rias Baixas, "the low rivers" region of Galicia on the northwest coast, is among the front-runners for its beautifully crisp, citrus, orchard fruit and floral-scented whites from the local Albariño variety. The finest are fresh, vibrant and unoaked. The other front-runner is Rueda, a region specializing in the Verdejo grape. Verdejo has the same pungent, herbal qualities as Sauvignon Blanc. Indeed, the two are often blended together in the area. Either wine's liveliness and moderate alcohol content would be a fine choice for the Spicy Lemon Edamame, Grilled Shrimp in Smoked Paprika and the tangy Sun-dried Tomato Garbanzo Dip.

The pleasantly bitter flavour of Swiss chard and the umami earthiness of the mushrooms and cheese in the hand pies call for an oaked aged white. Travel to the famous region of Rioja for its less famous white wines made in the traditional manner. Lengthy aging in American oak imbues the wines with an unmistakable spicy, toasted and coconut flavour that will harmonize magically with the hand pies as well as the artichoke dip.

Before lighting the grill and dipping into the reds, pause for a moment to sample some of the delicious *rosados* that Spain has to offer. Often based on Garnacha, these light, fragrant, strawberry-scented wines are among the best rosés in the world. Look for labels from the ancient kingdom of Navarra, Catalonia or the Castilian region of Cigales.

No Spanish party is complete without the uncorking of a few red wines. For this occasion, choose one of the modern-style, new-wave Tempranillos from Ribera del Duero, La Mancha or Rioja. These *jóven* (young) wines are aged very briefly, if at all, in oak, leaving them fairly brimming with ripe red and black fruits reminiscent of raspberries and strawberries. Meant for early consumption, these wines feature tannins that are soft, round and ripe, and a texture like plush velvet. Their inherent impression of sweetness will greet the salty flavours of the feta and the Tomato Olive Tapenade and the richness of the lamb, as Don Quixote dreamed of greeting his beloved Dulcinea.

Keep the fino sherry, rosados and whites on ice all afternoon and into the evening. The reds should also be dipped in the ice bath every so often on a sultry day to keep them at the ideal temperature of about 16°C. They will party on well into the early hours of the morning alongside the paella and the hanger steaks, as any good Spaniard would.

1 WEEK AHEAD

- Order the steaks for HANGER STEAKS GRILLED WITH DIJON-BBQ SAUCE.
- Make the FETA-STUFFED LAMB MEATBALLS and freeze, uncooked.
- Make the SWISS CHARD, MUSHROOM AND EMMENTAL HAND PIES and freeze.
- Make sure the barbecue grill is in working order and you have enough fuel.
- Organize music and decor, serving platters, cutlery, glassware, dishes and napkins.

2 DAYS AHEAD

- Make the COCONUT CAYENNE ALMONDS and ORANGE AND FENNEL SPICED OLIVES.
- Make the LEMON-HERB AIOLI for the PAELLA SALAD.
- Make the dressing for the SPICY LEMON EDAMAME.
- Make the CITRUS PEEL DIP for GRILLED SHRIMP IN SMOKED PAPRIKA.
- Make the TOMATO OLIVE TAPENADE for FETA-STUFFED LAMB MEATBALLS.
- Marinate the hanger steaks.

THE DAY BEFORE

- Make ARTICHOKE, ASIAGO AND ROASTED HAZELNUT DIP.
- Make SUN-DRIED TOMATO GARBANZO DIP.
- Bake ORANGE AND ALMOND SHORTCAKE.
- Macerate the fruit for the sangrias.
- Make the gazpacho mix for the GAZPACHO SLINGS.
- Thaw FETA-STUFFED LAMB MEATBALLS and SWISS CHARD, MUSHROOM AND EMMENTAL HAND PIES overnight.

THE MORNING OF

- Set up the decor and the music.
- Slice the fruit for ORANGE AND ALMOND SHORTCAKE and macerate.
- Make the cream for the shortcake.
- Make the PAELLA SALAD to the "hold" point.
- Bake SWISS CHARD, MUSHROOM AND EMMENTAL HAND PIES.
- Assemble the bocconcini and tomato skewers for the GAZPACHO SLINGS.
- Make SPICY LEMON EDAMAME.

1½ HOURS BEFORE GUESTS ARRIVE

- Combine the macerated fruit with wine for BRANDIED RED SANGRIA.
- Arrange SWISS CHARD, MUSHROOM AND EMMENTAL HAND PIES on a serving platter.
- Bake FETA-STUFFED LAMB MEATBALLS, reheat TOMATO OLIVE TAPENADE and transfer to a serving bowl with a side bowl for the tapenade.
- Fry GRILLED SHRIMP and arrange on a serving platter with a bowl of CITRUS PEEL DIP.
- Arrange bowls of ARTICHOKE, ASIAGO AND ROASTED HAZELNUT DIP and SUN-DRIED TOMATO GARBANZO DIP with pita crisps and chips.
- Crisp COCONUT CAYENNE ALMONDS in the oven, if necessary. Put out in several small dishes with small bowls of SPICED OLIVES.

15 MINUTES BEFORE DINNER

- Combine the macerated fruit with wine for SPARKLING WHITE SANGRIA.
- Light the barbecue (or earlier if using charcoal or firewood).
- Put out small plates.
- While the barbecue is heating, assemble the paella and serve from a big platter onto small tasting plates.
- Grill hanger steaks, allow them to rest, then slice and serve them from a platter or steak board onto small tasting plates.

1 HOUR BEFORE GUESTS LEAVE

- Make tea and coffee.
- Assemble shortcake.

Sun-dried Tomato Garbanzo Dip

Garbanzo beans are chickpeas in Spanish, and combined with the tomatoes, they make hummus with a very Spanish twist. Serve this dip with baskets of pita crisps.

1 can (19 oz/540 mL) chickpeas, drained,
    ¼ cup juice reserved
½ cup (packed) sun-dried tomatoes in oil,
    slightly drained
4 tsp minced garlic

1 Tbsp tahini (sesame seed paste)
⅛ to ¼ cup olive oil
juice of ½ lemon
¼ cup chopped basil leaves
⅛ tsp salt

In a food processor, purée chickpeas (without their juice) until smooth and transfer to a large bowl. Purée sun-dried tomatoes and add them to the chickpea purée. Stir in chickpea juice, garlic, tahini, olive oil, lemon juice, basil and salt. Stir until well combined. Transfer to a bowl and refrigerate, covered, until ready to serve.

Makes 3½ cups

ARTICHOKE, ASIAGO *and* ROASTED HAZELNUT DIP

Pulverized roasted hazelnuts are the secret ingredient that puts a new spin on a trendy dipping favourite. Serve this dip with baskets of pita crisps and chips.

½ cup hazelnuts
1⅓ cups marinated artichoke hearts in oil,
    roughly chopped, drained, marinade
    reserved

½ cup grated Asiago cheese
8 oz cream cheese, room temperature,
    cubed
1½ tsp freshly ground black pepper

Preheat the oven to 350°F. Place hazelnuts on a baking sheet and roast until skins are dark brown, about 15 minutes. (The hazelnuts should be well roasted so their skins peel off easily.) Using a kitchen towel, rub nuts while still warm to remove as much skin as possible.

Using a food processor, pulverize nuts. Add artichoke hearts (without their marinade), Asiago cheese, cream cheese and pepper. Process, adding as much of the reserved artichoke marinade as necessary, until dip is smooth and creamy.

Makes 2½ cups

COCONUT CAYENNE ALMONDS

This delectable, unusual nut mixture combines sweet and salty with the unexpected bite of cayenne. Make these almonds up to 1 week in advance and store them, uncovered, at room temperature. Crisp the nuts in a 350°F oven for 5 minutes before serving, then place them around the room in small bowls. These almonds are great to snack on with drinks.

¼ cup sweetened shredded desiccated coconut	1 Tbsp water
4 cups raw unsalted almonds	1½ Tbsp honey
¼ cup sugar	1½ tsp cayenne pepper
	1 tsp salt

Preheat the oven to 350°F. Place coconut and almonds on separate baking sheets. Toast coconut until lightly coloured, 2 to 3 minutes. Roast almonds until golden, 8 to 10 minutes. Set toasted coconut aside, and pour hot almonds into a medium bowl. Leave the oven on.

Line a baking sheet with parchment paper. In a small saucepan on medium heat, bring sugar, water and honey to a boil, stirring occasionally to make sure all sugar is dissolved.

Pour hot syrup over warm almonds and toss until well combined. Add toasted coconut, cayenne and salt and mix well. Pour nuts onto the parchment-lined baking sheet and roast for another 20 minutes, stirring occasionally. Remove from the oven and allow to dry and cool, breaking up any pieces that stick together.

Makes 4 cups

ORANGE *and* FENNEL SPICED OLIVES

Classic Spanish accents, orange zest and fennel seeds, give these olives a fresh flavour. Place bowls of olives around the room as a snack for guests to munch on with drinks.

2 lbs black kalamata olives, whole, drained

zest of 2 large oranges, in long strips

¼ cup fennel seeds

4 cloves garlic, peeled

4 sprigs fresh thyme

2 tsp red pepper flakes (optional)

2 Tbsp extra-virgin olive oil

In a medium bowl, combine olives, orange zest, fennel seeds, garlic, thyme, red pepper flakes and olive oil, and mix well. Cover and marinate in the refrigerator for at least 48 hours. Bring to room temperature before serving in small bowls.

Makes 4 cups

Spicy Lemon Edamame

Many supermarkets stock whole soybean pods, called *edamame*, in the specialty frozen section. You can also find them in most Asian food stores.

4 lbs frozen green soybeans (edamame)

zest and juice of 2 lemons

2 Tbsp olive oil

4 Tbsp sea salt or to taste

½ to 1 tsp Tabasco sauce or to taste

In a large pot of boiling, salted water, blanch soybean pods in batches for 3 minutes per batch, until beans are hot but still al dente. Using a slotted spoon, remove from the water and keep warm in a covered bowl. When all soybeans have been blanched, toss with lemon zest and lemon juice, olive oil, sea salt and Tabasco. Serve in a large bowl with a matching side bowl for emptied pods.

Makes 8 cups

Swiss Chard, Mushroom and Emmental Hand Pies

Empanar is Spanish for "to roll in pastry," and these fit-in-your-palm turnovers are a tasty vegetarian take on the traditional meat-filled empanada. Make these pies up to 1 month in advance and freeze them, or make them 2 days ahead and store them, covered, at room temperature. Reheat them in a 350°F oven for 10 to 15 minutes, until warm.

WINE PASTRY

1 cup butter, cold, in 1-inch cubes

3½ cups all-purpose flour

½ tsp salt

1 egg

6 Tbsp white wine

2 Tbsp freshly squeezed lemon juice

4 Tbsp vegetable oil

zest of ½ lemon

SWISS CHARD, MUSHROOM AND EMMENTAL FILLING

1 Tbsp olive oil

2 Tbsp butter

1 to 1½ lbs Swiss chard, ribs removed, finely sliced (or spinach to substitute)

2 tsp nutmeg

1 tsp salt

1 tsp freshly ground black pepper

¼ cup whipping cream (35%)

2 shallots, minced

2 cloves garlic, minced

6 cups sliced mixed mushrooms (shiitake, portobello, oyster, button)

¾ cup pizza sauce

1 cup grated Emmental or Swiss cheese (8 oz)

1 egg, beaten with ¼ tsp cold water (for egg wash)

WINE PASTRY: In a food processor fitted with a steel blade, combine butter, flour and salt. Pulse, on and off, for 1 to 2 minutes, or until the texture resembles oatmeal. Transfer to a large bowl and make a well in the middle of the mixture. Set aside.

In a small bowl, beat together egg, white wine, lemon juice, vegetable oil and lemon zest and pour into the well in the butter-flour mixture. Mix lightly until dough holds together. Form into a ball, wrap with plastic wrap and refrigerate for at least 20 minutes.

FILLING: In a large sauté pan on medium heat, melt half of the oil and half of the butter. Add Swiss chard, nutmeg, half of the salt and half of the black pepper and cook, stirring frequently, until well wilted, about 5 minutes. Add 2 Tbsp of the whipping cream and stir until combined. Transfer to a medium bowl.

In a sauté pan on medium-high heat, melt the remaining oil and butter. Add shallots, garlic and the remaining salt and pepper and cook until softened, about 2 minutes. Add mushrooms and cook until soft and liquid has been expelled and reduced, about 5 minutes. Stir in the remaining whipping cream until combined. Add the mushroom mixture to the Swiss chard mixture. Stir in pizza sauce and cheese until thoroughly combined.

Preheat the oven to 350°F. Line two baking sheets with parchment paper.

On a lightly floured board, roll out dough to ⅛-inch thickness. Cut circles using a 3-inch round cookie cutter. Place rounds on baking sheets and mound about 2¼ tsp of the filling on each round, leaving a ¼-inch border around the edges. Moisten the edges of each round with egg wash, then fold dough in half to form a half-moon shape and crimp the edges with a fork. Prick pastry all over with a fork and brush with more egg wash. Bake for 25 to 30 minutes until golden brown, turning the baking sheets at least once to ensure even baking. Serve warm, piled high on platters.

Makes about 50 hand pies

GRILLED SHRIMP *in* SMOKED PAPRIKA *with* CITRUS PEEL DIP

Foodies are always jumping on and off the latest flavour wagon that rolls into town, but smoked paprika from Spain is one of the most enduring imports of the last few years. Available in bitter, sweet and hot, it adds complexity and character to the simplest preparation. These shrimp can be cooked up to 24 hours in advance and stored, covered, in the refrigerator.

DIP

1 cup mixed-citrus marmalade

1 cup freshly squeezed lime juice

SHRIMP

3 lbs uncooked black tiger shrimp (16 to 20 shrimp per lb), deveined and peeled, tails left intact

2 Tbsp smoked paprika

1 Tbsp minced garlic

1 tsp salt

½ cup olive oil

DIP: In a small saucepan on medium heat, combine marmalade and lime juice and bring to a boil, stirring occasionally. Remove from the heat and set aside.

SHRIMP: In a large bowl, toss shrimp, paprika, garlic, salt and half of the olive oil until shrimp are well coated.

In a large sauté pan, heat the remaining oil on high heat. Add enough shrimp to cover the bottom of the sauté pan in a single layer. Sear for 60 seconds, then turn over and cook until shrimp are cooked through and opaque in the centre, about 2½ minutes more. Transfer cooked shrimp to a serving platter. Repeat until all shrimp are cooked.

Serve shrimp hot or cold, layered around the bowl of dip.

Makes 48 to 60 shrimp

SMOKED SPANISH PAPRIKA

Made from the smoked, dried and stone-ground *pimentón*, a variety of red pepper, smoked Spanish paprika is terrific with chicken and seafood and is an essential ingredient in such Spanish dishes as paella, hot pepper sauce and chorizo sausage. If it is not available in your local markets, it can be found and ordered through the Internet.

FETA-STUFFED LAMB MEATBALLS
with TOMATO OLIVE TAPENADE

These juicy meatballs are quick, they freeze well and they can be turned into Mini Feta-stuffed Lamb Burgers with baby brioche buns (page 218). Both the meatballs and the tapenade can be made up to 1 month in advance and frozen. Use fresh lamb if you make the meatballs in advance, as they should be frozen raw to retain their juiciness. Thaw the meatballs and roast them in a 350°F oven for 15 minutes before serving. The tapenade can be defrosted and reheated in a microwave oven on high power for 2 to 3 minutes.

MEATBALLS

2 Tbsp vegetable oil

1 large onion, minced

2 large cloves garlic, minced

2 eggs, beaten

4 tsp Worcestershire sauce

2 Tbsp Dijon mustard

1 bunch flat-leaf parsley, roughly chopped

6 sprigs fresh rosemary, stems removed, roughly chopped

1 cup bread crumbs

¼ tsp salt

½ tsp freshly ground black pepper

2 lbs fresh ground lamb

8 oz feta cheese, in ½-inch dice

½ cup chopped flat-leaf parsley, for garnish (optional)

TAPENADE

20 plum tomatoes

4 cloves garlic, peeled

12 anchovy fillets

2 Tbsp capers, roughly chopped

1 ½ cups black kalamata olives, pitted and roughly chopped

juice of 2 lemons

2 tsp smooth Dijon mustard

¼ cup olive oil

1 tsp chopped fresh thyme

MEATBALLS: Preheat the oven to 375°F. Heat oil in a medium sauté pan on medium-high heat. Add onion and garlic and sauté until soft and golden, about 5 minutes. Transfer to a large mixing bowl. Stir in eggs, Worcestershire sauce, Dijon mustard, parsley, rosemary, bread crumbs, salt and pepper. Add lamb and mix until well combined.

(continued over)

Spoon one heaping tablespoon of the lamb mixture into your hands and form into a ball. Push one cube of feta into the ball, re-rolling it if necessary so feta is completely covered. Transfer to a baking sheet with raised edges. Repeat with the lamb mixture and feta. You should have 50 to 60 meatballs. Roast for 15 to 20 minutes, or until golden brown.

TAPENADE: Preheat the oven to 375°F. Place tomatoes and garlic in a roasting pan and roast until soft and fragrant, about 45 minutes. Allow to cool slightly.

Peel and seed tomatoes over a large bowl, reserving any juice. Discard peel and seeds. Roughly chop tomatoes and place them in the bowl of a food processor or blender. Add reserved tomato juice, garlic, anchovies, capers, olives, lemon juice, Dijon mustard, oil and thyme. Pulse until ingredients are smooth and well combined.

TO SERVE: Arrange hot meatballs on a deep platter. Spoon tapenade over the meatballs and garnish with chopped parsley.

Makes 50 to 60 meatballs and 5 cups of tapenade

LA TOMATINA

You have to love a culture that institutionalizes food fights. Annually, on the last Wednesday of August, the Spanish city of Buñol in Valencia celebrates La Tomatina, a day on which all citizens and tourists of like spirit can throw tomatoes at whatever or whomever they want. Like all good food fights, the first one broke out among friends for no apparent reason and soon half the town was pitching the red ones. That was in the '40s, and they had so much fun, they started doing it every year. Now around 30,000 people gather in Buñol every year to hurl about 150,000 tomatoes at each other. If you go, don't wear the white shirt.

Paella Salad with Lemon-Herb Aioli

This is a lovely summer version of the Spanish classic. All ingredients are cooked to perfection hours ahead of time and simply assembled at the last minute and served at room temperature, so there's no threat of overcooking the tender shellfish.

If you're preparing this dish ahead of time, the rice can be cooked up to 4 hours in advance and stored, covered, at room temperature. Seafood can be cooked up to 4 to 6 hours in advance and stored, covered, in the refrigerator. Aioli can be made 2 days ahead and stored, covered, in the refrigerator.

Most commercially available stocks are oversalted to compensate for thinness of flavour, but it is very easy to make your own. This stock can be refrigerated for up to 3 days, but should be boiled vigorously for 5 minutes before using it, to destroy any harmful bacteria that might have formed. The stock can also be frozen immediately in small resealable freezer bags and kept for up to 2 months. Just thaw frozen stock when needed.

STRONG CHICKEN STOCK

4 lbs chicken bones

4 qts cold water

MARINATED SCALLOPS

4 Tbsp olive oil

2 Tbsp freshly squeezed lemon juice

2 cloves garlic, crushed

1 lb scallops

PAELLA

2 cups parboiled rice

3 cups strong chicken stock

4 large tomatoes, coarsely chopped

8 green onions, chopped

½ tsp crushed saffron

4 cloves garlic, minced

1 Tbsp ground cumin

4 Tbsp olive oil

4 Tbsp butter

cayenne pepper and salt to taste

2 cups white wine

2 lbs clams in the shell, scrubbed clean

2 lbs mussels in the shell, scrubbed clean

½ lb cooked diced chicken and/or cooked
    diced spicy sausage

1 cup chopped fresh cilantro

(continued over)

4 large egg yolks

1 tsp salt

¼ tsp freshly ground black pepper

1 tsp dry mustard

3 Tbsp white wine vinegar

3 ¼ cups olive oil

lemon juice to taste

1 Tbsp grated lemon zest

¼ cup finely chopped flat-leaf parsley

STRONG CHICKEN STOCK: Place chicken bones in a large pot and cover with water. Bring to a boil on high heat, then immediately reduce the heat to medium-low, cover and simmer for 4 to 6 hours.

Remove and discard the bones. Pour stock into a clean bowl. Rinse the pot to remove any coagulated protein. Return stock to the pot, and simmer uncovered on medium-low heat until reduced to 4 cups. Cool to room temperature and refrigerate, covered, until ready to use.

MARINATED SCALLOPS: In a medium bowl, combine olive oil, lemon juice and garlic. Add scallops, combine well and marinate, covered with plastic wrap in the refrigerator, for at least 1 hour.

PAELLA: Combine rice and chicken stock in a small saucepan on high heat. Bring to a boil, reduce heat to low and simmer, covered, for 15 to 20 minutes. When rice is cooked, stir in tomatoes, green onion, saffron, garlic, cumin, 2 Tbsp of the olive oil, 2 Tbsp of the butter, cayenne and salt. Set aside, covered, at room temperature, for up to 4 hours.

In a large sauté pan with a tight-fitting lid, bring wine to a boil on medium-high heat. Add clams and mussels, cover and steam just until shells open, about 5 minutes. Transfer seafood to a medium bowl, cover and refrigerate. Strain cooking juices into a small container, cover and refrigerate.

Drain scallops, discarding marinade, then sprinkle with salt and pepper. Place the remaining olive oil and butter in a sauté pan on very high heat. Sauté scallops for 2 to 3 minutes, until just cooked. Transfer scallops to another small bowl and refrigerate for at least 30 minutes and up to 3 hours.

LEMON-HERB AIOLI: With a whisk, beat egg yolks in a small bowl until frothy. Add salt, pepper, dry mustard and half of the vinegar, and whisk to combine. Add olive oil, a drop at a time, whisking constantly until the mixture begins to thicken. Add the remaining oil in a slow, steady stream, thinning the aioli occasionally by adding a little vinegar. Continue whisking until all the oil and vinegar have been incorporated. Season with salt and pepper and add lemon juice to taste. With a spatula, fold in lemon zest and parsley. Refrigerate until needed.

TO SERVE: Add reserved seafood cooking juice to the room-temperature rice and mix well. Spread rice on a large platter. Remove some mussels and clams from their shells. Scatter mussels, clams, scallops, chicken (and/or sausage) over rice, drizzle with some of the lemon-herb aioli and sprinkle liberally with fresh cilantro. Decorate the perimeter of the dish with the remaining mussels and clams in their shells. Pour the remaining aioli into a small bowl and serve it on the side for guests who want an extra dollop.

Makes 16 to 20 tapas-sized servings and 1 quart of lemon-herb aioli

PAELLA ON THE ROCKS

You can re-create our paella salad as a hot paella *aire libre* anywhere that open fires are allowed.

Make the fire's perimeter with several large rocks of the same height, or an iron tripod brought along for the purpose of providing level support for your paella or deep sauté pan. Build a wood fire under the pan.

When the flames are hotly licking at the sides of the pan, fry up all the ingredients except the rice. Throw in the glass of wine you've been drinking and simmer until ingredients are just cooked.

With a slotted spoon, scoop out the meat and seafood and set aside. Add the rice and enough liquid (water, stock, wine or Bloody Caesar) to equal twice the measure of rice. Allow all to boil gently. (If the mixture is boiling too rapidly, spread the wood away from the centre of the fire.) Boil until the top of the liquid is level with the top of the rice. Scoop out all flaming wood under the pan to lower the temperature, stir rice quickly and cover. Continue cooking until rice is tender. Return meat and seafood to the pan, cover and cook just until hot.

HANGER STEAKS GRILLED
with DIJON-BBQ SAUCE

Since there is only one pair of hanger steaks on each steer, it's advisable to order these ahead of time—you need two pairs for this party. Also called butcher's tender, this cut is the V-shaped muscle at the end of the skirt that "hangs" between the last rib and the loin. It has long been a favourite cut of butchers because of its intense flavour and heavy grain, but these days, all the hanger steaks are going to hip restaurants and upscale caterers.

Butchers in France refer to the hanger as *onglet* and in Italy as *lombatello*. If you cannot get the hanger cut, flank is an excellent alternative and skirt will do as well in this recipe. None of these cuts should be overcooked, and they all benefit from marinating, as they have a tendency to dry out and become tough, especially when pan-fried or grilled. Rare and medium-rare are best, as always.

MARINATED STEAK

4 lbs hanger (or flank or skirt) steaks
1 onion, sliced
2 cups red wine (or enough to cover steaks)
½ tsp salt

½ tsp pepper
handful of fresh herbs (rosemary, thyme,
     oregano) or baby arugula leaves,
     for garnish

DIJON-BBQ SAUCE

2 cups store-bought bottled smoky tangy
     barbecue sauce

1 cup smooth Dijon mustard

MARINATED STEAK: In a large glass baking dish, combine steak, onion and red wine. Cover and marinate overnight or up to 48 hours for a more intense wine flavour.

DIJON-BBQ SAUCE: In a medium bowl, combine barbecue sauce and Dijon mustard. Set aside.

FINISH STEAK: Preheat a barbecue to high heat. Remove steak from marinade and pat dry with paper towels. Sear for 2 minutes per side. Brush one side with Dijon-BBQ sauce and cook for another 2 minutes. Turn steak over, brush with Dijon-BBQ sauce and cook for another 2 minutes. Continue turning and glazing steak every 2 minutes until cooked (about 8 minutes total for rare). Season with salt and pepper and allow steak to rest for at least 15 minutes. Cut each steak on the bias into thin slices.

TO SERVE: Fan steak slices on a serving platter. Garnish with fresh herbs (or baby arugula leaves). Serve hot, cold or at room temperature.

Makes about 20 small-plate servings

Orange and Almond Shortcake with Berries and Cream

This cake gets its intense orange flavour from frozen concentrate and fresh zest, which are added to the batter before baking, and it is further enhanced with a sweet-tart glaze of freshly squeezed juice. Densely textured like a typical Spanish almond cake, it is irresistible topped with berries and cream. Since the cream topping contains gelatin, you can make it several hours ahead of serving.

ORANGE AND ALMOND SHORTCAKE

½ cup cake flour

¼ cup cornstarch

8 egg yolks

1 cup sugar

¼ cup frozen orange juice concentrate, thawed

2 tsp grated orange zest

2 tsp vanilla extract

8 egg whites

1 tsp cream of tartar

4 cups ground almonds, toasted and cooled

CITRUS GLAZE

¼ cup icing sugar, sifted

½ cup freshly squeezed orange juice

¼ cup freshly squeezed lemon juice

FRUIT TOPPING

6 cups mixed berries (raspberries, blueberries, blackberries, sliced strawberries) or any other cut fruit

⅓ cup sugar

½ cup orange liqueur, such as Grand Marnier

CREAM TOPPING

4 cups whipping cream (35%)

2 Tbsp unflavoured gelatin

⅔ cup sugar

1 cup medium-dry sherry

ORANGE AND ALMOND SHORTCAKE: Preheat the oven to 325°F. Line two 10-inch round cake pans with parchment paper (cut 2 rounds to fit the bottoms, then strips the height of the pans to fit against the sides).

Sift together flour and cornstarch in a small bowl.

In the large bowl of an electric mixer, beat egg yolks on medium speed until thick. Add ⅔ cup of the sugar and beat until light lemon-coloured and tripled in volume, 5 to 10 minutes. Slowly add orange juice concentrate, while beating continuously. Blend in orange zest and vanilla and beat until fluffy. Transfer to a large bowl and set aside.

Clean and dry the mixer bowl and beaters very well. Beat egg whites on medium-high speed until foamy. Add cream of tartar, increase the speed to high and beat until soft peaks form. Gradually add the remaining sugar, beating continuously until the mixture forms stiff peaks. Set aside.

Using a wide spatula, gently fold the flour mixture into the beaten egg yolks just until traces of flour disappear. Gently fold in half of the beaten egg whites. Fold in almonds, then fold in the remaining egg whites.

Divide the batter equally between the prepared pans. Using the spatula, smooth the batter to level the tops. Bake until nicely browned and a toothpick comes out clean, 25 to 30 minutes. Cool for about 30 minutes.

CITRUS GLAZE: In a small bowl, combine icing sugar and freshly squeezed juices. When cakes have cooled but are still slightly warm, brush glaze over both.

FRUIT TOPPING: In a large bowl, combine fruit with sugar and liqueur. Cover with plastic wrap and refrigerate until ready to serve.

CREAM TOPPING: In the medium bowl of an electric mixer, beat cream, starting on low and increasing the speed to medium as cream begins to thicken. Slowly sprinkle in gelatin while beating continuously. Gradually add sugar and increase the speed to medium-high, beating just until stiff. Do not overbeat. Using a spatula, fold in sherry. Refrigerate until ready to serve.

TO ASSEMBLE: Cut cake into 16 wedges. Place each wedge on a plate, top with fruit (and its juices) and a dollop of cream.

Serves 16

Sangria Pitchers

Perhaps the most famous of Spanish drinks, sangria is deserving of its international reputation; it is fresh, fruity and perfect for summer refreshment.

SPARKLING WHITE SANGRIA

In our white sangria, we use Segura Viudas, a delicious Spanish sparkler made in the Champagne method, mixed with diced peaches, pineapples, strawberries, raspberries, blueberries and sliced grapes.

> 7 cups mixed diced fruit
> ½ bottle (375 mL/13 oz) orange liqueur, such as Grand Marnier
> 4 bottles (each 750 mL/26 oz) sparkling wine
> GLASSWARE: 3 pitchers or a punchbowl; twenty 12-oz balloon wine glasses

In a large bowl or plastic pail, stir together fruit and liqueur and allow to macerate, covered and refrigerated, for a minimum of 4 hours. Just before serving, combine macerated fruit with wine in large, colourful pitchers or in a punchbowl with a ladle.

TO SERVE: Scoop half a ladleful of fruit into the bottom of each glass and top up with sangria until the glass is ¾ full.

Makes twenty 10-oz drinks

BRANDIED RED SANGRIA

In our red sangria, we use a Spanish Rioja or a Merlot mixed with diced plums, apples, pears, melon and sliced grapes.

> 7 cups mixed diced fruit
> ½ bottle (375 mL/13 oz) brandy
> ½ cup sugar
> 4 bottles (each 750 mL/26 oz) fruity full-bodied wine
> GLASSWARE: 3 pitchers or a punchbowl; twenty 12-oz balloon wine glasses

In a large bowl or plastic pail, stir together fruit, brandy and sugar and allow to macerate, covered and refrigerated, for a minimum of 4 hours. One hour before serving, combine macerated fruit with red wine in large, colourful pitchers or in a punchbowl with a ladle. Refrigerate.

TO SERVE: Scoop half a ladleful of fruit into the bottom of each glass and top up with sangria until the glass is ¾ full.

Makes twenty 10-oz drinks

Gazpacho Sling with a Caprese Skewer

This drink combines two summertime party favourites: cool, refreshing gazpacho (a traditional cold Spanish soup) and smooth, peppery tequila. The swizzle stick is a mini-kebab of baby bocconcini and cherry tomatoes and is a toothsome appetizer in itself!

GAZPACHO

16 cups tomato juice

2½ cups diced unpeeled English cucumber

2½ cups diced green pepper

4 large cloves garlic, crushed

1 cup white wine vinegar

2 tsp salt

2 tsp freshly ground black pepper

2 tsp Tabasco sauce (optional)

24 oz (700 mL) white tequila

¼ cup celery salt

1 lime, cut in half

twenty thick straws

GLASSWARE: three 2-qt pitchers; twenty 14-oz sling glasses

CAPRESE SKEWERS

20 grape cherry tomatoes

20 pieces baby bocconcini

3 green peppers, seeded, in 1-inch slices (need 20 pieces)

twenty 10-inch decorative skewers

GAZPACHO: In a blender or food processor, combine a third of the tomato juice, a third of the cucumber and green pepper, a quarter of the garlic, ⅓ cup of the vinegar, salt, pepper and Tabasco. Blend until very smooth, then pour into a pitcher. Repeat twice, filling each remaining pitcher with one batch. Top up each pitcher with 8 oz tequila and refrigerate.

CAPRESE SKEWERS: Thread a grape tomato, a piece of bocconcini and a slice of green pepper on each decorative skewer. Set aside.

TO SERVE: Sprinkle celery salt into a glass pie plate or dish. Rub lime around the rim of each glass, then dip rim of glass in celery salt.

Fill each glass with crushed ice and pour in 8 oz chilled gazpacho. Garnish with a skewer and a thick straw.

Makes twenty 10-oz drinks

FROM THE MASTER SOMMELIER

Drinking wine is increasingly becoming a part of North American culture, and interest in sampling new varieties has skyrocketed in recent years. The secret to appreciating wine is experimenting. With the wide range of wine-producing regions, styles and grape varieties available today, the possibilities can seem overwhelming. But this is the beauty of wine. It is a journey of exploration that can last a lifetime.

Understanding wine means being able to compare the glass in front of you to another glass of the same style, price and/or region, so that relative assessments can be made. With this knowledge, you will come to understand your own palate and your personal preferences will come into sharper focus. But it can be hard to remember the look, smell and taste of a wine you've tasted a few days, months or even years before. Enter the wine tasting event. There is no better way to gain experience than by tasting several examples side by side and making direct comparisons. Sharing this exploration with others is both fun and informative, as opinions can be exchanged and each person brings his or her own experience to the table. A greater number of wines can be tasted in a group, and all your guests can get involved if you ask them to bring a bottle or two each.

HOW SERIOUS SHOULD IT BE?

Wine is tasted, and consumed, for many reasons. Wine professionals may taste wines in order to make purchasing decisions, write reviews, assess quality and value and create food- and wine-pairing menus. This type of tasting demands a measure of rigour and professionalism. Home wine-tasting parties, though, need not be so formal. The idea here is to have fun, share your discoveries and enjoy learning about different varieties and different regions. How seriously you go about it is up to you and your group of friends. In our experience, however, the spittoon is rarely used.

1. THE CASUAL APPROACH

A casual wine-tasting party requires just a little thought and preparation. Select a few wines on a certain theme (see below), pull the corks, set out the wines on a table and have your guests taste as they please. Make sure you have at least one glass per person, though a few backups are a good idea in case someone loses a glass in the fray. You might also provide your guests with a little information about the theme of the tasting, such as some background on the region, grape variety or winery being exposed.

A bite of food is recommended whenever alcohol is served. This can be as simple as a basket of cheese gougères (page 214) or as involved as one of the full menus provided in this book. Or, choose one of the seasonal small-plates menus that Dinah has provided for a light post-tasting meal (pages 144–47). Make sure you have

plenty of water on hand; bottled water is preferable, as the strong chlorinated taste of tap water can interfere with the enjoyment of the wines.

2. THE SERIOUS APPROACH

For a more serious approach, you will want to arrange a place where guests can sit down and taste multiple glasses. Provide notebooks and pens for guests to record their impressions, and provide some background research and tasting notes on each of the wines. The Internet is a great resource for this type of information. Many wineries have their own Web sites, with technical details on all of their products.

Serious groups like to rank the wines and come up with a consensus on the winning wine of the night. This can be done by asking each taster to rank his or her three favourite wines in order from one to three. You can then tally up the results at the end of the tasting, awarding 3 points for each wine ranked number one, 2 points for second-place wines and 1 point for third-place ones.

LIGHT, ODOURS AND FOOD

A source of bright light is necessary to inspect a wine's visual attributes properly. Many key points regarding a wine's origins, grape variety, winemaking methods, age and alcohol level can be discerned from its appearance. Fluorescent lights, for example, will alter the appearance of wines, making them seem more green-tinged.

Since strong smells will interfere with the aromas of wine, perfumes, smoke and other intrusive odours should be avoided, or at least minimized. Strongly flavoured foods eaten before (or during) a wine tasting will desensitize your palate and significantly affect your impressions. It is a good idea, however, to have some food in your stomach before diving into a flight of wine, as hunger will also alter your perceptions of taste. Offer slices of plain baguette or water crackers during the tasting, and reserve the more serious food for the after party. Serve neutral, low-mineral bottled water such as Evian during the tasting. It's a good idea to rinse out your mouth every few sips, especially when tasting young tannic reds or sweet wines.

GLASSWARE

Use a colourless, totally transparent glass with a long stem so that you can hold it without warming the bowl with your hands or smudging the glass. The bowl of the glass should be larger than the rim, as in the shape of a tulip. This will concentrate the aromas like an inverted funnel, and permit the gentle rotation of the glass to aerate the wine without risk of spilling.

Convention has it that white-wine glasses are generally smaller than red-wine glasses only because of the temperature issue. As whites are served and appreciated chilled, smaller glasses are used and refilled more frequently so that the wine is always refreshingly cool. Whites are not,

however, any less aromatic, complex or deserving of full-sized glassware than reds are. For wine tastings, one size of glass is suitable for both reds and whites. The International Standards Organization (ISO) has a purpose-built 7-oz (21.5 cl) tasting glass often used by professionals, though any tapered glass of 8 to 12 oz will work perfectly well. If sparkling wine is to be tasted, a narrow flute is the best choice. The small surface area of wine in contact with the air will keep the bubbly bubbling much longer than the flat-bottomed, wide-rimmed coupe. If you have any of these lurking in your sideboard, save them for the sorbet course!

A 2-oz serving is usually sufficient for tasting, so you can count on one bottle of wine to serve about twelve people.

Ideally you should have a separate glass for each wine to be served, so you can go back and forth and compare. With twelve people tasting eight wines, for example, you would need 96 glasses. Since very few of us have that many stems in the sideboard, rent the necessary glassware. You will also avoid having to wash and polish the glasses at the end of a long night. At the very least you will need one glass per person.

When going from one wine to the next it is not necessary to rinse the glass with water each time, as long as you are pouring the same style of wine or going from less intense to more intense. If you are going from red back to white, or sweet back to dry, rinse with a little bottled water.

THE RATIO OF WINES TO GUESTS

The number of wines included in the tasting really depends on the theme, the availability of the wine, the budget and how many guests will be attending. Anything less than three wines doesn't really constitute a tasting, and anything more than eight to ten can be too much for all but the most diehard tasters. With a large number of wines you should provide a spittoon of some kind—a Champagne bucket or a ceramic pitcher is perfect; transparent pitchers look unattractive when filled with expectorated wine—for guests who don't want to drink it all. Indeed, you may insist that your guests leave their vehicles at home or that a designated driver be nominated. One bottle of wine is enough for twelve people to taste, so for more than twelve guests you will need a second bottle. More than twenty-four guests calls for three bottles, and so on in multiples of twelve.

OPEN OR BLIND?

The first consideration is whether the tasting will be open or blind. An open tasting means that the wines are known upfront: the vintage, grape variety, region and producer are all revealed as the wines are tasted. A blind tasting, in contrast, means that all or part of the wine's identity is concealed until after the wine has been tasted and judgements made.

Blind tastings force you to concentrate on what's in the glass, not what's on the label or any preconceived notions you may have. So a humble wine often comes out ahead of many more expensive wines in blind tastings, bringing surprise and, occasionally, some embarrassment. Blind tasting is a humbling experience, but there is no more true and accurate way to taste wine.

Each of the tasting themes below can be conducted open or blind. If the tasting is blind, simply cover each bottle with a paper bag and number it. Alternatively, you can pour each wine into a numbered carafe and keep the bottles out of sight. If your guests are bringing bottles for a blind tasting, ask them to bag the wines before arriving. You can also have someone in the group bag the bottles and a different person number them, so that no one will be able to identify the wine they brought.

WINE-TASTING THEMES

The only limit to the theme of a wine tasting is imagination, as any selection of multiple wines constitutes a tasting. We have outlined a few common themes here to get you started. Each has a certain focus, allowing you to gain a bit of experience in a particular area by comparing wines that have something in common rather than just a jumble of wildly different wines.

1. VARIETAL TASTINGS

A varietal tasting focusses on a single grape variety or on similar blends of varieties from anywhere in the world. How does Chardonnay made in Burgundy compare to Chardonnay from California's Sonoma County, Canada's Niagara Peninsula or Chile's Casablanca Valley? Or how about Bordeaux-style blends (Cabernet Sauvignon, Cabernet Franc and Merlot, a.k.a. Meritage) from France's Bordeaux, California's Napa Valley and Argentina's Mendoza region?

Comparing the same variety grown in different parts of the world can be a fascinating exercise. It will give you an idea of the breadth of flavours possible in a single variety, as well as its immutable, characteristic traits. What marks the style of the wine more? Is it the region or the grape? Or perhaps the producer has the most influence over style? Serve each sample blind and allow the wine, not the region, the producer or the price, to speak. There may be as many winning wines as there are guests in attendance. One thing is for sure: you will be surprised.

Varietal tastings are easy to organize. Pick your favourite grape, one you would like to get to know a little better, or perhaps even a grape you've never tasted before. Purchase several different bottles and set up a wine tasting. For a truly international experience, pick a grape that is widely planted all over the world. Chardonnay, Sauvignon Blanc, Pinot Gris/Grigio or Riesling are good bets for white varieties, and Pinot Noir, Merlot, Cabernet Sauvignon, Cabernet Franc and Syrah/Shiraz work well for reds.

When looking for examples from the Old World (Europe), you may need to enlist the aid of your local product consultant, as the grape variety does not often appear on the label. (White Burgundy, for example, is made from Chardonnay, but you would be hard-pressed to find Chardonnay written anywhere on the label.) More obscure, local varieties without international distribution might be more suitable for a different kind of tasting.

2. REGIONAL TASTINGS

A regional tasting focusses on the range of wines available from a distinct wine-producing area. It's like a virtual vacation, giving you the opportunity to taste a wide array of wines that you might find if you were on holiday in the region. You can include wines of the same or different vintages; the focus is more on the diversity within the region. The Italian regions of Tuscany and Sicily, western Australia and South Africa—the possibilities are limitless. Just browse through one section of the liquor store and pick up several bottles, or better yet, let your guests know the theme ahead of time and have each of them bring a bottle from that region.

3. HORIZONTAL TASTINGS

In a horizontal tasting, guests sample wines from the same vintage year, either from many different producers in the same region or from producers in many regions making the same style of wine. An example would be, say, 2003 Ontario Rieslings or 1994 vintage ports or 1998 wines from Châteauneuf-du-Pape. This is an ideal way to compare the production styles of several producers working under similar climatic conditions.

Differences in winemaking techniques, specific blends (where permitted) and quality levels become much more evident when making this kind of direct comparison. If you wish to do this tasting blind, tell your guests the theme but not the specific producers or bottle prices. If everyone is bringing a bottle, give your guests some parameters such as the theme and the price range.

4. VERTICAL TASTINGS

In a vertical tasting, several different vintages from one particular producer are sampled. This is a great way to get a sense of how weather affects wine styles from year to year, as well as how wines change in the bottle over time. This type of tasting is usually done with well-known wine producers from classic growing regions with significant variations in vintage, such as Bordeaux, Burgundy or the Rhône Valley in France, Barolo in Italy, or the Napa Valley in California to name but a few. In more stable warm-climate areas, vintage variation is less pronounced.

A minimum of three different vintages is a good start, though six or eight is even better! A little legwork is often necessary to track down the wines, unless you or your friends have been collecting wines from a particular producer for a number of years. Given the rarity of older wines, it is also a little more expensive to put on this kind of tasting.

A vertical tasting is usually done open, and the wines are often tasted from most recent to oldest, or vice versa. The oldest tends to be the most prized and anticipated and is frequently served last. Some believe, however, that the more delicate and fragile older wines should be served first, before the young bruisers overwhelm your palate.

5. SEASONAL TASTINGS

As our food cravings tend to follow seasonal patterns, so too do our wine preferences. What could top fresh, herbal-scented whites to welcome asparagus in the spring, or well-chilled rosés for a summer picnic? Fall demands earthy, gamey reds and oak-aged whites to accompany wild-mushroom, truffle and game season, while winter calls for big, brooding reds and luscious sweet dessert and fortified wines over which to meditate while sitting fireside.

Hosting a wine-tasting party based on a seasonal menu of food and wine is a guaranteed success. Select several wines to match the season: the warmer the weather, the cooler and lighter the wines; the cooler the weather, the richer and more full-bodied the wines should be. The first few warm days of springtime would be an ideal occasion for a varietal Sauvignon Blanc tasting; summer is perfect for a regional tasting of fresh and delicate whites and reds from Ontario. In the fall, look to the earthy reds and whites of France's Burgundy and Rhône Valley regions for inspiration, perhaps along a horizontal theme; winter's deep freeze calls for a selection of heart-warming ports, or bold, luscious reds from Australia and California to remind us of warmer climes. Yet another choice would be a tasting based on the theme of dried-grape wines from the Old World—like Veneto's Amarone, which has been known to humankind since antiquity.

6. POTLUCK FOOD AND WINE TASTINGS

This is the best and easiest way to combine your love of food, wine and friends. Ask each guest to bring one wine and a matching dish, and prepare for a night of uninhibited tasting and talking. Or, assign each participant a specific course, from appetizer through to dessert, in order to create a full menu.

HIRE A SOMMELIER

If you think these ideas sound wonderful, but you wonder who has the time and the resources to source ten vintages of a Bordeaux *cru classé* or the top eight super-Tuscans of 1997, or if your friends know even less about wine than you do, consider hiring a sommelier. A sommelier is a service professional dedicated to wine, and you can hire one for the evening, much as you might hire a caterer to handle the dining details. He or she will know the latest trends, top producers, best buys and, importantly, where to find them. Your sommelier can source and purchase the wine on your behalf according to your budget and theme, handle glassware rentals, provide background information on the wines and lead you and your guests through the tasting. The perspective of a wine professional is always valuable, and you and your guests will learn while enjoying. They will also be impressed.

REQUIREMENTS FOR A WINE TASTING FOR 20

2 BOTTLES *of* EACH WINE

20 *to* 40 **ISO** *or* 8- *to* 10-OZ WINE GLASSES

20 WATER GLASSES

10 BOTTLES (EACH 750 ML/26 OZ) WATER

1 DECANTER *per* WINE (*for* OLD RED WINES, AERATING YOUNG WINES *or* SERVING WINES BLIND)

1 ICE BUCKET *and* ICE (*for* KEEPING WINE CHILLED)

6 *to* 10 SPITTOONS (OPTIONAL)

20 NOTEBOOKS *and* PENS (OPTIONAL)

BACKGROUND INFORMATION *on* WINES *to be* SERVED (OPTIONAL)

BREAD *or* CRACKERS (2 SLICES *of* BREAD *and* 3 CRACKERS *per* PERSON)

20 SANDWICH *or* TASTING-SIZED PLATES

20 DINNER FORKS

TWO SMALL-PLATE MENUS *for a* POST WINE-TASTING SUPPER

WINTER:

BEEF TENDERLOIN *à la* BOURGUIGNONNE *served with* RICE *or* MASHED POTATOES

SUMMER:

WILD MUSHROOM *and* ASPARAGUS RISOTTO *served with a* LEAFY GREEN SALAD

SETTING THE SCENE

DECOR IDEAS

Regardless of your theme, you need to set up the room for your wine tasting by allocating groups of wine to separate tables. But wine tastings can range from studious to serendipitous, so it's a good idea to use decor to set your intended tone.

If the tasting is to be a very serious matter, you will want to provide chairs with tables so oenophiles can sit with their assorted glasses and make copious comparative notes. Fairly bright lighting and white table linen will enable them to judge physical aspects of the wine, such as colour, brilliance and viscosity.

Wine lovers at the informal extreme will prefer strolling from table to table without writing too many notes. In this case, chairs and writing tables won't be required. Perhaps needing only to discern white from red, this group will appreciate the softer kind of lighting that enhances tasters' credibility by hiding dribbles of wine, pinkness of nose and bleariness of eye.

MUSIC PICKS

Musician, actor, arranger and composer Joe Sealy is a *force majeure* in this country's jazz industry. He has won many awards, including a Juno for best jazz album and a Dora for musical direction, and he has toured with jazz greats like Joe Williams and Milt Jackson.

In our early catering days, we were lucky to get Joe to perform at some of our more extravagant parties. Now he's impossibly busy touring, running Triplet Records and hosting his popular jazz interview show, *Joe Sealy's Duets*. But he paused long enough to compile this list of favourites for your wine-tasting.

- Charlie Haden, *Nocturne* (Verve)
- Etta James, *Mystery Lady* (Private Music)
- Miles Davis, *Kind of Blue* (Columbia)
- Modern Jazz Quartet, *No Sun in Venice* (Atlantic)
- John Coltrane Quartet, *Ballads* (MCA/Impulse)
- Ellis and Branford Marsalis, *Loved Ones* (Columbia)

GET AHEAD SCHEDULE

1 MONTH BEFORE

- Send out invitations.

1 WEEK BEFORE

- Double check that you have all the wine, glassware and non-alcoholic beverages you need.
- Finalize the post-tasting menu.

THE DAY BEFORE

- Place any white, rosé or sparkling wines in the refrigerator to chill.
- Stand old red wines upright to allow the sediment to precipitate to the bottom of the bottle.
- Print out background information on the wines and make enough photocopies to go around.
- If serving BEEF TENDERLOIN, make red wine sauce.

THE DAY OF

- Set out glassware.
- Place crackers or sliced bread in baskets.
- Set out bottles of water.
- If making RISOTTO, prepare asparagus and mushrooms. Make salad dressing. Par-cook rice.
- If making BEEF TENDERLOIN, prepare the beef and vegetables. Make rice or mashed potatoes.

1 HOUR BEFORE

- Decant red wines, if necessary (older red wines are decanted to separate them from the sediment, young red wines to aerate them).
- Open all the wines, leaving whites, rosés and sparkling wines on ice.
- For a casual tasting, set out the wines on the tasting table.

- Serve low-alcohol aperitifs, sparkling wine or non-alcoholic beverages.

WHEN EVERYONE HAS ARRIVED

- Pour the wines, ensuring that everyone knows what order they have been poured in.
- Taste, discuss, enjoy!

30 MINUTES BEFORE THE TASTING ENDS

- If serving RISOTTO, combine stock, par-cooked rice and vegetables to finish cooking. Portion into soup plates and serve. Toss salad, portion onto small plates or salad bowls and serve.
- If serving BEEF TENDERLOIN, combine red wine sauce and beef and vegetables, and reheat. Reheat mashed potatoes or rice in microwave, portion onto small plates. Spoon hot sauce over the beef and serve.

Beef Tenderloin à la Bourguignonne

The term "à la Bourguignonne" means "as prepared in Burgundy," and this recipe retains all of the best classic French elements. The rich red-wine braising sauce, plump mushrooms and pearl onions are all traditional, but our version uses fine beef tenderloin instead of the heavier standard chuck. If you are making this recipe for a party, you can make the individual components separately ahead of time and assemble them at the last moment. Serve hot with crusty bread for dipping, or spooned over herbed rice or mashed potatoes.

RED WINE SAUCE

4 oz dried porcini mushrooms

4 cups red wine, such as Pinot Noir

2 tsp butter

1 lb smoked bacon, in ¼-inch slices

8 large shallots, minced

¾ cup all-purpose flour

6 cups beef stock

BEEF AND VEGETABLES

¼ cup olive oil

10 oz pearl onions, blanched and peeled

1 Tbsp butter

4 cups thinly sliced wild mushrooms

5 lbs beef tenderloin, patted dry with a paper towel, in 1-inch cubes

3 cups baby carrots, blanched

RED WINE SAUCE: Place mushrooms in a bowl, add red wine and soak for at least 4 hours. Using a slotted spoon, transfer mushrooms to a clean bowl and set aside. Line a fine-mesh sieve with a damp new disposable kitchen cloth. Strain wine through the cloth to remove any grit. Reserve wine.

Place butter in a medium saucepan on medium-low heat, add bacon and cook slowly, stirring, until fat is rendered, 8 to 10 minutes. Add shallots and increase the heat to medium, stirring, until shallots are soft and translucent, about 5 minutes. Reduce the heat to medium-low and add flour, stirring to make a roux. Cook for 10 minutes until roux is slightly browned. Stir in beef stock and reserved wine, increase the heat to medium and cook sauce, stirring occasionally, for 20 minutes. Add reserved mushrooms. Season with salt and pepper to taste.

BEEF AND VEGETABLES: In a large sauté pan on medium heat, place 2 tsp of the olive oil and sauté pearl onions until golden and translucent, about 5 minutes. Season to taste with salt and pepper and transfer to a medium bowl.

Add butter and another 2 tsp olive oil to the pan, stir in mushrooms and sauté until mushrooms are soft and liquid has been expelled and reduced, about 5 minutes. Season to taste with salt and pepper and set aside.

Season beef cubes with salt and pepper. Heat 1 Tbsp olive oil in a large sauté pan on high heat, then sear beef in batches, adding more oil as necessary, until just brown, 4 to 5 minutes. Be careful to leave the beef rare. Remove from the heat and set aside.

Bring sauce back to a boil, add pearl onions and carrots and simmer for 8 to 10 minutes. Add beef cubes and mushrooms and stir until well combined. Heat until beef has been warmed through but is still rare, about 5 minutes. Serve immediately on individual plates.

Serves 20

Wild Mushroom and Asparagus Risotto

Risotto is one of those dishes that demands constant attention and must be eaten the moment it is done. It means stirring the cauldron over a hot stove surrounded by guests waiting with spoons and bowls. This is not on for cocktail parties. But everyone loves risotto, so we have devised a way of preparing risotto ahead of time. This recipe shows how to par-cook it in advance and then finish it just before serving—turning risotto into the perfect party dish. Use high-quality Italian rice (such as Carnaroli, Arborio superfine or Vialone Nano) that will hold its shape. Served with a mixed green salad, this risotto makes a lovely light summer meal.

24 cups strong chicken stock (page 123)

3 Tbsp olive oil

1½ cups butter

12 shallots, diced

6 cups Carnaroli, Vialone Nano or Arborio superfine rice

1½ cups dry white wine

7½ cups asparagus, tough ends removed, in ½-inch diagonal pieces

7½ cups thinly sliced mixed wild mushrooms (such as shiitake, oyster, portobello or chanterelle)

3 cups grated Parmesan cheese

½ cup shaved Parmesan-Reggiano cheese, for topping

Coat 2 to 3 baking sheets with nonstick spray or line them with parchment paper. In a medium saucepan on high heat, heat 15 cups of the stock until simmering. Reduce the heat to low.

Place oil and ¼ cup of the butter in a large, shallow sauté pan on medium heat until foam subsides. Add shallots and sauté until soft, about 2 minutes. Add rice and cook, stirring, until grains are well coated and slightly translucent, about 5 minutes. Reduce the heat slightly and add a third of the hot stock (about 5 cups), stirring occasionally until the liquid is absorbed. Add another third of the stock and stir until absorbed. Add the last third of the stock and the wine, stirring until absorbed. The entire process should take 12 to 15 minutes.

Spread the par-cooked rice in a thin layer on the prepared baking sheets. Cool, transfer to a small bowl and refrigerate, covered with plastic wrap, for up to 1 day.

To cook the risotto, heat 1 Tbsp of the butter in a large sauté pan on medium heat. Add a third of the asparagus (about 2½ cups) and cook, stirring, until just soft, 4 to 5 minutes. Season to taste with salt and pepper, then transfer to a bowl and set aside. Cook the remaining asparagus in two batches, adding 1 Tbsp butter with each batch. Cool, then refrigerate, covered with plastic wrap, for up to 1 day.

Add another 1 Tbsp butter to the pan, stir in a third of the mushrooms (about 2½ cups) and sauté until mushrooms are soft. Remove from the heat, transfer to another bowl and set aside. Cook the remaining mushrooms in two batches, adding 1 Tbsp butter with each batch. Cool, then refrigerate, covered with plastic wrap, for up to 1 day.

Twenty minutes before serving, remove rice and vegetables from the refrigerator. Bring the remaining 9 cups of chicken stock to a boil in a medium saucepan on high heat, then reduce the heat to a simmer. Pour half of the hot stock into a large, wide saucepan. Bring it to a boil on medium-high heat, then add rice all at once and stir constantly until all the stock has been absorbed. Stir in mushrooms and asparagus. Gradually add the remaining hot stock, a ladleful at a time, stirring constantly until most of the liquid has been absorbed and the mixture is creamy. Remove from the heat and add the remaining ¾ cup butter and the grated Parmesan cheese. Season with more salt and pepper, if necessary. Garnish with shaved Parmesan-Reggiano cheese and serve immediately on individual plates.

Makes 20 small plates

NEW YEAR'S DAY RELAXER

condo brunch for 30

Great view, fabulous neighbourhood and urban lifestyle: condominium living means that the whole big city is your backyard. And how better to celebrate life than by having friends over for brunch. Maybe it's a birthday or New Year's Day or your own condo-warming—whatever the occasion, entertaining is easy and elegant on Sunday afternoon in the city.

This brunch is designed for a New Year's Day celebration. Certain elements are in play that afternoon that are unique to the holiday. These elements can be summed up in one phrase: the night before. Some of your guests will show up slightly hungover. Others will arrive well rested and ravenous. A few may drop in on their way home from First Night revelling. All will straggle in at various times according to the where and when of their respective New Year's Eve bedtimes.

Designed for an open kitchen and loft-o-minimum space, this brunch menu requires very little last-minute cooking. That leaves the kitchen open for bartending. Everything is served at room temperature or from warming trays to accommodate varied arrival times. The menu is made up of fork food served on small plates so guests can stand and mingle. That way, you won't need lots of seating—your usual furniture set-up should work just fine.

MENU FOR A DAY OF RELAXATION, REFLECTION AND RECOVERY

OYSTER SHOOTERS

TANGY TOMATO-BEER MIX

TEQUILA CEVICHE MIX

VODKA CUCUMBER MIX

CRISPY CHEESE *and* PEPPER STRAWS

AS-YOU-PLEASE EGGS BENEDICT

HOME FRIES *with* SPANISH ONIONS

CROISSANT QUICHE LORRAINE

ENDIVE CITRUS SALAD *with* HONEY-LEMON DRESSING

TOP BANANA CREAM PIE

COCKTAILS

CINNAMON APPLE COLLINS

ESPRESSO CRAIC MARTINI

SETTING THE SCENE

DECOR IDEAS

Your condominium view is all the decor you need for a midwinter afternoon. Just add a big vase of fresh-cut flowers. Their artless beauty is a welcome sight after the month-long decor glut known as the Christmas-Dawali-Hanukkah-holiday season.

Since this is a low-energy day, with guests arriving at different times, the best way to serve this food is to put everything out on a big help-yourself buffet with a separate station for dessert and coffee. If you have an open kitchen, serve the drinks, including the Oyster Shooters, from the counter.

MUSIC PICKS TO START THE YEAR

Journalist and architecture critic Christopher Hume may win awards for his insightful and erudite writings on heritage architecture and urban issues, but his most talked-about columns have been his condominium critiques in the *Toronto Star*. A former bass player whose second calling is music, he has selected these CDs as music for your condo party.

- Dave Brubeck Quartet, *Time Out* (Columbia/Legacy)
- Penguin Café Orchestra, *Preludes Airs and Yodels* (Virgin)
- *Ravel and Debussy: The String Quartets* (Philips)
- The Beatles, *Rubber Soul* (Capitol)
- Stevie Wonder, *Songs in the Key of Life* (Motown)

SZABO'S WINE ALTERNATIVES

A DROP-IN PARTY on the first day of the year is the perfect opportunity to uncork a variety of weird and wonderful wines to encourage a year of new discoveries and adventures. Most of the egg-based dishes to be served, contrary to the wintry conditions outside, call out for light, crisp whites, preferably with bubbles. Despite our seasonal lust for heart-warming reds during midwinter darkness, lighter-style whites may not be such a bad idea given the previous night's, and probably month's, revelry. They can also call forth the distant days of spring and the return of warm sunshine.

An eclectic tasting should include some sparkling wine, a morning-after pick-me-up for those hungover friends who believe the best thing for what ails you is more of what ails you. For the Champagne, choose some of the smaller grower Champagnes instead of the usual Grandes Marques big-brand labels, and include some Blanc de Blancs, Blanc de Noirs and vintage cuvées for extra diversity and interest. For sparklers from other parts of the world, intrigue your weary guests' palates with a traditional-method sparkling wine from Ontario or similarly styled cool-climate examples from New Zealand or Tasmania. Northern Italy offers us the fun and fruity Prosecco (also perfect for mimosas), as well as the frothy, sweet low-alcohol Moscato d'Asti that could be just the ticket.

Riesling in all its wonderful guises is the ideal white: low to moderate alcohol, vibrant acidity and sweetness levels ranging from bone dry to lusciously sweet. Try a varietal tasting of Rieslings from around the world. Alternatively, browse the dark, unfamiliar corners of your local wine shop and pick up a selection of white grapes you've never heard of. You might try a Grüner Veltliner from Austria, Furmint from Hungary, Robola from Greece, Encruzado from Portugal, Verdelho from Australia or Vidal from Ontario, to choose just a few obscurities. Open and compare them in the comfort of your own home, surrounded by close friends.

CHAMPAGNE COCKTAILS

If New Year's ebullience has you in the mood for popping corks, you can spread the cheer a little more fancifully and a little bit farther in classic Champagne cocktails like the Bellini (Champagne mixed with white peach purée), Mimosa (Champagne mixed with freshly squeezed orange juice and Cointreau) and Kir Royale (Champagne mixed with Crème de Cassis).

Although the sound of their names may evoke images of jetting from Venice to Ibiza and Monte Carlo, you don't really have to break the bank to enjoy Champagne cocktails. There are many quality sparkling wines that are less expensive than true French Champagne, and perfect for mixing into very special drinks. Prosecco and Spanish Cavas are wonderful in signature Champagne cocktails like our elegant Pear Sparkle and Raspberry Royale (page 231) or stirred into party pitchers of Sparkling White Sangria (page 130) and pints of rich Black Velvet (page 86). Still more extravagant are sweet sparklers like the Pink Pussycat (page 104).

These Champagne cocktails bubble over with elegant exuberance and are an extra special treat for the last hours of the holiday—after which all resolutions will be in effect.

3 WEEKS AHEAD

- Rent glasses, china, cutlery and chafing dishes, if necessary (be sure to confirm your order during this busy season).

1 WEEK AHEAD

- Make CRISPY CHEESE AND PEPPER STRAWS.
- Order fresh oysters (page 43) for OYSTER SHOOTERS.

2 DAYS BEFORE

- Get and arrange the flowers.
- Make HONEY-LEMON DRESSING for ENDIVE CITRUS SALAD.
- Make the filling for TOP BANANA CREAM PIE.
- Organize the music.

THE DAY BEFORE

- Finish TOP BANANA CREAM PIE and refrigerate.
- Make CROISSANT QUICHE LORRAINE and refrigerate.
- Make APPLE-ONION CURRY and CHEDDAR MORNAY sauces for EGGS BENEDICT and store in tightly covered containers in the refrigerator.
- Sauté mushrooms and spinach for EGGS BENEDICT toppings and refrigerate.
- Boil potatoes and sauté onions for HOME FRIES WITH SPANISH ONIONS and refrigerate.
- Cut fruit for ENDIVE CITRUS SALAD, wrap tightly and refrigerate.
- Make espresso for ESPRESSO CRAIC MARTINIS and chill.
- Make TANGY TOMATO-BEER, VODKA CUCUMBER AND TEQUILA CEVICHE mixes for OYSTER SHOOTERS, cover tightly and refrigerate.
- Organize layout of the buffet table, oyster station and bar.

1½ HOURS BEFORE

- Arrange slices of smoked salmon on a platter, cover and refrigerate until ready to serve.
- Finish HOME FRIES WITH SPANISH ONIONS, keep warm in the oven.
- Finish ENDIVE CITRUS SALAD and place on buffet.
- Toast half of the muffins for EGGS BENEDICT.
- Prepare the eggs for baking.
- Shuck oysters and set up OYSTER SHOOTER station.
- Slice and fry half of the beef and ham toppings for EGGS BENEDICT and arrange over warmers on buffet.
- Make HOLLANDAISE SAUCE.

30 MINUTES BEFORE

- Reheat CROISSANT QUICHE LORRAINE in the oven.
- Pre-mix ESPRESSO CRAIC MARTINIS, if desired.
- Pre-mix CINNAMON APPLE COLLINS.

1 HOUR LATER

- Bake more eggs as necessary.
- Toast the remaining English muffins, as necessary.
- Sauté the remaining beef fillets and ham slices (or bacon), as necessary.
- Reheat the remaining mushrooms and spinach, as necessary.
- Replenish sauce bowls, as necessary.
- Make coffee and tea.
- Slice and set out TOP BANANA CREAM PIE.

10 MINUTES BEFORE GUESTS ARRIVE

- Reheat half of the vegetable toppings and the APPLE-ONION CURRY, CHEDDAR MORNAY and HOLLANDAISE sauces for EGGS BENEDICT. Set out half of each sauce and the mushroom and spinach toppings.
- Bake half of the eggs and put them on warming trays on the buffet.
- Place the platter of smoked salmon on the buffet with the other toppings.
- Set out half of the HOME FRIES, CHEESE STRAWS and CROISSANT QUICHES to complete the buffet.

Oyster Shooters

Nothing adds sophistication to a menu quite like raw oysters. These fun, flavourful shooters will bring out the adventurer in even the most modest foodie at your party. They are our riff on those venerable hangover antidotes, the Prairie Oyster and the Hair of the Dog. Do a few of these shooters with your first guests and word of mouth will take care of the rest.

This recipe will serve twelve guests with three oysters each. If your friends are big raw oyster fans, multiply quantities accordingly. Be sure not to shuck the oysters more than 2 hours before serving them.

TANGY TOMATO-BEER MIX

½ cup store-bought seafood sauce

¼ cup beer (your favourite)

2 tsp freshly squeezed lemon juice

TEQUILA CEVICHE MIX

½ cup freshly squeezed lime juice

½ cup good-quality tequila

⅓ cup finely chopped fresh cilantro

1 tsp minced jalapeño pepper

2 tsp minced garlic

¾ tsp salt or to taste

VODKA CUCUMBER MIX

½ cup freshly squeezed lemon juice

¼ cup good-quality vodka

3 Tbsp finely diced English cucumber, unpeeled

3 tsp horseradish, bottled or freshly grated

2 tsp smooth Dijon mustard

¾ tsp salt or to taste

36 fresh oysters, on the half shell, liquor drained and all shell fragments removed (pages 43–44)

3 to 5 lbs crushed ice

GLASSWARE: thirty-six 1-oz shot glasses

TANGY TOMATO-BEER MIX: In a measuring cup, mix seafood sauce, beer and lemon juice until well combined. Season to taste with salt and pepper. Pour 1 Tbsp of mix into each of 12 shot glasses.

TEQUILA CEVICHE MIX: In a measuring cup, mix lime juice, tequila, cilantro, jalapeño pepper, garlic and salt until well combined. Pour 1 Tbsp of mix into each of 12 shot glasses.

VODKA CUCUMBER MIX: In a measuring cup, mix lemon juice, vodka, cucumber, horseradish, Dijon mustard and salt until well combined. Pour 1 Tbsp of mix into each of the remaining 12 shot glasses.

TO ASSEMBLE: On a large platter with sides deep enough to contain water from melting ice, make a bed of crushed ice and arrange oysters on the half shell on top.

On a matching platter or a tray, arrange the 36 shot glasses. For each guest, slip one oyster off its shell and into one of the shot glasses containing their preferred mix, make a toast and shoot it back.

Makes ¾ cup of each mix, enough for 36 oyster shooters

Crispy Cheese and Pepper Straws

These flaky, cheesy straws are super simple to make but look elegant enough to have come from your local gourmet grocer. Long, thin and golden, the straws look best when arranged upright in an attractive glass or a crystal vase.

The straws can be made up to 2 weeks ahead, allowed to cool and stored in a covered container in the refrigerator. You can also use frozen phyllo sheets for this recipe; just thaw them beforehand.

1 egg white

2 Tbsp olive oil

17 sheets fresh phyllo pastry, each
17 × 14 inches

1½ cups grated Cheddar or 1¼ cups grated Parmesan-Reggiano cheese

salt and cracked black pepper to taste

Preheat the oven to 400°F. Line a baking sheet with parchment paper or aluminum foil coated with nonstick spray.

In a small bowl, beat together egg white and olive oil until foamy. Set aside.

Place a phyllo sheet on a clean, dry work surface (keep the remaining phyllo covered with plastic wrap and a damp kitchen towel). Using a long sharp knife, cut the sheet lengthwise into four even strips. Work carefully, as the phyllo is very thin and tears easily.

Using a pastry brush, gently glaze one strip with the egg mixture. Sprinkle with 1 tsp Cheddar and a pinch of salt (or ¾ tsp Parmesan-Reggiano, a pinch of salt and a few grindings of pepper).

Fold up the phyllo strip in thirds lengthwise to make a loose roll about 14 inches long and 1 inch in diameter. Brush with the egg mixture. Holding one end of the strip stationary, gently wind the other end toward you 3 or 4 times to twist the strip into a long cigar shape. Place the twisted phyllo straw on the baking sheet and brush the top with more of the egg mixture. Repeat with the remaining phyllo strips, until all of the pastry and cheese is used up.

Bake straws for about 15 minutes, or until golden brown. Cool for 2 to 3 hours at room temperature before serving to give the pastry time to crisp.

Makes about 65 cheese straws

As-You-Please Eggs Benedict

Classic and elegant, Eggs Benedict is a welcome addition to any brunch menu. What will delight your guests is the effort you have made to please all palates with this smorgasbord of buttery poached eggs, three creamy sauces and several rich toppings. Set up this dish buffet-style and let guests help themselves. (We've given directions for preparing eggs and garnishes in two batches so you can refresh the buffet with hot selections at the halfway point of your brunch.) You'll need about forty-five 3-inch ramekins in which to poach the eggs.

You can prepare the Apple-Onion Curry and Cheddar Mornay sauces 1 or 2 days ahead, refrigerate them and reheat just before serving. For best results, make the Hollandaise Sauce the same day.

APPLE-ONION CURRY SAUCE

⅔ cup butter

7 onions, finely diced

⅔ cup mild curry powder

7 apples, cored, in ½-inch dice

⅔ cup all-purpose flour

7 cups strong chicken stock (page 123)

3 tsp salt or to taste

CHEDDAR MORNAY SAUCE

8 cups milk

½ cup unsalted butter

¼ cup minced onion

¾ cup all-purpose flour

1 tsp salt

½ tsp white pepper

1 Tbsp nutmeg or to taste

6 cups grated Cheddar cheese

HOLLANDAISE SAUCE

9 egg yolks

6 Tbsp warm water

2 Tbsp freshly squeezed lemon juice

½ tsp cayenne pepper or to taste

3 cups butter, heated to bubbling

(continued over)

(make at least 3 cups each of cooked spinach and mushrooms)

4 Tbsp unsalted butter

4 Tbsp olive oil

30 oz baby spinach, washed, stems
    removed and dried

8 cups thinly sliced mushrooms

MEAT TOPPINGS

2 to 4 Tbsp olive oil

3 lbs beef tenderloin, in ¼-inch slices
    (about 2 slices or 3 oz beef per muffin),
    seasoned lightly with salt and pepper

3 lbs smoked blackforest ham or good-
    quality peameal bacon, in ½-inch
    slices (about 1 slice or 3 oz per muffin)

2 lbs thinly sliced smoked salmon (2 slices
    per muffin)

ENGLISH MUFFINS

25 English muffins, split in half

1 cup softened butter

BUTTER-POACHED EGGS

45 large eggs

1½ cups butter, melted

APPLE-ONION CURRY SAUCE: Heat butter in a large sauté pan on medium-high heat until foam subsides. Add onion and sauté until soft and translucent, about 5 minutes. Stir in curry powder and cook for another minute. Add apple and cook, stirring, for 3 minutes. Add flour and stir to combine, then cook for 1 minute. Pour in chicken stock and bring to a boil, then reduce the heat to medium-low and allow to simmer uncovered, stirring occasionally, for 5 minutes. Season to taste with salt. Transfer sauce to a stainless steel bowl and refrigerate, covered with plastic wrap, for up to 2 days.

CHEDDAR MORNAY SAUCE: In a 4-qt saucepan, heat milk on medium-high for about 4 minutes, just until bubbles begin to form at the edges. Remove from the heat and set aside.

To make the roux, place butter in a medium heavy-bottomed saucepan on medium-low heat. Add onion and cook until soft and translucent, 2 to 3 minutes. Using a wooden spoon, stir in flour and cook, stirring constantly, for about 3 minutes, being careful not to let the mixture brown.

(continued over)

Gradually add the hot milk to the roux, stirring constantly with a whisk to prevent lumps from forming. Bring to a boil. Reduce the heat to a simmer and add salt, pepper and nutmeg. Simmer, uncovered, for 10 minutes, or until the sauce thickens. Add Cheddar cheese to the hot mixture, stirring with a whisk to incorporate. Transfer to a bowl and cover with plastic wrap, pressing it directly onto the sauce to prevent a skin from forming. Cool, then refrigerate.

HOLLANDAISE SAUCE: In a blender, place 3 of the egg yolks, 2 Tbsp of the water, 2 tsp of the lemon juice and a pinch of the cayenne. Season to taste with salt and pepper. Cover and blend for 3 seconds, open the lid, scrape down the sides and blend for another 3 seconds. With the motor on high, pour ⅓ of the hot butter over the egg mixture in a steady stream (about 30 seconds). The sauce should be smooth and well emulsified. If it is not quite combined, blend for another 5 seconds on high. Transfer the sauce to a stainless steel bowl. Place the bowl over a saucepan of hot but not simmering water on low heat until ready to serve. Repeat with the remaining egg yolks, water, lemon juice, cayenne and butter in two batches, adding each to the stainless steel bowl.

VEGGIE TOPPINGS: Melt ½ Tbsp of the butter and ½ Tbsp of the olive oil in a large, heavy-bottomed sauté pan on medium-high heat. Add 10 oz of the spinach and sauté gently until spinach is wilted but still bright green, about 2 minutes. Season to taste with salt and pepper, mix well, transfer to a microwave-safe container and cover with plastic wrap. Repeat twice with the remaining spinach.

Melt ½ Tbsp butter and ½ Tbsp olive oil in a large sauté pan on medium-high heat. Add 2 cups of the mushrooms and sauté until liquid has been expelled and reduced, 5 to 6 minutes. Season with salt and pepper, mix well, transfer to a microwave-safe container and cover with plastic wrap. Repeat three times with the remaining mushrooms.

MEAT TOPPINGS: Warm a large serving platter in the oven at 200°F. Heat a large sauté pan on high heat. Add 1 Tbsp of the olive oil. Place 4 to 8 beef slices in the pan (be sure they're not crowded) and sear for 1 minute per side. Transfer beef to the warm platter and keep covered with heavy aluminum foil. Repeat with half of the beef slices, adding more oil as necessary. Sear the remaining half of the beef slices when required.

Add another 1 Tbsp of the oil to the pan. Place ham (or bacon) slices in the pan (be sure they're not crowded) and sear for 1 minute per side. Transfer ham (or bacon) to the warm platter and keep covered. Repeat with half of the ham (or bacon) slices, adding more oil as necessary. Sear the remaining half of the ham (or bacon) when required.

Arrange salmon slices on a medium serving platter.

ENGLISH MUFFINS: Preheat the oven to 450°F. Spread muffin halves with butter and place on a baking sheet. Just before serving, toast half of the muffins for 3 to 5 minutes until golden. Place in baskets. Toast the remaining muffins as required.

BUTTER-POACHED EGGS: Preheat the oven to 375°F. Coat forty-five 3-inch ramekins with nonstick spray. Pour 1 tsp melted butter into each ramekin. Place half of the ramekins in a large baking pan. Crack one egg into each ramekin and top with another ½ tsp butter. Add enough hot water to the baking pan to come halfway up the sides of the ramekins. Bake until whites have just set, about 10 minutes. Sprinkle with a little salt and pepper. Repeat with the remaining eggs when required.

TO SERVE: Bring two saucepans of water to a simmer on medium heat. Place the bowl of Cheddar Mornay Sauce over one saucepan and the bowl of Apple-Onion Curry Sauce over the other and allow to reheat, about 15 minutes. Reduce the heat to low. Spoon half of the Mornay sauce and half of the curry sauce into separate serving bowls and place on the buffet. Return the remaining sauce to the heat over the saucepans of simmering water to hold until the buffet needs replenishing. Bring a third saucepan of water to a simmer on low heat. Spoon half of the hollandaise sauce into a serving bowl and place it on the buffet. Place the remaining hollandaise sauce in a bowl over the third saucepan of simmering water and turn heat off to hold.

If necessary, reheat vegetable toppings in a microwave on high power for 2 to 3 minutes. Arrange English muffins, eggs, vegetable and meat toppings on the buffet. Allow guests to assemble their own Eggs Benedict: place two halves of an English muffin on each plate, top with eggs, vegetable and/or meat toppings and sauces. Replenish the buffet with the remaining muffins and ingredient toppings, as required.

Makes 45 servings of Eggs Benedict

HOME FRIES WITH SPANISH ONIONS

The secret to a crunchy, crisp home fry is to boil the potatoes the day before and chill them overnight in the refrigerator. That, combined with a slow cook in a generous amount of olive oil, will yield absolutely perfect home fries.

10 lbs russet (baking) potatoes, unpeeled	¾ cup olive oil
1¼ cups unsalted butter	¾ cup finely chopped fresh parsley, for
10 Spanish onions, thinly sliced	garnish

Place potatoes in 2 or 3 large pots and cover with cold, salted water. Bring to a boil on medium-high heat and cook until tender when pierced with a fork, 20 to 25 minutes. Drain and cool potatoes, transfer to a bowl, cover with plastic wrap and refrigerate for at least 2 hours or overnight.

Cut potatoes into ½-inch chunks. Set aside.

Preheat the oven to 200°F. Heat two large sauté pans on medium heat, then add 2½ Tbsp of the butter to each pan. Add onion, season with salt and pepper, then reduce the heat to medium-low and sauté until golden, 12 to 15 minutes. Divide onion between two large bowls and keep warm in the oven.

Add another 1 Tbsp butter and 1 Tbsp olive oil to each pan and melt on medium heat. Add enough potatoes to just cover the bottom of the pan. Season to taste with salt and pepper and sauté until golden, 15 to 20 minutes. Add half the potatoes to each bowl of onion and keep warm. Continue adding butter and olive oil to the two pans and cooking potatoes, seasoning as you go, until all potatoes have been cooked and added to the onion.

Transfer half of the home fries to a serving dish, sprinkle with half of the parsley and serve immediately. Cover the remaining home fries with aluminum foil. They will hold at room temperature for 2 hours. When required, heat in a 425°F oven, uncovered, for 8 to 10 minutes, stirring occasionally.

Makes 30 servings

Croissant Quiche Lorraine

The grande dame of quiches, Lorraine, does not traditionally have cheese, but to provide a vegetarian version we have added a blend of Swiss cheeses to the classic recipe, deleted the bacon and enhanced the nuttiness with gratings of nutmeg. The croissant crust looks and tastes gorgeous, circling the cheesy centre like the petals of a sunflower. Although these quiches are best made fresh, they can be made up to 2 days ahead and reheated in a 250°F oven for 20 minutes, or just until warm.

20 eggs	1 tsp salt
6 cups half-and-half cream (10%)	8 croissants, cut crosswise diagonally in
⅓ cup finely chopped fresh mixed herbs	¾-inch slices
(such as parsley, sage, rosemary,	2 cups grated Swiss Emmental cheese
chives)	2 cups grated Swiss Gruyère cheese
1 tsp nutmeg	1 cup grated Parmesan-Reggiano cheese

Preheat the oven to 350°F. Coat four 9-inch pie pans with nonstick spray, then brush the sides and bottom with butter.

In a large bowl, beat eggs lightly. Add cream, herbs, nutmeg and salt and beat until well blended.

Dip croissant slices in the egg mixture, coating them lightly, and line the sides of each pie pan with these slices, placing them side by side with the curve of each crust rising above the sides of the pan so they look like the petals of a flower. Use any extra slices to line the bottom of the pan.

Spread Emmental, Gruyère and Parmesan-Reggiano in the bottom of each pan, dividing evenly among the four pans. Divide the egg mixture evenly among the four pans, adjusting croissant slices, if necessary, to keep them against the sides of the pans in a petal-like formation. Grind black pepper on top of each pie, to taste. Bake for 25 to 30 minutes, or just until a knife inserted in the centre of the quiche comes out clean or any liquid that clings to the knife is clear, not yellow.

Allow to rest at room temperature at least 15 minutes before serving.

Makes four 9-inch pies or 24 servings

ENDIVE CITRUS SALAD
with HONEY-LEMON DRESSING

A perfect fruity accompaniment for brunch, this bright salad, with its slight acidity, balances the richness of the Eggs Benedict perfectly.

HONEY-LEMON DRESSING

2½ cups freshly squeezed lemon juice

1½ cups olive oil

¾ cup honey

2 tsp finely minced garlic

1 tsp salt

ENDIVE CITRUS SALAD

1 sweet red onion, thinly sliced (optional)

8 navel oranges

5 ruby-red grapefruit

4 lbs mixed salad greens (such as mesclun)

8 to 10 heads fresh endive, thinly sliced

HONEY-LEMON DRESSING: Combine all ingredients in a bowl and whisk together, or place all ingredients in a blender and process until thoroughly mixed.

ENDIVE CITRUS SALAD: Place onion in a small bowl, cover with cold water and soak for 1 hour. Drain and blot dry with paper towel. Set aside.

Using a small, sharp serrated knife and holding the fruit over a bowl, cut away all pith and zest from oranges and grapefruit. Avoid cutting into the flesh as much as possible. Remove segments by carefully cutting between membrane and flesh, keeping segments whole. Discard pith, zest and membrane. Set aside.

Arrange salad greens and endive on 2 serving platters. Top each platter with half of the red onion. Arrange half of the orange and grapefruit segments atop the onion on each platter. Drizzle with dressing and serve immediately.

Makes 4 cups Honey-Lemon Dressing and enough greens to serve 30 to 35

Top Banana Cream Pie

Not just any banana pie, this one goes over the top with caramel and white chocolate, which, like wishes for your New Year, are sweet and rich. Use the best-quality chocolate you can find, such as Callebaut.

BANANA CRUST

4 cups graham wafer crumbs

¼ cup brown sugar

1 cup melted butter

1 very ripe banana, mashed

BANANA CREAM FILLING

6 cups milk

¾ cup sugar

¾ cup sifted cornstarch

8 egg yolks, beaten

8 oz good-quality white chocolate, grated

2 tsp vanilla extract

8 large ripe bananas, in ¼-inch slices

CARAMEL

⅔ cup sugar

1 cup light corn syrup

1⅓ cups whipping cream (35%)

2 Tbsp cold water

2 tsp cornstarch

1 tsp vanilla extract

TOPPING

4 cups whipping cream (35%)

½ cup icing sugar, sifted

6 oz shaved good-quality white chocolate, for garnish

BANANA CRUST: Preheat the oven to 375°F. In a medium-large bowl, mix together graham wafer crumbs, brown sugar, butter and banana until thoroughly blended. Divide the mixture evenly among three 9-inch pie pans, pressing firmly to completely cover the bottom and sides. Bake for 15 minutes, or until crisped and lightly browned. Set aside to cool.

BANANA CREAM FILLING: Place 5 cups of the milk in a medium heavy-bottomed pot on medium heat and bring to a boil. Remove from the heat and set aside.

(continued over)

In a medium bowl, combine sugar and cornstarch. Add the remaining 1 cup milk and whisk until thoroughly combined. Add egg yolks and whisk until well blended. Slowly add half of the hot milk, whisking constantly.

In a steady stream, pour the egg mixture into the remaining hot milk in the saucepan, whisking constantly. Using a wooden spoon and stirring constantly, cook on low heat until thickened, about 10 minutes. Remove from the heat, add white chocolate and stir to melt and combine. Add vanilla. Set aside to cool.

When completely cool, fold in banana slices. Place a sheet of plastic wrap directly on the surface of the filling, pressing it gently against the filling to prevent a skin from forming.

Chill in the refrigerator for at least 2 hours and up to 6 hours.

CARAMEL: In a very dry heavy-bottomed skillet on medium heat, slowly cook sugar without stirring until melted and golden brown, 5 to 8 minutes. Swirl the skillet occasionally to keep the caramel from burning. When sugar is completely melted and golden, add corn syrup, stirring slowly with a wooden spoon until combined. Pour in cream (the mixture may harden slightly, but it will melt again as cream heats), and stir occasionally. Cook until a candy thermometer registers 210°F, or until the caramel runs in a thin thread when dropped from a spoon.

In a small bowl, add water to cornstarch and stir until smooth. Add to the sugar-cream mixture. Boil for 1 minute, stirring constantly, then remove from the heat and cool for 10 minutes. Stir in vanilla and cool completely.

TOPPING: In the large bowl of an electric mixer fitted with wire beaters, whip cream until thickened and soft peaks start to form. Add icing sugar and beat until stiff peaks form.

TO ASSEMBLE: Spread a thin layer of caramel over each crust, reserving about ½ cup of the mixture for drizzling. Pour a third of the banana filling into each crust, spreading evenly. Top with dollops of whipped cream, swirling to form little peaks, or pipe rosettes using a piping bag. Drizzle the remaining caramel over the whipped cream and sprinkle with white chocolate shavings. Chill for at least 6 hours.

Makes three 9-inch pies or 24 small wedges

CINNAMON APPLE COLLINS

Goldschlager is elegance in a bottle with its flecks of gold leaf languidly drifting about in cinnamon-scented schnapps. Gold has long been touted as a curative and although its health benefits have not been proven, at least you can count on it to increase your inner bling.

> 3 bottles (each 750 mL/26 oz) brandy
> 9 oz Goldschlager
> 3 cans (each 355 mL/12 oz) frozen apple juice concentrate, thawed
> 10 lbs crushed ice
> 6 bottles (each 750 mL/26 oz) soda water
> 30 long cinnamon sticks, for garnish
> 90 thinly sliced apple wedges, brushed with acidulated water to prevent browning, for garnish
> GLASSWARE: three 3-qt pitchers; thirty 10-oz Collins glasses

Combine brandy, Goldschlager and apple concentrate and refrigerate in pitchers until ready to serve.

To serve, fill each Collins glass with crushed ice. Pour in 4 oz of the brandy mixture and top with soda water. Garnish with a cinnamon stick and 3 slices of apple. Serve with a straw.

Makes thirty 4-oz drinks

ESPRESSO CRAIC MARTINI

Craic is the Irish term for fun and enjoyment, and this espresso–Irish Cream combination is sure to revive even the groggiest of partygoers.

> TO MAKE AS A PARTY PRE-MIX:
> 2 bottles (each 750 mL/26 oz) Irish Cream liqueur (such as Bailey's)
> 1 bottle (750 mL/26 oz) Amaretto
> 6 cups espresso, chilled
> GLASSWARE: two 2-qt pitchers; thirty 5-oz martini glasses

To pre-mix, combine Irish Cream, Amaretto and espresso, stir well and refrigerate in large pitchers. Fill a shaker with crushed ice and 2½ oz of the pre-mix per serving. Cover and shake until beads of condensation form on the sides and the shaker is very cold to the touch. Strain into chilled martini glasses.

To make to order, mix one to four at a time in these proportions. For one drink:

> 1 oz Irish Cream liqueur (such as Bailey's)
> ½ oz Amaretto
> 1 oz espresso
> GLASSWARE: one 6-oz martini glass

Chill a martini glass by filling it with crushed ice. Fill a shaker with crushed ice and add Irish Cream, Amaretto and espresso. Cover and shake until beads of condensation form on the sides and the shaker is very cold to the touch. Discard ice from glass and strain in the drink. Alternatively, strain into shooter glasses.

Makes thirty 2½-oz martinis

PAN-ASIAN BEACH PARTY

cocktail supper for 40

Forget about the travel agent. You can escape to your own exotic beach right in your own backyard...or on your condo's rooftop patio...or at your family cottage. A bit of Oceania-inspired decor and a menu of pan-Pacific pleasures is all it takes to transport you and forty of your closest friends to a tropical paradise.

Whether your style is campy Kon-Tiki, Somerset Maugham Plantation or elegant Island Retreat, you'll love this menu. The cocktails are deliciously fun, and our new Asian-fusion recipes offer something addictive for everyone.

Designed as a cocktail supper party, this gathering is an all-evening event and the food is substantial, so make it clear on your invitations that guests are invited for a full-length food fest. If you don't want to hire help, set out all the food on a grazing buffet, replenishing the hot food once or twice during the evening, and ask a couple of close friends to take turns tending the bar. Most of the cocktails are pre-mixed in big pitchers, so bartending will be a breeze. All they will have to do is pour and smile.

MENU

TO BE PASSED ON PLATTERS

BEEF *and* SPINACH ROLLS *with* TERIYAKI DRIZZLE

CHICKEN POT STICKERS *with* HOT AND SOUR DIPPING SOY

SHRIMP AND MANGO SALAD ROLLS *with* WASABI MAYONNAISE

CRISPY TRIANGLES *of* SATAY CHICKEN *with* PEANUT SAUCE

TAKE-OUT STATIONS

ASIAN GRAVLAX *with* GINGERED FOCACCIA

DECONSTRUCTED VEGETABLE SUSHI *in a* TAKE-OUT BOX

VIETNAMESE-STYLE BARBECUED RIBS

PEKING DUCK QUESADILLAS

TARO FRITES *with* COCONUT CILANTRO DIPPING SAUCE *in a* NEWSPAPER CONE

DESSERT TABLE

SOUPÇON *of* CHOCOLATE MOUSSES

CHOCOLATE FORTUNE COOKIES

TROPICAL FRUIT PLATTER

COCKTAILS

TO GREET THE GUESTS:

LYCHEE SNOW MARTINI

AT THE BAR:

SHANGHAI LILY SLING

FLAMING PASSION

SAKE MARTINI

SETTING THE SCENE

INVITATION IDEAS

E-mail: If your theme is Kon-Tiki, type "Party Invitations" into your Internet search engine and browse the many snappy designs that are good campy fun. Choose one design or several, fill in the details for your party and your guests' e-mail addresses, and let the computer do the rest.

Postcards: Have a friend who lives in a tropical country send you a few dozen blank postcards. Handwrite your invitation on the back in the "message" area, address and mail.

Snail mail: Buy seashells at a specialty store, write each invitation on a long strip of paper and stuff it inside a shell with the tip sticking out, fortune-cookie style. Wrap each shell in a box with shell-motif gift paper. Mail from the post office in order to have boxes weighed for correct postage, and, where possible, try to buy unusual or colourful postage stamps that match your theme.

MUSIC PICKS

Throbbing away in the heart of Toronto's Kensington Market amid the European sausage makers, vegetable vendors, West Indian curry houses and Mexican spice shops is the supercool Supermarket Restaurant and Bar. This supper club has wild cocktails, hot music and a mouth-watering menu of tapas with an Asian accent. Owners Greg Bottrell and Rob Eklove have created a scene that celebrates the spirit of socializing. John Kong is their music programmer and a great DJ with his own independent record label, Do Right Music. Who better to suggest music for your Pan-Asian Beach Party?

- Various artists, *Ready or Not: Deep Jazz Grooves from the CBC Radio Canada Archive 1967–1977* (Do Right Music): Deep and mellow.
- Various artists, *Keb Darge presents Funk for the 21st Century* (Do Right Music): Good funk for party socializing.
- Various artists, *On the Right Track* (Do Right Music): Bossa Nova, Jazz—a Supermarket fave.

DECOR IDEAS

Go on a treasure hunt in your local Chinatown and Little India. You'll find beaded curtains, paper lanterns, parchment parasols, bamboo trays, fans, bowls and yards of brilliantly coloured silks. The hard part of decorating is deciding which way to go: wild or posh. Here are some ideas to help you decide:

STYLE FILE 1: TONGUE IN CHIC

- *Ambience:* If you're having a Kon-Tiki patio party, hang colourful plastic patio lanterns and Japanese paper kites in the trees. Cover the tabletops with bamboo curtains and rattan thatching. Place bamboo torches everywhere.
- *Food:* Use rattan baskets and trays or line plates with banana leaves (available frozen in Asian food markets). Tropical fruits make great decorations that you can eat later.
- *Bar:* This may be the only occasion when you will be encouraged to decorate drinks with paper umbrellas and flaming fruit kebabs. The bar itself can be decorated with a large parchment umbrella or a piece of canvas painted with Asian calligraphy. Make terrific cups by sawing the tops off coconuts ¼ of the way down. Discard this top bit. Pour out the coconut water and saw each coconut in half at the midway point, parallel to your original cut. This will leave you with some half-coconut cups and some ring-shaped pieces. Knock the coconut meat out of the rings. Place the

bottom (closed) end of each coconut cup in the hollow of a ring-shaped piece. Be sure the cups are well balanced. Then, using a ridiculous amount of hot glue, fasten the two parts together.

STYLE FILE 2: URBAN SLEEK

- *Ambience:* Summon the serene spirituality of the East with saffron-coloured candle pillars in red lacquered dishes, orange silk cushions, giant seashells, stalks of bird-of-paradise flowers and scatterings of purple orchids. Create tropical mystique with mosquito netting canopies draped from the ceiling.
- *Food:* Use gold-leafed platters, little Japanese sake cups at the bar for shooters, trays decorated with river rocks, seashells and mother-of-pearl.
- *Bar:* A skirting of sunset-coloured silk will hide all the bar supplies that have to be stashed under the table.

SZABO'S WINE AND BEER ALTERNATIVES

ASIAN CUISINE is generally high on the flavour-intensity scale, and this menu is no exception. Intense, contrasting taste sensations are often combined in the same dish: saltiness and sweetness, acidity and spicy heat—the flavours mingle together to a funky backbeat of umami, playfully balancing one another as they jostle for your palate's attention. Although this may delight the diners, it would horrify the sommeliers. This is not the party for refined and complex old wines. They will not be welcome here.

Since Asian cuisine is not traditionally tied to any wine-producing region, this is your chance to step outside the box and experiment a little with your wine choices. The challenges here, however, are many. The sauces—the inherent sweet-saltiness of teriyaki, the saltiness of soy, the spicy heat of chilies preserved in acid vinegar and the natural oily-salty-sweetness of peanuts—are just a few of the tricky elements to contend with when selecting an appropriate wine—or, more likely, wines—and we haven't even made it past the appetizers yet. There is no single wine that will match happily with all the dishes on this menu.

The diversity of flavours may send you running to the beer section, and beer is a simple and suitable choice. Look for lagers, or even better, Pilsner-style beers. They are generally low in alcohol, meaning that the spicy elements won't cause a three-alarm fire in your mouth. Properly served well chilled, the refreshing quality of these beers also contrasts nicely with salty tastes, crisp textures and hot temperatures. The pleasant bitterness contributed by the hops marries beautifully with these high-umami creations.

The most likely candidates for general refreshment are fresh, crisp, unoaked whites. Sparkling wines are wonderfully versatile with their light body, low alcohol and high acidity, which is made to seem even brighter by the "lifting" effect of carbon dioxide. Although the matches may not take you and your guests to a higher plane, they will certainly offend no one. Otherwise, look for cool-climate whites such as Sauvignon Blanc from France's Loire Valley or from New Zealand. Fairly neutral Pinot Grigio from the northern Italian regions of Trentino–Alto Adige or Friuli Venezia Giulia would also work.

If you can get beyond the memory of cheap, soft and sweet wines from your early days of drinking, wines with a touch of residual sugar work even better with the many sweet and spicy flavours, as well as contrasting nicely with salty elements. The king of off-dry grapes is undoubtedly Riesling; *kabinett* and *spätlese*-designated examples from Germany often have a hint of sweetness, low alcohol and deceptively intense flavours that can hold their own even when fighting up a weight category. More full-bodied examples from Ontario, New York State, France's Alsace and Australia's Clare and Eden Valleys are often a little drier (unless otherwise stated on the label) and bring a bit more heft to the ring.

Red wines, with their lower acidity and higher levels of tannin, are somewhat tougher to match here. Avoid high-tannin monsters: the salty flavours will make them even more astringent and bitter. Soft, round and fruity wines with at least moderate acidity are the way to go. Beaujolais or other nouveau-style wines (released immediately after the vintage) may not rock the house but make for fruity, juicy, pleasant companions. Serve lightly chilled. Higher-octane Zinfandel will be comfortable with the Vietnamese ribs and the Peking duck, though beware excessive alcohol levels. Alternatively, New World Pinot Noir (New Zealand, Oregon, Russian River Valley in California), lighter-style Cabernet Franc (Loire Valley, Ontario) or Dolcetto from Piedmont, Italy, are all solid options.

The dessert table poses fewer challenges. Here the exotic fruits, smooth-textured mousse and chocolate would all sing in harmony with an aromatic, fortified Muscat-based wine. Look for fresh, young wines from the appellations of Muscat de Rivesaltes or Muscat de Beaumes-de-Venise from France. Serve well chilled.

GET AHEAD SCHEDULE

4 WEEKS AHEAD

- Send out invitations.
- Source special items such as Chinese food take-out containers, chopsticks, porcelain soup spoons and exotic decor items.
- Order fortune cookies. Ask about personalized fortunes. If you have trouble finding a supplier, try to order them from your friendly neighbourhood Chinese restaurant.

3 WEEKS AHEAD

- Rent decor props, dishes and glasses.
- Hire servers, either professional (2 waiters, 1 bartender, 1 grill cook) or 6 clever young friends.
- Arrange for a kitchen helper for the day before and the day of the party. The recipes are simple, but you'll need help with the quantities.

1 WEEK AHEAD

- Make paper cones out of Chinese newspapers for TARO FRITES.
- Make BEEF AND SPINACH ROLLS and freeze uncooked.
- Make CHICKEN POT STICKERS and freeze uncooked.
- Make CRISPY TRIANGLES OF SATAY CHICKEN and freeze uncooked.

3 DAYS AHEAD

- Check with people who have not replied to your invitation in order to confirm your guest count.
- Plan and set up music.
- Marinate lychees for LYCHEE SNOW MARTINIS.
- Make LYCHEE SNOW MARTINI and SAKE MARTINI, freeze in large containers.
- Dip FORTUNE COOKIES in chocolate.
- Make lime shells for FLAMING PASSION cocktails.
- Marinate VIETNAMESE-STYLE BARBECUED RIBS and refrigerate.

2 DAYS AHEAD

- Purchase fresh flowers and arrange in vases.
- Make WASABI MAYONNAISE for SHRIMP AND MANGO SALAD ROLLS.
- Make PEANUT SAUCE for CRISPY TRIANGLES OF SATAY CHICKEN.
- Make COCONUT CILANTRO DIPPING SAUCE for TARO FRITES.
- Make HOT AND SOUR DIPPING SOY for CHICKEN POT STICKERS.

THE DAY BEFORE

- Make the ASIAN GRAVLAX.
- Make SOUPÇON OF CHOCOLATE MOUSSES, cover tightly and refrigerate.
- Make TARO FRITES.
- Make PEKING DUCK QUESADILLAS and refrigerate.
- Slice vegetables for SHRIMP AND MANGO SALAD ROLLS and refrigerate.
- Make fruit purée and juice combinations for SHANGHAI LILY SLINGS.
- Arrange for one of the waiters to bring bags of ice to the party.
- Move furniture as required to make space.
- Set up as much decor as possible.
- Set out trays and platters.
- Set up system for music.

THE MORNING OF

- Thaw BEEF AND SPINACH ROLLS, CHICKEN POT STICKERS and CRISPY TRIANGLES OF SATAY CHICKEN.
- Finish decor as pre-arranged with helper.
- Pre-mix pitchers of FLAMING PASSION cocktails.
- Cool the wine as necessary.
- Make SHRIMP AND MANGO SALAD ROLLS, cover with plastic wrap and refrigerate.
- Make DECONSTRUCTED VEGETABLE SUSHI.
- Boil and fry CHICKEN POT STICKERS.
- Fry CRISPY TRIANGLES OF SATAY CHICKEN.
- Make GINGERED FOCACCIA.
- Arrange ASIAN GRAVLAX on a platter. Cover well with plastic wrap and refrigerate.
- Arrange the fruit platter and bowl of CHOCOLATE FORTUNE COOKIES.

1½ HOURS BEFORE

- Familiarize staff with duties. From this point, they should take over almost all the food preparation and serving.
  Set up the bar, chill the glasses, cut the garnishes and show the bartender how to finish and serve the drinks.

1 HOUR BEFORE

- Grill VIETNAMESE-STYLE BARBECUED RIBS to three-quarters doneness.
- Toast GINGERED FOCACCIA.
- Set up the ASIAN GRAVLAX station with baskets of GINGERED FOCACCIA.
- Portion some of the DECONSTRUCTED VEGETABLE SUSHI into take-out containers or martini glasses with chopsticks on the side, and set up station so guests can dish out their own glass or box of rice if they wish.
- Light the candles and adjust the lighting.
- Start music.

AS THE FIRST GUESTS ARRIVE

- Spoon out the LYCHEE SNOW MARTINIS, garnish and serve.
- Arrange SHRIMP AND MANGO SALAD ROLLS on a platter with WASABI MAYONNAISE and begin passing.
- Fry one-third of the BEEF AND SPINACH ROLLS, arrange on platters, drizzle with sauce, sprinkle with sesame seeds and begin serving, repeating with the balance as required.
- Preheat the oven to 375°F for reheating.
- Reheat one-third of the CHICKEN POT STICKERS, arrange on platters with the HOT AND SOUR DIPPING SOY and begin passing.
- Reheat a third of the CRISPY TRIANGLES OF SATAY CHICKEN and arrange on platters, each with a bowl of PEANUT SAUCE.
- Reheat about ten PEKING DUCK QUESADILLAS. Cut in half, arrange on platters and serve, heating the balance as required.
- Reheat one-third of the TARO FRITES, portion into paper cones and serve with COCONUT CILANTRO DIPPING SAUCE. Continue heating and serving as required.
- Reheat and finish cooking half of the par-cooked VIETNAMESE-STYLE BARBECUED RIBS in the oven or on a low grill. Arrange on a platter and place at station, grilling (reheating) the balance as required to replenish platter.
- Replenish GINGERED FOCACCIA at ASIAN GRAVLAX station when necessary.

1 HOUR BEFORE THE PARTY ENDS

- Start to brew coffee.
- Set up the dessert table with SOUPÇON OF CHOCOLATE MOUSSES, TROPICAL FRUIT PLATTER, CHOCOLATE FORTUNE COOKIES, tea and coffee.

Beef and Spinach Rolls with Teriyaki Drizzle

Tender, rich and juicy, these bite-sized mignons of beef are interpreted with Japanese elegance. You can make the teriyaki drizzle up to 1 month in advance and freeze it. Although the rolls are best when they're cooked just before serving, you can brown them quickly on the outside up to 3 hours ahead, keep them covered, then reheat them in a 450°F oven for about 5 minutes or until hot.

TERIYAKI DRIZZLE

¾ cup soy sauce

1½ Tbsp sherry

⅓ cup brown sugar

1½ tsp crushed garlic

1 Tbsp minced fresh ginger

2 Tbsp sesame oil

BEEF AND SPINACH ROLLS

3 lbs beef tenderloin, centre cut, frozen

three 10-oz bags spinach

1½ cups Teriyaki Drizzle

⅓ cup sesame seeds, lightly toasted

30 toothpicks

1 Tbsp vegetable oil or more

TERIYAKI DRIZZLE: In a medium bowl, combine soy sauce, sherry, brown sugar, garlic, ginger and sesame oil. Refrigerate until needed, up to 1 week.

BEEF AND SPINACH ROLLS: Place beef in a shallow pan and partially thaw for 6 to 8 hours in the refrigerator. (You want the beef to be frozen but thawed enough to slice with a sharp knife.)

Cut 24 sheets of parchment paper, each 12 × 14 inches, or tear off 12 × 14-inch sheets of plastic wrap as you work.

Slice beef ⅛ inch thick. Place a sheet of parchment paper (or plastic wrap) on a clean, dry work surface. Arrange 6 to 8 beef slices on top, overlapping the pieces by ½ inch to make a single layer of beef about 10 inches long × 4 inches wide. Cover with another sheet of parchment paper (or plastic wrap) and press gently with your fingers to flatten beef to an even ⅛-inch thickness. Transfer to a baking sheet that will fit in the freezer.

Repeat until all beef has been layered, 10 to 12 sheets. Place beef in the freezer to firm up slightly, about half an hour.

Place spinach in a resealable food storage bag, seal and microwave on high power, shaking the bag every 30 seconds, for about 2 minutes or until well wilted. Squeeze out excess moisture and set aside.

Place one layer of beef slices on a clean, dry work surface, with the long side toward you. Remove the top sheet of parchment paper (or plastic wrap). Spread beef evenly with 1 tsp of the teriyaki drizzle. Cover with a thin, even layer of spinach and spread another 1 tsp of the teriyaki drizzle on top. Sprinkle with 1½ tsp sesame seeds.

Starting at the bottom edge and using the bottom layer of parchment paper (or plastic wrap) to lift the beef so it doesn't fall apart as you work, tightly roll the beef into a cylinder about 1 inch in diameter and 10 inches long, trimming the top edge with a knife to even it out. Discard the parchment paper (or plastic wrap). Secure the roll with 6 toothpicks evenly spaced along its length. Cut between the toothpicks to make 6 beef rolls. Repeat with the remaining beef slices, teriyaki drizzle, spinach and sesame seeds. You should have 60 to 70 beef rolls.

Preheat the oven to 250°F. Heat vegetable oil in a large sauté pan on high heat. Cover the bottom of the pan with a single layer of beef rolls (be sure they're not crowded) and sauté for about 30 seconds on each side, adding more oil if needed. Transfer cooked rolls to a roasting pan, cover and keep warm in the oven. Repeat with the remaining beef rolls. Just before serving, arrange on serving platters, drizzle with any remaining teriyaki drizzle and sprinkle with any remaining sesame seeds. Serve immediately.

Makes 60 to 70 rolls

CHICKEN POT STICKERS *with*
HOT *and* SOUR DIPPING SOY

A Chinese dim sum specialty, these homemade dumplings are vastly superior to the store-bought varieties found in the frozen food section of your supermarket. The traditional shape is pleated and bonnet-like, but to lessen your work, we have shaped these like lovely moon-inspired half-rounds. If you cannot find the round dumpling wrappers, use the square wonton wrappers and make triangles.

Like the Vegetable Pot Stickers (page 52), these can be made ahead and stored, on the parchment-lined baking sheets, covered and uncooked, in the refrigerator for up to 2 days or in the freezer for up to 1 month. Cook and reheat them as you would the Vegetable Pot Stickers. Kim chee is Korean spicy preserved cabbage, which is sold in jars in Asian food stores.

HOT AND SOUR DIPPING SOY

2 cups light soy sauce

½ cup red wine vinegar

2 Tbsp minced fresh ginger

1 Tbsp Asian chili sauce

1 Tbsp sugar

POT STICKERS

2 whole boneless, skinless chicken breasts (about 1 lb), in ½-inch dice

2 Tbsp soy sauce

1 tsp chopped garlic

2 tsp sake (Japanese rice wine)

1 cup finely diced fresh shiitake mushrooms, or dried Chinese mushrooms, rehydrated, stems removed then finely diced

1 cup corn kernels, fresh or frozen

1 cup coarsely chopped kim chee, or 1 cup diced celery with 1 tsp chili sauce

½ cup finely chopped green onion

1 cup coarsely chopped bamboo shoot strips

2 Tbsp oyster sauce

pinch of salt

60 round dumpling wrappers, 3-inch diameter

2 Tbsp vegetable oil for brushing (or more)

HOT AND SOUR DIPPING SOY: In a medium bowl, combine soy sauce, vinegar, ginger, chili sauce and sugar. Set aside.

POT STICKERS: In a food processor, coarsely chop chicken breasts. Place chicken in a medium bowl. Add soy sauce, garlic and sake and set aside to marinate for at least 20 minutes and up to 12 hours.

In a large bowl, combine mushrooms, corn, kim chee (or celery), green onion, bamboo shoots, oyster sauce and salt. Add chicken and stir to combine.

Lightly dust 3 to 4 baking sheets with sifted cornstarch. Place a dumpling wrapper on a clean, dry work surface (keep the remaining wrappers covered with a damp towel). Mound 1 heaping teaspoon of filling in the centre of the wrapper, then, using your finger or a pastry brush, moisten the edges of the wrapper with water. Fold the top half of the wrapper over the bottom half to make a half-moon shape, being careful to completely enclose the filling. Press the edges together tightly. Transfer the filled dumpling to the baking sheet. Repeat with the remaining wrappers and filling.

Lightly oil a baking sheet. Bring a large pot of water to a boil on high heat. Cook dumplings, 10 to 12 at a time, until they float to the top and the wrappers look almost translucent (3 to 4 minutes). Using a slotted spoon, transfer the dumplings to the baking sheet. Brush dumplings with 2 Tbsp of the vegetable oil. If desired, heat ⅛ inch vegetable oil in a shallow sauté pan on medium-high heat. Add boiled dumplings and sauté on both sides. Drain on paper towel. Serve immediately with hot and sour dipping soy.

Makes about 150 dumplings

THE FABLE OF THE POT-STICKER DUMPLING

Chinese legend has it that two young sisters working in the royal kitchen were preparing dumplings for the king's tea. There was so much to do that the girls forgot they had left the dumplings steaming in a shallow pan of water. By the time tea was to be served, the water had boiled away completely and the bottoms of the dumplings had scorched. Little Sister was afraid to serve them, but it was too late to make more, so Big Sister said, "We have to serve them. We've burnt the whole batch. If we put them scorched side up, the king will see that we are not trying to conceal anything and our punishment will be lighter."

To everyone's surprise, the upturned bottoms of the dumplings were very crisp and the king pronounced them delicious. He asked that the cook responsible be presented, and when the girls appeared, he requested the name of the new dish so that it could be entered into the royal menu. Little Sister nervously blurted, "Wo Tip," which translates to "Pot stick," hence "Pot stickers."

This is but one legend. Is it possible that, unbeknownst to the Chinese court, at the very same time, two Tatar defectors working in a kitchen in Kiev were inventing fried perogies?

SHRIMP AND MANGO SALAD ROLLS
with WASABI MAYONNAISE

A fresh and light counterpoint to the richer hors d'oeuvres of this menu, these flavourful salad rolls can be made strictly vegetarian by excluding the shrimp. The wrapper is made from rice flour and is great for guests who have wheat allergies. Rice paper wrappers and Szechwan peppercorns are available from Asian food stores.

The wasabi mayonnaise can be made up to 3 days in advance and stored, covered, in the refrigerator. The salad rolls should be made no more than 4 to 6 hours in advance and stored, covered well with plastic wrap, in the refrigerator.

WASABI MAYONNAISE

4 Tbsp wasabi powder (Japanese horseradish)

3 Tbsp cold water

1 cup mayonnaise

3 tsp light soy sauce or to taste

SALAD ROLLS

3 cups sake (Japanese rice wine) or white wine

1 Tbsp minced fresh ginger

1 Tbsp Szechwan peppercorns

30 black tiger shrimp, raw, unpeeled

1 large firm mango

1 medium jicama or 1 large carrot

1 English cucumber

75 round rice paper wrappers, 6-inch diameter

4 cups mixed salad greens (such as mesclun), roughly chopped

WASABI MAYONNAISE: In a medium bowl, combine wasabi powder with water until a smooth paste forms. Add mayonnaise and mix until well combined. Set aside.

SALAD ROLLS: In a large, heavy-bottomed pot on medium-high heat, bring sake (or wine), ginger and Szechwan peppercorns to a simmer. Add shrimp and poach until shrimp are just cooked through, about 3 minutes. Using a slotted spoon, transfer shrimp to a bowl and set aside to cool.

Peel and slice mango and jicama (or carrot) into thin matchsticks about 3½ inches long. Using a paring knife, cut cucumber into lengths of 3½ inches. Peel the skin off each length in one piece. Cut cucumber skin into thin matchsticks. Discard the cucumber flesh or save for another use. Peel poached shrimp and slice in half lengthwise. Set aside.

Place a clean tea towel on the counter. Fill a medium bowl with warm water. Using scissors, trim rice paper wrappers to a width of 3 inches (maintain the original length). Dip one wrapper at a time into the water for about 15 seconds. As soon as the wrapper becomes a little pliable, lay it on the tea towel to continue softening.

Transfer one softened rice paper wrapper to a clean, dry work surface. Mound 1 Tbsp of the salad greens on the bottom half of the wrapper, leaving 1 inch along the bottom edge uncovered by filling. Top with ¼ tsp of the wasabi mayonnaise and 3 strips each of mango, cucumber and jicama (or carrot), laying each strip parallel to the bottom edge of the wrapper so it extends from the sides.

Fold the bottom of the wrapper over the filling, then roll once so the filling is completely covered by the wrapper. Place half a shrimp, pink side out, on the wrapper, then roll up into a snug cylinder about 1 inch in diameter. Cover the filled roll with a damp cloth to keep it from drying out. Repeat with the remaining wrappers, soaking, filling and rolling them until all shrimp have been used. Arrange the salad rolls on a serving platter, making sure to leave enough room so they do not touch each other, and leaving enough space for a small bowl of dipping sauce in the middle. Reserve any extra Wasabi Mayonnaise in a small bowl.

Add soy sauce to the Wasabi Mayonnaise to make a dip. Mix well. Transfer the dip to a serving bowl and place it in the middle of the platter.

Makes 60 salad rolls

Crispy Triangles of Satay Chicken with Peanut Sauce

Shaped like baby samosas and tasting of peanuts and hot sauce, these plump chicken mouthfuls will disappear in a flash. They can be made well ahead of time: the peanut sauce can be made up to 1 month ahead and frozen, or up to 1 week ahead and kept refrigerated. The triangles can be assembled 2 weeks ahead and frozen, uncooked, or you can fry them up to 24 hours ahead, refrigerate and reheat in a 375°F oven for 5 to 10 minutes.

PEANUT SAUCE

1½ cups peanut butter, smooth or crunchy

½ cup soy sauce

1 Tbsp sesame oil

1 Tbsp minced garlic

2 Tbsp minced fresh ginger

½ cup red wine vinegar

2 tsp brown sugar

2 cups coconut cream (page 55)

2 to 3 Tbsp Asian chili sauce

SATAY CHICKEN

½ cup soy sauce

½ tsp minced fresh ginger

½ tsp minced garlic

2½ lbs chicken breast, bone in (or 3 lbs thigh or drumstick, bone in)

2 Tbsp vegetable oil

4 cups celery (1 bunch), in ¼-inch dice

2 large onions, in ¼-inch dice (2 cups)

2 tsp Asian chili sauce

2 cups peanuts, coarsely chopped

¼ tsp salt

¼ tsp pepper

75 spring roll wrappers, 6-inch diameter (½ lb/200 g)

1 egg beaten with 1 tsp water, for egg wash

vegetable oil for deep-frying

PEANUT SAUCE: In a large bowl, combine peanut butter, soy sauce, sesame oil, garlic, ginger, vinegar, brown sugar, coconut cream and chili sauce. Using a whisk, blend until smooth. Set aside.

SATAY CHICKEN: In a large resealable food storage bag or a baking dish, combine soy sauce, ginger and garlic. Add chicken, tossing well to coat, and marinate in the refrigerator for at least 1 hour and up to 24 hours.

Preheat the oven to 350°F. If necessary, transfer the marinated chicken plus the marinade to an ovenproof baking dish. Roast chicken until juices run clear when pricked, 20 to 25 minutes. Transfer chicken to a plate, cover and refrigerate until completely cool.

Heat oil in a large sauté pan on medium heat. Add celery and onion and sauté, stirring occasionally, until lightly browned, 2 to 3 minutes. Set aside.

Remove chicken meat from the bone. Discard bones and cut chicken meat in ¼-inch dice. In a large bowl, combine chicken, onions and celery, 1¼ cups peanut sauce, Asian chili sauce, peanuts, salt and pepper. Mix well. (Reserve the remaining peanut sauce to use as a dip.)

Place one spring roll wrapper on a clean, dry work surface (keep the remaining wrappers covered with a damp towel). Cut the wrapper in half to make two 3 × 6-inch rectangles. With the short side of one rectangle toward you, mound 1 Tbsp of the chicken mixture along the bottom edge of the wrapper. Fold one corner over the filling at 45° to form a triangle, then fold the triangle at 90° onto the rectangle. Continuing folding like this, retaining the triangle shape, until you reach the end of the wrapper. Brush the edges of the wrapper with egg wash and press them together tightly to seal. Place the filled triangle along the bottom edge of the second half of the wrapper. Folding as before, rewrap the entire filled triangle in the second half of the wrapper. Brush egg wash along the edges and seal well. Repeat with the remaining wrappers and chicken filling until all have been used. You should have about 75 triangles.

Line a baking sheet with paper towels. Heat a deep fryer filled with vegetable oil to 375°F. Place 6 to 8 triangles in the deep fryer and fry until crisp and golden, 3 to 4 minutes. Lift the fryer basket out of the oil, shake off any excess and transfer satay triangles to the paper towel–lined baking sheet to drain. Serve hot with the reserved Peanut Sauce.

Makes about 75 triangles

Asian Gravlax with Gingered Focaccia

You'll love the simplified technique we have devised for making cold-cured salmon, and your guests will love the exotic Thai twist on a Nordic classic. Use a food processor to finely chop the herbs for the gravlax marinade. We recommend that you follow this recipe and slice the salmon very thinly; however, if you are really short for time, cut fresh salmon in ¼-inch dice and toss with marinade 1 hour before serving. Alternatively, make the gravlax ahead of time. It can be marinated, then arranged on the platter 6 to 8 hours in advance and kept refrigerated, covered tightly with plastic wrap. Gingered focaccia can be made up to 6 hours in advance and stored, uncovered, at room temperature.

ASIAN GRAVLAX

2½ cups finely chopped fresh mint

2½ cups finely chopped Thai basil

2½ cups grated fresh ginger

grated zest of 10 limes

2½ cups vodka (orange-infused, if desired) or sake

1 cup fish sauce

¼ cup Asian chili sauce

¾ cup sugar

1 Tbsp salt

5 lbs fresh cleaned salmon fillet

10 to 15 sprigs mint, for garnish (optional)

10 to 15 sprigs Thai basil, for garnish (optional)

GINGERED FOCACCIA

2½ cups sesame oil

¼ cup grated fresh ginger

1½ Tbsp salt

8 to 10 square loaves of focaccia, sliced ½ inch thick × 2 inches long

ASIAN GRAVLAX: In a large bowl, combine mint, basil, ginger, lime zest, vodka, fish sauce, chili sauce, sugar and salt.

Line 2 baking sheets with plastic wrap or parchment paper and brush a very thin layer of marinade on top. Using a very sharp knife and keeping the blade at a 45° angle, slice salmon ⅛ inch thick against the grain. Arrange salmon slices on top of marinade, slightly overlapping the pieces in a row. Using a pastry brush, baste salmon with a very thin layer of marinade. Cover with more plastic wrap (or parchment paper) and another layer of salmon, being sure to brush the tops and bottoms of each salmon slice with marinade. Continue layering and brushing salmon with marinade until all salmon has been used. Cover with plastic wrap and refrigerate for at least 12 hours and up to 24 hours.

GINGERED FOCACCIA: Preheat the oven to 400°F. In a small bowl, combine sesame oil, ginger and salt. Brush one side of each bread slice with the oil mixture. Arrange bread in a single layer on baking sheets and toast oil-side up until golden, 5 to 7 minutes.

TO SERVE: Arrange marinated salmon on a large platter and brush with more marinade. Garnish with mint and Thai basil if desired. Serve with Gingered Focaccia on the side.

Makes 60 to 80 servings

This recipe calls for fish sauce, which is a vestige of *liquamen,* a sauce made by fermenting fish that was so ubiquitous it was called for in almost every ancient Roman recipe. Although many varieties of fish sauce are available at Asian food stores, only one has been awarded an AOC (appellation d'origine contrôlée) designation: nuoc mam from Phu Quoc in Vietnam. The AOC assures quality and authenticity, which is comforting when you are purchasing a product made from fermented fish.

DECONSTRUCTED VEGETABLE SUSHI
in a TAKE-OUT BOX

This colourful rice dish is scented with sesame and dotted with vitamin-rich nori (toasted seaweed), shiso (an Asian herb that is part of the mint and basil family) and mirin (a sweet, golden Japanese cooking wine). All ingredients can be purchased at Japanese and Korean food stores. To save time, marinate the carrots and ginger the day before.

4 cups sushi rice (Japanese short-grain rice)

2 cups grated carrot (4 to 5 large)

2 cups Japanese pickled ginger, juice reserved

2 cups asparagus, cut on the diagonal in ½-inch lengths (or green beans, cut diagonally, or fresh peas)

1 Tbsp vegetable oil

5 cups thinly sliced fresh shiitake mushrooms, stems discarded

1½ cups mirin

2 Tbsp sugar

2 Tbsp salt

2 Tbsp sesame oil

three 8-inch sheets nori

7 to 8 large shiso leaves or 6 green onions, thinly sliced

2 Tbsp black sesame seeds

2 Tbsp white sesame seeds

Place rice and 5 cups water in a rice cooker and cook until all water has been absorbed, 15 to 20 minutes. (Or, using a stovetop method, bring 5 cups water to a boil, add rice, cover and simmer until all water has been absorbed, 15 to 20 minutes.)

In a medium bowl, combine carrot, ginger and ½ cup of the reserved ginger juice and marinate for at least 30 minutes.

Fill a bowl with cold water. Bring a medium pot of salted water to a boil. Blanch asparagus (or green beans or fresh peas) for 1 minute, then immediately plunge in cold water to stop the cooking and preserve the bright green colour. Drain asparagus (or green beans or peas) into a colander and reserve until needed.

Heat vegetable oil in a large sauté pan on medium-high heat and sauté mushrooms until soft, 2 to 3 minutes. Set aside and allow to cool.

(continued over)

In a large bowl, combine the warm cooked rice, 1¼ cups of the mirin, sugar and 1 Tbsp of the salt. Mix well until all grains are glossy and separated. Allow rice to cool to room temperature.

To cooled rice, add the remaining mirin and salt, and the sesame oil, 2 cups of the carrot-ginger mixture, ½ cup cooked mushrooms and ½ cup blanched asparagus (or green beans or peas) and mix well. Adjust seasoning, if necessary.

Preheat the oven to 375°F. Place nori on the rack for 1 to 2 minutes to crisp. With scissors, cut sheets in 1-inch lengths, then in ⅛-inch slivers.

Spoon rice onto a large platter or a 12-inch diameter Chinese steamer and garnish with the remaining carrots, mushrooms and asparagus (or green beans or peas). Top with shiso (or green onions) and garnish with black and white sesame seeds. Sprinkle nori slivers over top. Serve portioned into small Chinese take-out boxes.

Makes 14 cups, or forty-two ⅓-cup servings

Vietnamese-style Barbecued Ribs

Spicy and sweet, these ribs do well par-cooked for 10 minutes several hours ahead, covered with aluminum foil, then reheated at the last minute in the oven or on the grill. For the marinade, use the lime juice reserved from the Flaming Passion cocktails. You can make the marinade up to 1 week ahead and refrigerate it, covered, or if you're very organized, make the marinade 1 month ahead and freeze it.

5 to 7 lemon grass stalks	½ cup vegetable oil
12 shallots	½ cup Asian chili sauce
2 onions	2 cups fresh lime juice
8 cloves garlic	½ cup grated lime zest
2 Scotch bonnet or habañero chilies	2 cups medium-dry sherry
7 cups demerara (or raw) sugar	2 Tbsp pepper
1 cup water	8 racks meaty pork back ribs, 16 to 18 lbs
3 cups fish sauce	

Using a sharp knife, remove roots, withered tops and outer layers from lemon grass stalks and trim off the top quarters. Slice stalks lengthwise into thin threads and chop into a very fine mince. Peel and mince shallots and onions and crush garlic. Wearing latex gloves to prevent the chilies from burning your fingers, mince chilies. Set aside.

In a medium saucepan on low heat, combine sugar, water and fish sauce, stirring to dissolve sugar crystals, and slowly bring to a boil. Stir in lemon grass and remove from the heat.

Heat oil in a medium sauté pan on medium-high heat and sauté shallots, onion and garlic until fragrant, lightly browned and translucent, about 3 minutes. Remove from the heat and add chilies.

In a medium bowl, combine the sugar and onion mixtures. Stir well to combine and allow to cool slightly. Stir in chili sauce, lime juice, lime zest, sherry and pepper and allow to cool completely.

(continued over)

Using a sharp knife, peel the thin skin off the backs of the rib racks and separate into individual ribs. Discard the skin. Divide ribs among four large resealable plastic food storage bags. Cover the ribs in each bag with one-quarter of the marinade and allow ribs to marinate in the refrigerator for at least 48 hours, turning the bags occasionally to recoat ribs.

Line several baking sheets with aluminum foil, then coat with nonstick spray. Heat a grill to medium-high or preheat the oven broiler. Remove ribs from the marinade, shaking off any excess, but reserve the marinade for basting. If broiling, place ribs on baking sheets. Grill (or broil) ribs slowly until browned, about 10 minutes. Remove from the grill (or broiler).

Turn the oven to 350°F. If grilled, transfer ribs to the baking sheets. Baste ribs with marinade and bake for 10 minutes, basting once after 5 minutes.

To make more sauce for serving, bring the remaining marinade to a boil in a small saucepan and cook on medium-high heat for about 5 minutes. Serve immediately.

Makes about 40 servings

PEKING DUCK
QUESADILLAS

This is one of the most requested appetizers from Dinah's Tiger Lily's Noodle House. The recipe calls for flour tortillas, which are available in most supermarkets, and Chinese barbecued duck, which can be found in barbecue shops and noodles house in Chinatown. These quesadillas can be made 1 day in advance and stored, wrapped in aluminum foil, in the refrigerator. Reheat them in a 375°F oven for 10 to 15 minutes until warmed through.

32 flour tortillas, 6 inches in diameter	8 to 10 large carrots, peeled and shredded
1 cup sesame oil	8 cups bean sprouts
2 cups hoisin sauce	8 to 10 green onions, thinly sliced
1 cup sesame seeds, toasted	4 Tbsp butter, melted
4 whole roasted Chinese barbecued ducks (each about 2½ lbs), meat removed and shredded	4 Tbsp vegetable oil

Place one tortilla on a clean, dry work surface. Brush one side evenly with ½ tsp of the sesame oil, followed by 2 tsp of the hoisin sauce. Sprinkle with ½ tsp of the sesame seeds. On the bottom half of the tortilla, arrange ½ cup of the duck meat. Top with ¼ cup of the carrot, a handful of bean sprouts and 1 Tbsp of the green onion. Fold the top half of the tortilla over the toppings and brush both sides with butter. Repeat with the remaining tortillas and fillings.

Line a baking sheet with paper towels. Heat 1 tsp of the vegetable oil in a large sauté pan on medium-high heat. Two at a time and using metal tongs to hold the filling and wrapper together, brown tortillas until golden brown on both sides, 2 to 3 minutes. Transfer to the paper towel–lined baking sheet and cover with aluminum foil. Pan-fry the remaining tortillas, adding more oil as necessary to prevent the tortillas from sticking. Keep covered with aluminum foil until all quesadillas have been browned and heated. Cut quesadillas in half and serve warm.

Makes 64 servings

Taro Frites with Coconut Cilantro Dipping Sauce

Taro is a starchy, potato-like tuber that has a subtly nutty flavour and makes an interesting substitute for potato. It's a favourite ingredient in Chinese cuisine and a staple of Hawaiian cooking. Taro frites can be made a day ahead and reheated in a 375°F oven for 15 to 20 minutes until heated through. For a festive touch, serve the frites in newspaper cones.

DIPPING SAUCE

⅓ cup Asian chili sauce

2 cups coconut cream (page 55)

3 large bunches cilantro (leaves only), finely chopped

6 Tbsp finely minced fresh ginger

5 green onions, thinly sliced

1½ tsp salt

TARO FRITES

vegetable oil for deep-frying

12 egg whites

6 cups coconut cream (page 55)

4½ cups cornstarch

2 Tbsp salt

⅓ cup sugar

6 cups sesame seeds, lightly toasted

15 large taro roots (about 1½ lbs each), peeled, in ¼ × ¼ × 2½-inch pieces

DIPPING SAUCE: In a large bowl, combine chili sauce and coconut cream. Stir in cilantro, ginger, green onion and salt and set aside.

TARO FRITES: Heat a deep fryer filled with vegetable oil to 400°F.

Line a baking sheet with paper towels. In a wide bowl, beat egg whites lightly with a fork until frothy. Add coconut cream, cornstarch, salt, sugar and sesame seeds. Dip one handful of taro strips into the batter at a time and coat well. Shake off excess batter and deep-fry until golden brown, 3 to 5 minutes. Lift the fryer basket out of the oil, shake off any excess oil and transfer frites to the paper towel–lined baking sheet to drain. Repeat with the remaining frites, skimming the oil occasionally to remove bits of batter.

Season with salt to taste and serve hot, either on a plate or in individual newspaper cones. Place dipping sauce in a small bowl and serve on the side.

Makes enough for 60 people (10 frites per cone), and 1 qt dipping sauce

Soupçon of Chocolate Mousses

This recipe takes advantage of the stylish functionality of white porcelain Chinese soup spoons. You will need 8 dozen spoons for this party, and they can be purchased quite inexpensively in Chinatown. The gold leaf makes a lovely garnish for dark chocolate and can be purchased from art supply stores.

These mousses will keep, covered and refrigerated, for 2 to 3 days. Fill and decorate the individual spoons up to 1 hour before serving.

WHITE CHOCOLATE MOUSSE

12 oz white chocolate	2 tsp vanilla extract
¼ cup tropical fruit–flavoured liqueur, such as Alize or Galliano	1½ cups whipping cream (35%)
1 Tbsp unflavoured gelatin	½ pt fresh raspberries or blueberries, for garnish
1 cup milk	

DARK CHOCOLATE MOUSSE

12 oz bittersweet dark chocolate	1 cup milk
¼ cup orange liqueur, such as Triple Sec or Grand Marnier	2 tsp vanilla extract
	1½ cups whipping cream (35%)
1 Tbsp unflavoured gelatin	2 to 3 sheets gold leaf, for garnish

WHITE CHOCOLATE MOUSSE: Using a vegetable peeler or a sharp, heavy knife, shave chocolate into thin strips over a medium bowl. Set aside.

Bring a shallow saucepan of water to a simmer, not a boil, on medium-low heat. Combine liqueur and gelatin in a small stainless steel bowl and place the bowl over the saucepan of simmering water. When just combined, remove bowl from the heat, leaving the saucepan of water to simmer.

Place milk in a small saucepan on medium-high heat and bring to a gentle boil. Pour hot milk over chocolate, add the gelatin mixture and stir to combine. If the chocolate doesn't melt completely, place the bowl over the simmering saucepan of hot water and stir just long enough to melt, 2 to 3 minutes. The mixture should not get hot. Whisk vanilla into the melted chocolate and cool slightly. Refrigerate, stirring occasionally, until completely cool, 20 to 30 minutes. The mixture should be slightly jelled but not set.

Place whipping cream in a medium bowl. By hand or using an electric mixer, whip cream until it forms soft mounds (not stiff peaks) and fold into the cooled chocolate.

Arrange Chinese spoons on a flat serving tray and spoon 1 Tbsp of mousse into each one. Top each spoon with a berry.

DARK CHOCOLATE MOUSSE: Using a vegetable peeler or a sharp, heavy knife, shave chocolate into thin strips over a medium bowl. Set aside.

Bring a shallow saucepan of water to a simmer, not a boil, on medium-low heat. Combine liqueur and gelatin in a small stainless steel bowl and place the bowl over the saucepan of simmering water. When just combined, remove bowl from the heat, leaving the saucepan of water to simmer.

Place milk in a small saucepan on medium-high heat and bring to a gentle boil. Pour hot milk over chocolate, add the gelatin mixture and stir to combine. If the chocolate doesn't melt completely, place the bowl over the simmering saucepan of hot water and stir just long enough to melt, 2 to 3 minutes. The mixture should not get hot. Whisk vanilla into the melted chocolate and cool slightly. Refrigerate, stirring occasionally, until completely cool, 20 to 30 minutes. The mixture should be slightly jelled but not set.

Place whipping cream in a medium bowl. By hand or using an electric mixer, whip cream until it forms soft mounds (not stiff peaks) and fold into the cooled chocolate.

Arrange Chinese spoons on a flat serving tray and spoon 1 Tbsp of mousse into each one. Gently tear a small shard from a leaf of gold. Using a piece of paper or a chicken feather, carefully transfer gold leaf to the top of the mousse in each spoon. (The gold leaf is very delicate and thin, so work slowly, as abrupt movement will cause the sheets to crumple irreparably.)

Makes 48 servings

CHOCOLATE
FORTUNE COOKIES

To make this recipe, you will need a double boiler or a heatproof medium bowl that hangs easily inside a medium saucepan. You will be filling the bottom part of the double boiler or the saucepan with water and you want the top part or the bowl to rest above, not in, the water. Use the best-quality chocolate you can find, such as Valrhona or Callebaut.

2 lbs good-quality dark chocolate	4 dozen fortune cookies
½ tsp vegetable oil	½ cup candy sprinkles (optional)

Fill a saucepan with enough water to come within ½ inch of a bowl placed above it. Remove the bowl and dry it thoroughly.

Using a vegetable peeler or a sharp, heavy knife, chop or shave chocolate into thin shards over the bowl.

Bring the water in the double boiler or saucepan to a boil, then reduce the heat to very low. When water ceases to ripple from the heat, place bowl over the water. (The tiniest bit of water will cause molten chocolate to "seize" or harden irreversibly, so take care not to splash any water into the bowl of chocolate.) Allow the heat of the water to melt the chocolate, 5 to 10 minutes depending on the size of the shards. Stir in oil. Allow chocolate to cool to about 85°F on a candy thermometer.

Line several baking sheets with parchment paper. Dip one side of each fortune cookie in chocolate, sprinkle lightly with candy sprinkles and place on a baking sheet, chocolate-side up, to dry. Try to keep the temperature of the chocolate between 85°F and 90°F, or tepid to the touch. Repeat until cookies are all dipped.

If chocolate does not harden at room temperature once cookies have been dipped, cool them in the refrigerator for a couple of hours. Serve in a large glass fishbowl or a wide-topped glass vase.

Makes 48 cookies

Tropical Fruit Platter

The time of year will determine the varieties and quantities of fresh fruits, but you can always count on pineapples, papayas, kiwis, mangos, tangerines and grapes to provide a solid foundation for your tropical fruit platter. Strawberries will also provide great colour year-round. For variety, a visit to your local Chinatown's fruit vendor will often reveal such exotica as branch lychee, custard apple, rambutan, mangosteen, dragon fruit, persimmon and mango varietals, all fragrant reminders of perpetually sunny climates.

Arrange the fruits on a platter, leaving them whole, as if they're starring in a still-life painting. Place a few knives on a round wooden board and set out some grape scissors so guests can cut off pieces as they wish. Abundance always looks spectacular, so heap your tray with a variety of fruit. Use contrast to make the colours jump— frame the fruit with clusters of green leaves such as salal or grape ivy, available from your local florist.

WHERE DID ALL THESE FRUIT FLIES COME FROM?

You'll have to ask Dr. Suzuki where they come from, but we can tell you how to get rid of them. Pour a splash of bourbon or brandy into a glass snifter. Cover the top with plastic wrap, using a rubber band to secure it as tightly as a drum skin. With the tip of a sharp pen, poke three or four pinhead-sized holes in the plastic. Leave this snare out on the counter for a day and you will be morbidly thrilled with the results.

Lychee Snow Martini

Make the pre-mix ahead of time in pitchers and freeze in plastic containers that can be stacked in the freezer. The mix can be spooned out of the containers directly into glasses, garnished and served slushy. If the bar is not near the freezer, store the containers in a cooler filled with a combination of ice and dry ice. Do not use dry ice alone or allow too much of it to contact the containers as it will freeze the mixture too hard.

12 cans (each 565 g/12 oz) lychees
2½ bottles (each 750 mL/26 oz) orange vodka
4 bottles (each 750 mL/26 oz) vodka
4 oz orange liqueur, such as Cointreau
4 oz lychee liqueur, if available
GLASSWARE: forty 10-oz martini glasses

Strain liquid from lychees into a large container and reserve.

Place lychees in a large bowl. Add ½ bottle of the orange vodka, cover with plastic wrap and refrigerate overnight or longer, stirring occasionally to macerate evenly.

To the reserved lychee liquid, add vodka, the remaining 2 bottles of orange vodka, orange liqueur and lychee liqueur. Mix well, pour into plastic bottles and store in the freezer.

One hour before serving, chill the martini glasses.

To serve, spoon 8 oz of the partially frozen mixture into each martini glass. Drop in 2 or 3 macerated lychees or thread them onto a decorative bamboo toothpick, and serve.

Makes forty 8-oz cocktails

Shanghai Lily Sling

For more than ten years, Dinah's Zagat-listed restaurant, Tiger Lily's Noodle House, was a cozy den of noodle nirvana in Toronto's hot Queen Street West entertainment district. One of the most popular drinks on the menu was Lily's layered sling. Serve these drinks in the tallest, slimmest sling glasses possible and float each layer lovingly, one upon the next, to create a rainbow that tastes and looks like a ten-day tropical holiday. (Before you begin, test the capacity of your glass to ensure that all the layers and ice will come up to the rim without overflowing. Adjust the quantities slightly, if necessary.)

2 cups (480 mL) frozen lime juice concentrate, thawed

4 kiwis, peeled and quartered

30 oz frozen raspberry juice concentrate, thawed

15 to 16 oz (600 mL) Chartreuse

20 oz mango purée, available in cans

30 oz (900 mL) dark rum

5 to 7 lbs cracked ice

20 long straws

20 long skewers

60 pieces of fruit (strawberries, gooseberries, pineapple chunks, grapes, star fruit slices)

GLASSWARE: twenty 14-oz tall, slim sling glasses

In a blender, purée lime juice concentrate with kiwi until smooth. Transfer to a pitcher and set aside.

To serve, fill a glass with crushed ice. Using a 1-oz measure, pour each layer gently over the back of a spoon into the sling glass, building the drink one layer at a time. Start with 1½ oz raspberry concentrate, followed by 1 oz lime-kiwi purée, ¾ oz Chartreuse, 1 oz mango purée and finish with 1½ oz dark rum. Float each layer on top of the previous one, taking care to pour slowly to keep the layers separate. Carefully add more ice to the top of the glass, as necessary.

Thread 2 or 3 pieces of fruit onto the end of a skewer and slide the other end into the drink, close to the side of the glass, taking care not to shift the ice or disturb the layers. Serve with a long straw.

Makes twenty 8-oz drinks

FLAMING PASSION

No truly adult tropical beach party is complete without a flaming pineapple drink. This one is so out-there that it's in. Sighting this cocktail, served in a large saucer-type glass with a flaming lime shell floating in a vast sea of rum, you can almost feel your shipwreck coming in. A delicious way to go. Prepare the lime cups several days ahead, as they need time to dry out.

> 12 limes
> 3 bottles (each 750 mL/26 oz) white rum or vodka
> 3 bottles (each 750 mL/26 oz) passion fruit liqueur, such as Alize
> 4½ cups passion fruit juice or fruit juice blend containing passion fruit
> 4½ cups frozen pineapple juice concentrate, thawed
> 1 bottle (750 mL/26 oz) brandy
> GLASSWARE: three 3-qt pitchers; twenty 12-oz saucer-shaped cocktail glasses

Cut each lime in half lengthwise from blossom end to stem end. Juice limes and reserve liquid (use it for the Vietnamese-style Barbecued Ribs marinade, page 193). Using the tip of a teaspoon, scrape membranes out of limes, taking care not to make any holes in the peel. Discard membranes and any broken peels, as the cups must not leak. Dry the inside of the cups with paper towel and refrigerate them uncovered for a few days to dry.

Combine rum (or vodka), Alize, juice and juice concentrate in a large container or in pitchers. Refrigerate until ready to serve.

Just before serving, warm brandy in a saucepan on medium heat. Warm a heat-resistant glass or stainless steel measuring cup, then fill with warmed brandy.

To serve, pour 1½ cups of the rum mixture and ½ cup crushed ice in a blender. Blend for 30 seconds. Pour into two cocktail glasses. Half-fill 2 lime cups with warm brandy and gently float them in each drink. Dim the lights and, using a long barbecue lighter, light the brandy. (The flame is blue and shows best in a darkened room.)

Makes twenty 9-oz cocktails

SAKE MARTINI

Pre-mix this elegant drink in pitchers and keep it refrigerated until you're ready to serve, or leave the mix in the freezer for an hour before serving. Do not shake with ice when serving as the subtle flavour gets overly diluted. Instead, pour into delicate 5-oz martini glasses directly from chilled pitchers or decanters.

The garnish is made from Japanese pickled baby ginger, which is sold in jars at most Asian food stores. You can find it in the sushi cooler in many larger supermarkets.

> 2 bottles (each 1 L/40 oz) sake (Japanese rice wine)
> 4 oz gin
> 20 thin slices English cucumber, unpeeled
> ½ cup sliced preserved pink ginger, in ⅛-inch strips
> GLASSWARE: three 3-qt pitchers; twenty 5-oz martini glasses

In a large container, mix together sake and gin. Pour into pitchers, or back into the sake bottles, and refrigerate to chill.

To serve, measure 4 oz into a martini glass and garnish with a slice of cucumber and a few slivers of ginger.

Makes twenty 4-oz cocktails

ENGAGEMENT CELEBRATION

cocktail hour for 60

When you want to celebrate with a large number of people in a casual but sophisticated way, a cocktail party is best. We've designed this one as an engagement celebration, so it's extra splashy and hip yet still romantic. You may want to simplify the menu by choosing five of the items and doubling the recipes. Or drop one and substitute take-out sushi.

Guests are only attending for two or three hours, so it seems unnecessarily mean-spirited to make them spend half of that time searching for food. Have plenty of waiters circulate with trays of hors d'oeuvres. And keep the portions bite-sized: you know how restless people get when someone is about to tell all but can't talk because they've just bitten into a large, chewy forkful.

This is a big menu of little hors d'oeuvres. Although they are easy to make, because of the variety and the quantity involved, we recommend dividing the cooking duties among several friends. Or, if you are feeling ambitious, follow the Get Ahead Schedule for preparing and freezing almost everything in advance.

MENU OF PASSED HORS D'OEUVRES

CHEESE GOUGÈRES

CHICKEN *and* VEGETABLE NORI ROLLS

MINI LOBSTER ROLLS

BABY BOCCONCINI *in* PROSCIUTTO ROSEBUDS

SHRIMP *and* SMOKED SALMON HEARTS

WILD MUSHROOM SPRING ROLLS *with* CREAMY CHIVE DIP

WILD RICE *and* SCALLION PANCAKES

TOASTED ASPARAGUS ROLLS

CAVIAR ON SHRIMP *and* POTATO BLINIS

RATATOUILLE *and* CHÈVRE-TOPPED ENDIVE SPEARS

COCKTAILS

PEAR SPARKLE *or* RASPBERRY ROYALE

PINK PEARL

MARTINI BAR

CITRUS MARTINI

BLACKBERRY MARTINI

LADY GODIVA

SETTING THE SCENE

INVITATION CONSIDERATIONS

Time: For a cocktail party, specify the time with the knowledge that no one will arrive on time and everyone will stay late. If you want the party to go from 6 to 9 PM, specify 5:30 to 8 PM. Only your hard-core friends will show up on time and they will be happy to engage in last-minute caviar testing and wardrobe consulting until the first surge of guests begins.

    Type of party: The time specified will indicate to most guests that no meal will be served. Calling the gathering a "reception" or a "cocktail party" or a "drinks party" further clarifies the type of food that will be served, so no guests will arrive expecting dinner and dessert.

    Dress: The style of the invitation should indicate the formality of the event, but for everyone's comfort, you might want to specify a dress code on the invitation. The iconoclasts will need to know what not to wear.

    Gifts: An engagement is often a gift-giving occasion. You may wish to use your printed invitations to say something about gifts. "Wine shower" indicates that the happy couple is building a wine collection and guests are encouraged to make wine their gift. "No gifts, please" printed at the bottom of the invitation makes it clear the happy couple does not want another toaster, no matter how aerodynamically designed or capacious. "Donation to [named charity] in lieu of gifts" is a postscript that seems more passive-aggressive than gracious, but reflects a rising trend in charity fundraising, so it can't be all bad.

DECOR NOTES

You may not have enough room in your home to host sixty people comfortably—especially if, in the process of preparing the food, you've converted your entire loft into a field kitchen. This is a good time to consider booking the party room in your own or one of your friend's condominiums.

    We know…a vast, windowless room clad in beige vinyl wallpaper, Group of Seven fakes and green broadloom is not the image spooling in the wedding movie of your mind. Fear not. Set decorating for movies has taught us that some of the best settings are illusions created by simple but transformative devices. Consider these:

Set Dec Trick #1: Install a large central decor feature. Create a focal point in the middle of the room to take attention away from the wallpaper. For example, you could rent a stage-set fountain from a party prop house (fill it with ice and wine and surround it with pots of flowers), order a big ice sculpture (use it as the backdrop for a raw bar) or obtain a chocolate fountain from a party rental company (elevate it on a high table and surround it with fresh fruit).

Set Dec Trick #2: Drape the walls. Swathing objects in miles of fabric has worked for land artist Christo and it can work for you, too. Hang panels of white sheers from floor to ceiling and throw coloured light on them with floor spots and gels rented from a staging or display company. Rent backdrops from a film prop house and add a few rented silk ficus trees to add a third dimension to the painted scene. Some party rooms have suspended ceilings, so you can use the T-bar structure to support your wall treatments; more likely, though, you will need to rent a pole-and-drape system from a display company—a fantastically simple and inexpensive option.

Set Dec Trick #3: Go minimalist and atmospheric. Remove every stick of furniture from the room and create a New York bar look with pin lights, linen-draped cruiser tables, high stools and tall, minimalist floral centrepieces.

Set Dec Trick #4: Change the lighting. For evening functions or in windowless rooms, try candlelight or lamplight. Check the fire regulations to confirm what kind of candles can be used. Cocktail glasses filled with water, rose petals and floating candles usually fit the fire code, the flirty atmosphere and the fiscal boundaries of any party.

Set Dec Trick #5: Get out on location. If the party room is absolutely awful, go outside—consider the roof garden. In the summer, it's an obvious option, but on a mild December night, it can be utterly and unexpectedly enchanting. Create a magical winter wonderland by renting a transparent party tent with plenty of heaters, hundreds of candles and Pashmina shawls for all. Instead of working against the elements, get the winter to work for you—and the element of surprise.

BIG PARTY MEMO

Big parties have special logistics. As well as reviewing the lists of party requirements (page 67), consider these items:

- Rent coat racks, boot bags and an umbrella stand.
- Hire a valet parking service or have several taxi phone numbers and your house address displayed by the phone or the coat rack.
- Board the animals or get a pet sitter.
- Alert your neighbours that there will be noise and parking, give them your phone number and a bottle of wine or a box of chocolates, if you can.
- Circulate waiters near the entrance with trays of cocktails with which to greet arriving guests. A welcome drink helps break the ice.
- Think about flow. Some furniture may have to be moved aside or small pieces taken away. Even though the room may look a little empty, making space for guests is more important.
- Set up the bar in an accessible place or make sure there is plenty of staff to pass drinks.
- Complete all party preparations at least 1 hour ahead of the announced start time of the party. A few guests may arrive early.
- Be sure to make introductions, especially at an engagement party when two different groups of people are being brought together. Remind key people at the party to do the same.
- Supply outdoor ashtrays or you will be picking cigarette filters out of the rhododendrons for months.
- Ensure you have a good supply of ice, mineral water, lemons, limes and cocktail napkins. You can never have too much.

MUSIC PICKS

As one of the early organizers of the Toronto International Film Festival and a one-time board member of the Ontario Film Development Corporation, André Rosenbaum knows the arts scene well. He opened the Queen Mother Café on Queen Street West with David Stern in 1978 and started a hipness tsunami for the street that has continued to roll west. For years, these two have showcased hot new bands and DJs at their perpetually cool resto-bar, the Rivoli. Now André, the king of Queen, and his consort Kelly St. John are calling the tune at Queen Mother Waterside Café in Victoria. Here's a short list of their "Young Love Cocktail Party" picks.

- *Ultra-Lounge* (Capitol)
- *Vintage Chill Vol. 4: Winter* (Kriztal Entertainment)
- *Saint Germain des Prés Café, Vols. 3 and 4* (FIP-Wagram Music)
- Molly Johnson, *Another Day* (Marquis/Universal)

WINE PICKS

For a big menu and a mixed crowd, it's best to serve good-value wines with wide appeal, such as:

Reds: Southern Rhone Valley, New World Pinot Noir, Shiraz, Valpolicella

Whites: Unoaked or lightly oaked Chardonnay, Sauvignon Blanc from France or New Zealand

GET AHEAD SCHEDULE

4 MONTHS IN ADVANCE

- Book the party room, if necessary.

4 WEEKS AHEAD

- Send invitations.

3 WEEKS AHEAD

- Make brioche buns for MINI LOBSTER ROLLS, and freeze.
- Make WILD MUSHROOM SPRING ROLLS, and freeze.
- Make SHRIMP AND POTATO BLINIS, and freeze.
- Order rentals, hire staff.

2 WEEKS AHEAD

- Make CHEESE GOUGÈRES, and freeze.
- Order flowers and decor items.

4 DAYS AHEAD

- Confirm guest list, rentals and staff.
- Marinate blackberries for BLACKBERRY MARTINIS. Freeze raspberries for RASPBERRY ROYALE.

2 DAYS AHEAD

- Make fillings for RATATOUILLE AND CHÈVRE-TOPPED ENDIVE SPEARS.
- Pre-mix pitchers of CITRUS MARTINI, BLACKBERRY MARTINI, PINK PEARL and LADY GODIVA cocktails.

THE DAY BEFORE

- Make TOASTED ASPARAGUS ROLLS but do not fry.
- Make CHICKEN AND VEGETABLE NORI ROLLS but do not slice.
- Make filling for MINI LOBSTER ROLLS.
- Make CREAMY CHIVE DIP for WILD MUSHROOM SPRING ROLLS.
- Cut out and butter heart shapes for SHRIMP AND SMOKED SALMON HEARTS, store in refrigerator layered on damp paper towel covered tightly with plastic wrap.
- Set out serving trays for hors d'oeuvres.
- Set up as much decor as possible.

THE MORNING OF

- Thaw WILD MUSHROOM SPRING ROLLS, SHRIMP AND POTATO BLINIS, CHEESE GOUGÈRES.
- Thaw brioche buns for MINI LOBSTER ROLLS.
- Receive rentals.
- Make pancakes for WILD RICE AND SCALLION PANCAKES.
- Finish making SHRIMP AND SMOKED SALMON HEARTS.
- Make BABY BOCCONCINI IN PROSCIUTTO ROSEBUDS.
- Fill MINI LOBSTER ROLLS.

1 HOUR BEFORE GUESTS ARRIVE

- Set up the bar and cocktails with the bartender.
- Review the food with the kitchen help.
- Review the menu and serving style with the wait staff. Make sure they are familiar with the key ingredients of menu items.

30 MINUTES BEFORE GUESTS ARRIVE

- Have the kitchen helpers start heating food and assembling two trays of each selection.
- Fill RATATOUILLE AND CHÈVRE-TOPPED ENDIVE SPEARS.
- Start music.

AS GUESTS ARRIVE

- Begin pouring and serving PEAR SPARKLE or RASPBERRY ROYALE CHAMPAGNE cocktails.

Cheese Gougères

This Burgundian treatment of choux pastry is baked in a medium oven so the dough does not puff up hollow, as it does when making éclairs. This version is bite-sized and so chock-full of delicious ingredients that a separate filling is not needed. (We've given you four fillings to choose from.) The puffs look so perfect you won't believe how simply and quickly they come together. Bake these gougères up to 1 week ahead and freeze them, or make them the morning of the party and reheat in a 350°F oven for 7 to 10 minutes just before serving.

GOUGÈRE DOUGH

2 cups water

½ tsp salt

2 tsp sugar

1 cup butter

2 cups all-purpose flour

8 large eggs

CHEDDAR-APPLE FILLING

4 cups old Cheddar cheese, in ⅜-inch cubes

4 cups baking apples (such as Royal Gala), peeled and cored, in ⅜-inch cubes

SPICY JACK FILLING

4 cups spicy Jack cheese, in ⅜-inch cubes

2 cups dry black olives, pitted and quartered

2 cups chopped green onion

FETA-OLIVE FILLING

4 cups feta cheese, in ⅜-inch cubes

1 cup slivered sun-dried tomatoes

2 cups green pepper, in ⅜-inch cubes

1 cup green olives, pitted and chopped

PROSCIUTTO-PARMESAN FILLING

½ cup thinly sliced green onion

½ cup prosciutto, in ⅜-inch cubes

½ cup grated Parmesan cheese

Preheat the oven to 400°F. Line several baking sheets with parchment paper.

In a medium saucepan on high heat, bring water, salt, sugar and butter to a full rolling boil until butter melts. Reduce the heat to medium. Add flour all at once and cook, stirring constantly, until the mixture forms a ball and comes away from the sides of the pan. Remove from the heat and cool for 4 minutes.

Transfer the mixture to a food processor, add eggs and process until completely incorporated. (If mixing by hand, beat in eggs one at a time, being sure to incorporate each egg before adding the next one.) Scrape the mixture into a large bowl. Mix the ingredients from your selected filling into the dough and stir until evenly incorporated.

Using two spoons, form the mixture into 1¼-inch balls and drop onto the baking sheets. Bake 10 minutes, reduce the heat to 350°F and bake for another 15 to 20 minutes, or until gougères are light and golden. Serve warm or at room temperature.

Makes about 80 gougères

CHICKEN *and* VEGETABLE NORI ROLLS

These rolls can be made up to 1 day in advance and kept whole, covered, in the refrigerator. To reheat them, slice rolls into individual pieces and heat on a parchment-lined baking sheet in a 375°F oven for about 5 minutes, until warm. Serve with Hot and Sour Dipping Soy (page 182).

12 boneless, skinless chicken breasts (about 6 lbs), in 1-inch dice
4 large carrots, peeled, in ⅛-inch dice
6 green onions, finely chopped
24 green beans, in ⅛-inch lengths
¼ cup grated fresh ginger
½ cup chopped fresh cilantro
6 eggs

¾ cup light soy sauce
1½ Tbsp whipping cream (35%)
2 tsp salt
2 tsp pepper
eighteen 8-inch sheets nori (page 191)
1 egg plus 1 tsp of water, for egg wash
vegetable oil for deep-frying

Place chicken in a food processor and pulse on and off every 10 seconds until chicken is coarsely chopped. Be careful not to over-process chicken or the texture will be too fine when cooked. Transfer chicken to a large bowl. Add carrots, onion, green beans, ginger, cilantro, eggs, soy sauce, whipping cream, salt and pepper and mix until well combined.

Place one sheet of nori on a clean, dry work surface. Place about 4 Tbsp of the filling along the bottom edge of the nori, or enough to form a log about 1 inch in diameter. Spread the filling across the entire width of the nori, leaving 1 inch at the bottom free of filling. Gently fold the bottom of the nori over the filling. Loosely roll up into a cylinder, being careful not to wrap too tightly or the roll will burst when cooked. Brush egg wash along the edges of the nori, then press together tightly to seal. Repeat with the remaining nori and filling until all the chicken mixture is used.

Line a baking sheet with paper towels. Heat a deep fryer filled with vegetable oil to 365°F. Place 2 to 3 rolls in the deep fryer and fry for 3 to 4 minutes, until rolls are firm and lightly brown. Lift the fryer basket out of the oil and drain off any excess oil, then transfer nori rolls to the paper towel–lined baking sheet. To serve, trim the edges of each roll, then cut into 3 equal-length logs. Slice each log on the diagonal into two pieces. Arrange rolls on a serving platter, slanted side up, and sprinkle with black sesame seeds.

Makes 108 pieces

Mini Lobster Rolls

From Peggy's Cove to Nantucket, lobster rolls are a favourite. Soft buttery buns loaded with warm, succulent chunks of freshly caught lobster, they are impossible to eat neatly. This version is just as luscious and tender but miniaturized into an elegant hors d'oeuvre. Unfilled mini-buns can be baked and frozen for up to 1 month. Defrost and bring them to room temperature before filling and serving.

BRIOCHE BUNS

2½ cups warm water	1 cup butter, softened
4 Tbsp active dry yeast	4 eggs
½ cup sugar	6½ cups sifted all-purpose flour
2 tsp salt	1 cup butter, melted

LOBSTER SALAD

6 cups fresh cooked lobster meat (page 88), in ¼-inch dice	1 bunch fresh tarragon leaves, roughly chopped
2 stalks celery, finely chopped	1 cup homemade mayonnaise (page 97)

BRIOCHE BUNS: Lightly grease several baking sheets with butter. In the bowl of an electric mixer, mix warm water with yeast and stir to dissolve. Add sugar, salt, softened butter, eggs and 4 cups of the flour and combine on low speed. Increase the speed to medium and beat for 2 to 3 minutes. Remove the bowl from the mixer and set aside.

Place the remaining 2½ cups flour in a bowl larger than the mixer bowl. Add dough and, using a wooden spoon, incorporate into flour. Pinch off 1-inch pieces of dough, form them into balls by hand and place them on baking sheets, about 1½ inches apart. Allow dough to rise in a warm room, 30 to 40 minutes, or until doubled in size.

Preheat the oven to 425°F. Brush the tops of the buns with melted butter and bake for 12 to 15 minutes or until golden brown.

LOBSTER SALAD: In a large bowl, combine lobster meat, celery, tarragon and mayonnaise. Season with salt and pepper and mix well to combine. To assemble, slice buns at a 45° angle, not quite severing the top from the bottom, and spoon 1 heaping teaspoon of the lobster salad into each bun. Serve immediately.

Makes about 100 mini-buns

BABY BOCCONCINI *in* PROSCIUTTO ROSEBUDS

Bocconcini is Italian for "mouthful," and these easy-to-assemble bites are perfect mouthfuls of flavour (from the prosciutto and pesto), texture (from the fresh cheese) and aroma (from the basil garnish). They will disappear in a flash. Make the rosebuds up to 2 hours in advance and store them, covered, in the refrigerator. Bring them to room temperature before serving.

40 to 50 paper-thin slices of prosciutto
120 baby bocconcini (about 2 lbs/
    four tubs) or 30 regular-sized
    bocconcini, in quarters

1 cup store-bought pesto
120 small fresh basil leaves

Cut prosciutto slices into 1 × 5-inch strips.

Using a sharp knife, make a small vertical slit in the top of a bocconcini, about ½ inch wide and about half the depth of the cheese. Dab ¼ tsp pesto in this slit, then insert a basil leaf, stem first, leaving the greenery visible.

Holding a slice upright with the folded edge at the top, loosely wrap prosciutto around the bocconcini, leaving the top of cheese exposed, with the basil leaf sprouting from the top. Serve at room temperature.

Makes 120 pieces

Shrimp and Smoked Salmon Hearts

Finger sandwiches are always crowd pleasers—dainty, easy to eat and versatile. These sandwiches are no exception, plus their beautiful heart shape is the perfect culinary symbol for the occasion. Make these sandwiches a day ahead and store them, separated with layers of damp paper towel and covered tightly with plastic wrap, in the refrigerator.

SHRIMP HEARTS

50 thin slices quality sandwich bread

½ cup butter, softened

2 lbs (800 g) frozen cooked baby shrimp, thawed and drained

1 cup mayonnaise, preferably homemade (page 97)

1½ Tbsp chopped fresh dill

SMOKED SALMON HEARTS

50 thin slices soft dark rye bread

½ cup butter, softened

50 thin slices smoked salmon (2½ lbs)

½ cup (250 g) plain cream cheese, softened

4 lemons, zested into 50 thin strips

50 small sprigs of dill weed

SHRIMP HEARTS: Using a 2-inch-long heart-shaped cookie cutter, cut 2 hearts from each piece of bread, for 100 hearts total. Set 50 of the cut hearts aside as bottoms.

Using a 1-inch-long heart-shaped cookie cutter, cut another heart into the centre of each of the remaining 50 hearts. (You will have 50 heart-shaped frames.) Discard the 1-inch hearts or save for another use.

Carefully butter one side of the whole hearts and one side of the heart frames, ensuring that you spread butter right to the edges. Place heart frames on top of whole hearts, buttered sides facing, and press the two pieces of bread together lightly.

In a medium bowl, combine shrimp, mayonnaise and dill. Spoon 4 to 5 baby shrimp, curved side up, into the heart-shaped opening on each sandwich. Arrange on a platter and serve.

SMOKED SALMON HEARTS: Using a 2-inch-long heart-shaped cookie cutter, cut 2 hearts from each piece of bread, for 100 hearts total. Set 50 of the cut hearts aside as bottoms.

Using a 1-inch-long heart-shaped cookie cutter, cut another heart into the centre of each of the remaining 50 hearts. (You will have 50 heart-shaped frames.) Discard the 1-inch hearts or save for another use.

Carefully butter one side of the whole hearts and one side of the heart frames, ensuring that you spread butter right to the edges. Set aside.

Using the 2-inch-long heart-shaped cookie cutter, cut out 100 smoked salmon hearts. Set aside.

Spread the buttered side of the whole hearts with cream cheese and top with two salmon hearts. Place heart frames on top of whole hearts, buttered side down, and press the two pieces of bread together lightly. Garnish each heart-shaped opening with lemon zest and dill weed. Arrange on a platter and serve.

Makes 50 of each sandwich, 100 total

WILD MUSHROOM SPRING ROLLS
with CREAMY CHIVE DIP

These crisp rolls are packed with mushroom flavour, and guests will appreciate your effort. The rolls can be assembled up to 1 month ahead and frozen, uncooked, or up to 2 days ahead, assembled, cooked and kept covered in the refrigerator. Bring the rolls to room temperature and reheat them in a 375°F oven until warm and crispy, 10 to 15 minutes, turning occasionally.

CREAMY CHIVE DIP

1½ cups mayonnaise, preferably homemade (page 97)

1½ cups sour cream

1 bunch chives, finely chopped

1 tsp salt or to taste

SPRING ROLLS

¼ cup olive oil

12 cups thinly sliced assorted wild mushrooms (shiitake, portobello, oyster)

4 cloves garlic, minced

½ cup white wine

½ cup whipping cream (35%)

1 Tbsp chopped fresh tarragon

¼ tsp salt

¼ tsp pepper

100 six-inch spring roll wrappers (two 400-g/14-oz packages)

1 egg beaten with 1 tsp water, for egg wash

vegetable oil for deep-frying

CREAMY CHIVE DIP: In a small bowl, combine mayonnaise with sour cream, chives and salt to taste. Mix until well combined and set aside.

SPRING ROLLS: Heat 1 Tbsp of the olive oil in a large sauté pan on medium-high heat and sauté 4 cups of the mushrooms and a third of the garlic until soft and fragrant, about 5 minutes. Add a splash of wine, 2 Tbsp of the whipping cream, 1 tsp of the tarragon, and a dash of salt and pepper. Cook until all liquid has been expelled and evaporated, 3 to 4 minutes. Repeat with the remaining mushrooms, garlic, wine, whipping cream and tarragon, in two more batches. Allow the mushroom mixture to cool to room temperature, covered.

When the mixture has cooled, place one spring roll wrapper on a clean, dry work surface (keep the remaining wrappers covered with a damp towel). Turn the wrapper so one corner is pointing toward you. Spoon 2 tablespoons of the filling onto the wrapper, about 2 inches from the bottom corner. Form the mixture into a sausage shape about 2 inches long. Fold the bottom corner of the wrapper over the filling and roll once so the filling is completely covered by the wrapper. Moisten the left and right corners of the wrapper with egg wash, fold in the sides to enclose the filling and press down to seal. Moisten the top corner of the wrapper with egg wash, then roll up into a snug cylinder about ¾ inch in diameter and 2 inches long. Press down on the top corner to seal the roll. Repeat with the remaining filling and wrappers.

Line a plate with paper towels. Heat a deep fryer filled with oil to 375°F. Place 6 to 10 rolls in the deep fryer and cook until crisp, 3 to 5 minutes. Lift out fryer basket, drain any excess oil and transfer rolls to the paper towel–lined plate to drain. Repeat with the remaining rolls. Serve immediately, mounded around bowls of cool, creamy chive dip.

Makes 90 rolls

Wild Rice and Scallion Pancakes

Wild rice and mushrooms add an earthy flavour and texture to these chewy sautéed cakes. They make the perfect base for a variety of savoury toppings such as smoked duck or chicken or, for vegetarians, smoked cheese, or chèvre and store-bought mango chutney. Make the pancakes up to 1 day ahead and store them, covered, in the refrigerator. Reheat in a 350°F oven for 5 minutes before serving.

2 cups wild rice, rinsed	½ cup half-and-half cream (10%)
2 tsp + 2 Tbsp olive oil, or more	2 tsp salt
1 cup thinly sliced mixed wild mushrooms (such as shiitake, chanterelle or oyster), roughly chopped	2 tsp pepper
	1 cup all-purpose flour
	1 cup rice flour
2 cups finely chopped green onion (or scallions)	1¼ lbs smoked duck breast, smoked turkey breast or smoked cheese, thinly sliced
4 eggs, lightly beaten	

In a medium saucepan, bring 4 cups of water to a boil on high heat. Add wild rice. Bring to a boil again, reduce the heat to low and simmer uncovered until all water has been absorbed, about 40 minutes. Drain and cool.

Heat 1 tsp of the olive oil in a sauté pan on medium-high heat. Add mushrooms and sauté until liquid has been expelled and reduced, about 5 minutes. Transfer to a small bowl. To the sauté pan, add another 1 tsp of the olive oil. Stir in green onion and sauté until soft and slightly coloured, 2 to 3 minutes. Remove from the heat and set aside.

In a medium bowl, whisk together eggs and cream and set aside.

In a large bowl, combine rice, mushrooms, green onion, salt, pepper and the egg-cream mixture. Add ½ cup of the flour and ½ cup of the rice flour and stir well to incorporate them into the mixture. Add the remaining flour and mix well.

(continued over)

Line a plate with paper towels. Heat a large sauté pan on medium heat and add 2 Tbsp of the olive oil. Using two spoons, drop heaping teaspoonfuls of the mixture into the pan. Form and flatten the mixture into round pancakes and cook until crisp and golden, 2½ minutes per side. Transfer to the paper towel–lined plate to drain. Repeat, adding more oil if necessary, until all batter is used.

To serve, arrange pancakes on a platter and top each with a slice of smoked duck, turkey or cheese.

Makes about 100 pancakes

TOASTED
ASPARAGUS ROLLS

This nosh of nostalgia should be eaten warm to ensure an oozy Cheddar cheese centre—a perfect foil for the green, crunchy asparagus spears. These roll-ups can be assembled the day before you plan to serve them, placed uncooked on a damp paper towel, then wrapped well in plastic wrap and refrigerated. They can be gently browned early in the morning on the day of the celebration and reheated just before serving in a 350°F oven for about 5 minutes or until warm throughout.

75 stalks fresh asparagus (about 4 bunches)
40 thin slices fresh quality sandwich bread

1 cup spreadable sharp Cheddar cheese
(such as MacLarens Imperial cheese)
1 cup butter, melted

Line a plate with paper towels. Fill a bowl with ice water. Bring a large pot of water to a boil and blanch asparagus for 30 seconds. Immediately plunge into ice water to stop the cooking and preserve the bright green colour. Drain well on paper towels and set aside.

Using a sharp knife, trim crusts from bread. With your fingers, gently compress bread to about ¼ inch thickness. Evenly cover one side of each slice with 1 tsp of the spreadable cheese. Cut slices in half.

Lay one half-slice short side toward you on a clean, dry work surface. Place 1 stalk of asparagus parallel to the bottom edge of the bread, leaving 1 inch of the asparagus tip showing on one side. Trim the bottom of the asparagus stalk flush with the other side of the bread. Tightly roll bread around asparagus and continue rolling until you reach the top edge. Set seam-side down on a baking sheet. Repeat with the remaining half-slices and asparagus. Brush roll-ups on all sides with melted butter.

Cook roll-ups in a large sauté pan on medium heat, turning frequently, until all sides are golden brown, 2 to 3 minutes. Arrange on a serving platter. Serve hot.

Makes 75 rolls

Caviar on Shrimp and Potato Blinis

Traditional blinis, thin yeast and buckwheat pancakes, are a Russian favourite featured on menus all over the world as a foundation for caviar. This version uses plump cakes of delicate shrimp, fluffy mashed potatoes and sautéed spring onion as sumptuous as the caviar they carry. The blinis can be cooked and frozen up to 1 month, or cooked and refrigerated, covered, for 2 days. Reheat them in a 350°F oven for 5 minutes until warm throughout, and top with caviar right before serving.

2 large (or 3 medium) Yukon Gold potatoes, peeled, in 2-inch dice	4 egg yolks, lightly beaten
2 tsp butter	2 tsp salt
1½ cups thinly sliced green onion	1 tsp Tabasco or other hot sauce
2 lbs raw black tiger shrimp, peeled and cut in thirds	1 cup all-purpose flour
1 large red bell pepper, in ¼-inch dice	⅓ to ½ cup vegetable oil for pan-frying
	⅓ cup salmon or black caviar

In a medium to large pot, cover potatoes with cold, salted water and simmer, uncovered, until tender (about 18 minutes). Drain potatoes well in a colander, return to the pot and mash with a fork or potato masher. Measure out 2 cups, set aside and allow to cool.

Heat butter in a medium sauté pan on medium heat until foam subsides. Add green onion and cook until soft and slightly coloured, about 2 minutes. Set aside to cool.

Place shrimp in a food processor and pulse, on and off, until roughly chopped (about 20 seconds). Transfer the shrimp to a large bowl. Add potato, red pepper, egg yolks, salt, Tabasco (or other hot sauce) and flour. Mix until well combined.

Line a plate with paper towels. Heat ⅛ inch vegetable oil in a large, heavy-bottomed sauté pan on medium-high heat. Using two spoons, drop heaping teaspoonfuls of the shrimp mixture into the pan. Form and flatten the mixture into ½-inch thick, 2-inch round cakes and cook, turning once, until cakes are just beginning to colour on both sides, about 4 minutes. Using a metal lifter, transfer cakes to the paper towel–lined plate to drain. Repeat until all batter is used. Top each with ⅛ tsp caviar and serve immediately.

Makes about 100 blinis

RATATOUILLE *and* CHÈVRE-TOPPED ENDIVE SPEARS

Colourful and elegant, this finger food is made from tiny diced vegetables that are sautéed separately and combined at the end to preserve their individual flavour, colour and texture. This dish can be prepared and assembled up to 1 hour ahead and kept uncovered at room temperature.

4 Tbsp olive oil

2 shallots, finely minced

peel of 3 large zucchini, in ⅟₁₆-inch dice

2 red bell peppers, seeded, sliced as thin as possible and cut in ⅟₁₆-inch dice

6 cups button mushroom caps, cut in ⅟₁₆-inch dice

juice of 1 lemon

¼ cup water

12 small heads Belgian endive (green and red, if available)

2 cups soft, unripened chèvre

¼ cup chopped fresh basil (optional)

Heat 2 tsp of the olive oil in a medium sauté pan on medium-high heat. Add shallots and sauté until soft and translucent, 2 to 3 minutes. Transfer these to a small bowl. Add another 2 tsp of the oil and sauté zucchini peel until just soft, about 2 minutes. Transfer to another small bowl. To the sauté pan, add 1 Tbsp of the olive oil. Add peppers and sauté until soft, 2 to 3 minutes. Transfer to another small bowl. Add another 1 Tbsp of the oil to the sauté pan. Add mushrooms and sauté until liquid has been released and reduced and mushrooms are soft, about 5 minutes. Transfer mushrooms to another small bowl. Allow vegetables to come to room temperature.

Combine lemon juice with water in a small bowl. Slice ends off endive, separate the leaves and dip the white ends of the leaves in the lemon water. Dry the ends, then arrange about 100 endive spears on platters and spoon ½ tsp of the chèvre onto the base of each leaf.

In a medium bowl, gently combine sautéed vegetables, mixing well. Season with salt and pepper and basil.

Sprinkle ½ tsp of the ratatouille mixture on top of the chèvre. Serve at room temperature.

Makes about 100 endive spears

Champagne Cocktails

Nothing elevates an occasion like Champagne: everything about it is magical, and greeting your guests with flutes of the elegant drink sets a celebratory tone from the very first moment.

For your party, we have created two Champagne cocktails from which to choose, because the selection of fruit hangs on the season. For sixty drinks, you will need twelve bottles of Champagne or sparkling wine such as Segura Viudas from Spain or Prosecco from Italy.

PEAR SPARKLE

Superbly elegant in autumn or winter and garnished with a cool slice of crisp Bosc pear.

> 1 bottle (750 mL/26 oz) Xanté (pear liqueur) or apple liqueur
> 12 bottles (each 750 mL/26 oz) Champagne, chilled
> 5 to 6 crisp ripe Bosc pears, in thin wedges, brushed with lemon water to prevent discolouration
> GLASSWARE: sixty 8-oz Champagne flutes

To serve, pour ¼ oz (or more to taste) Xanté (or apple liqueur) into the bottom of each flute. Top with 4 to 5 oz Champagne. Float one slice of pear on top and serve.

Makes sixty 8-oz drinks

RASPBERRY ROYALE

Raspberries are summer's most flirty fruit—a soft velvet exterior encasing intense, sweet and fragrant flesh. This recipe makes the most of raspberry's charms as a focal flavour point and garnish.

> 10 pts fresh raspberries
> 1 bottle (750 mL/26 oz) Chambord (raspberry liqueur)
> 12 bottles (each 750 mL/26 oz) Champagne, chilled
> GLASSWARE: sixty 8-oz Champagne flutes

Spread raspberries flat on a baking sheet and freeze, about 3 hours.

To serve, pour ¼ oz Chambord (or more to taste) into the bottom of a Champagne flute. Top with 4 to 5 oz of Champagne and float 3 frozen raspberries on top.

Makes sixty 8-oz drinks

PINK PEARL

Suavely flavoured, seductively pink and velvety textured, this signature cocktail is as luscious as a perfect romance. Garnish with decorative skewers of whole strawberries if you wish.

5 qts fresh strawberries, washed and hulled

6 cans (each 10 oz/340 mL) frozen cranberry juice concentrate, thawed

1½ bottles (each 750 mL/26 oz) vanilla vodka

1 bottle (750 mL/26 oz) + 4 oz Galliano (vanilla liqueur)

1 bottle (750 mL/26 oz) + 4 oz Cointreau (orange liqueur)

GLASSWARE: two 2-qt jugs or pitchers; sixty 10- or 12-oz Collins glasses

In a blender, combine 1 qt of the strawberries with 1 can cranberry juice concentrate and purée until very smooth. Pour into a large container. Repeat with the remaining strawberries and 4 cans cranberry juice concentrate. Add the remaining cranberry juice concentrate, vodka, Galliano and Cointreau and stir to blend well. Refrigerate in jugs or pitchers until ready to serve.

To serve, fill a Collins glass with crushed ice and fill to the top with the vodka mixture.

Makes sixty 8-oz drinks

Citrus Martini

Not just for tarts, this tangy aperitif really awakens the palate with fresh lemon oil and a blend of lively citrus liqueurs.

1½ bottles (each 750 mL/26 oz) orange vodka

1½ bottles (each 750 mL/26 oz) lemon vodka

20 oz Lemoncello (lemon liqueur)

10 to 12 lemons, cut in 40 large twists, for garnish

GLASSWARE: two 2-qt jugs or pitchers; forty 5-oz martini glasses

Mix orange and lemon vodkas and Lemoncello together and pour into large jugs or pitchers. Refrigerate until ready to serve.

To serve, rub a lemon twist around the rim of a chilled martini glass, then place it in the bottom of the glass. Fill a cocktail shaker half-full with cracked ice and measure in 2½ oz of the citrus vodka mix. Shake for 30 seconds or until condensation forms on the sides and it is very cold to the touch. Strain into a glass. Serve immediately.

Makes forty 3-oz drinks

Blackberry Martini

Communicate with this blackberry! The best way to stay in touch with this drink is to start early: the gin should be macerated with the blackberries for at least 24 hours before serving. Lillet is a fruity wine-based liqueur from France.

> 3 pts fresh blackberries
> ¾ cup sugar
> 3 bottles (each 750 mL/26 oz) premium dry gin
> 20 oz Lillet
> 40 sprigs fresh marjoram, for garnish
> GLASSWARE: forty 5-oz martini glasses

In a large container with a lid, combine blackberries and sugar and crush very softly to release some of the juices (don't bruise all of the berries, as it is nice to keep some whole for the garnish). Add gin, cover and refrigerate for 24 to 48 hours.

Strain gin into a large container, reserving the macerated blackberries for another use and setting aside some whole berries for the garnish. Add Lillet and mix well to combine. Refrigerate or freeze until ready to use.

To serve, fill a shaker half-full with crushed ice and measure in 2½ oz of the gin mixture. Shake until condensation forms on the sides and it is very cold to the touch. Strain into a chilled martini glass and garnish with 2 or 3 blackberries and a sprig of marjoram.

Makes forty 3-oz drinks

LADY GODIVA

For the love of chocolate and naked protest. For the ultimate garnish, pierce a Godiva chocolate truffle with a long toothpick and drop it into the drink like an olive.

> 3 bottles (each 750 mL/26 oz) premium vodka
> 1 bottle (750 mL/26 oz) Godiva white chocolate
>   liqueur
> 13 oz Grand Marnier
> ½ cup cocoa powder, sifted, for garnish
> 2 limes, for garnish
> 1 cup chocolate shavings, for garnish (optional)
> GLASSWARE: two 2-qt jugs or pitchers;
>   forty 5-oz martini glasses

Mix vodka, Godiva and Grand Marnier together and place in jugs or pitchers. Refrigerate until ready to serve.

To serve, sift a thin layer of cocoa onto a dinner plate. Rub the rim of a chilled martini glass lightly with half a lime and dip the rim of the glass into the cocoa. Shake off any excess.

Fill a shaker half-full with crushed ice and measure in 3 oz of the vodka mixture. Shake until condensation forms on the sides and it is very cold to the touch. Strain into the rimmed glass, being careful not to disturb the cocoa. Garnish with a few chocolate shavings, if desired.

Makes forty 3-oz drinks

ACKNOWLEDGEMENTS

Our gratitude to friends and associates who helped so much—every one as important as each ingredient in a very special recipe.

For making order of Dinah's creations, our appreciation to Meaghan Hardcastle (food recipes) and David Libbey (drinks recipes); thank you, always, to the team that makes Koo & Co soar: Jason, Shaan, Ron, Simon, Luke, Frankie, Lil, Nestor, Lux, Max, Enoch, Debbie, Susan, Jeannie and Evelyn; to Christopher for encouragement and Barry Koo for support on all levels; to Stewart Bailey of the LCBO, master product advisor and guiding light for over a decade; to Rob Jull of Vinifera Wine Services, master tester, taster and critic; to Alison Fryer, Jennifer and everyone at The Cookbook Store for invaluable insights; to Lucy Waverman, for always sharing connections and advice; to Nina Wright, for inspirational leadership; to Lynda Reeves, for all the TV appearances, magazine articles and parties; to Susan McIntosh, for opening the door; to Ingrid Paulson, for wow design and to Lucy Kenward, for her brilliant and unflagging attention to the form and detail of every aspect of our book.

INDEX

Photos are referenced in italics

aioli, lemon-herb, 124–25

almond and orange shortcake, 128–29

almonds, coconut cayenne, 115

apple

    -cheddar filling, for cheese gougères, 214–15

    cinnamon Collins, 169

    -onion curry sauce, for Eggs Benedict, 159–61

artichoke, asiago and roasted hazelnut dip, 114

Asian gravlax with gingered focaccia, 188–89

Asian walnuts, spiced, 49

asparagus

    and brie sandwich, 96

    rolls, toasted, 227

    and wild mushroom risotto, 146–47

as-you-please Eggs Benedict, 159–63, *160*

baby bocconcini in prosciutto rosebuds, 219

baguette, stuffed, 57

balsamic honey drizzle, for stuffed figs, 84

banana cream pie, 167–68

barbecued ribs, 193–94

basic spread, for tortilla crisps, 58

BBQ-dijon sauce, 127

beef

    hanger steaks, 127

    and spinach rolls with teriyaki drizzle, 180–81

    in stuffed baguette, 57

    tenderloin à la Bourguignonne, *132*, 144–145

beer-tomato mix, for oyster shooters, 156–57

Belgian endive spears, ratatouille and chèvre-topped, 230

bitter lemon Collins, 19

blackberry martini, 233

Black Velvet (stout and champagne), 86

blinis, shrimp and potato, 229

Blue Hawaiian snow cone, 21, *21*

bocconcini in prosciutto rosebuds, 219

bocconcini, tomato and green pepper skewer, 131

boiled lemonade, 17

brandied cherries, 18

brandied red sangria, 130

brie and asparagus sandwich, *90*, 96

brie strata with maple-cinnamon sausages, 89

brioche buns, 218

butter-poached eggs, 161–63

canapés, star fruit, with minced pork and cilantro, 56

canapés, stuffed baguette, 57

Caprese skewer, 131

caramel, for banana cream pie, 167–68

caramel nut clusters, 101

caviar and smoked salmon club sandwich, 96

caviar on shrimp and potato blinis, *228*, 229

ceviche tequila mix, for oyster shooters, 156–57

champagne cocktails, 230–32

chard, mushroom and Emmental hand pies, 118–19

Chartreuse margarita, 20, *20*

cheddar-apple filling, for cheese gougères, 214–15

cheddar mornay sauce, for Eggs Benedict, 159–61

cheese, buying and serving, 36–42

cheese, recipes

    asiago, artichoke and roasted hazelnut dip, 114

    baby bocconcini in prosciutto rosebuds, 219

    brie and asparagus sandwich, 96

    brie strata with maple-cinnamon sausages, 89

    Caprese skewer, 131

    cheddar-mornay sauce, for Eggs Benedict, 159–61

    chèvre and ratatouille–topped endive spears, 230

    chèvre and tapenade, prosciutto and roasted pepper flatbread, 58

    chèvre-stuffed figs, 84

Emmental, Swiss chard and
        mushroom hand pies, 118–19
feta-stuffed lamb meatballs, 121–22
gougères, 214–15
and lobster sandwiches, 87
mascarpone and fig sandwich, 96
parmesan pesto palmiers, 100
and pepper straws, 158
quiche Lorraine croissant, 165
stuffed baguette, 57
toasted asparagus rolls, 227
cherries, brandied, 18
chèvre
        and ratatouille–topped endive
                spears, 230
        -stuffed figs, 84
        and tapenade, prosciutto and
                roasted pepper flatbread, 58
chicken
        pot stickers with hot and sour
                dipping soy, 182–83
        skewers in three ways, 54–55
        stock, 123–24
        triangles, satay, 186–87
        and vegetable nori rolls, *216*, 217
        Waldorf salad sandwich, 96
chive dip, 222
chocolate
        fondue for two, 86
        fortune cookies, 200
        Lady Godiva martini, 233
        mousse, 198–99
chutney dipping sauce, mango, 51
cinnamon apple Collins, *148*, 169
citrus. *See also* lemon
        -berry cosmo, 16
        endive salad, 166
        glaze, for orange and almond
                shortcake, 128–29
        martini, 232
        orange and fennel spiced olives, 117
        peel dip, 120

classic martini, 10
cocktails, history and techniques, 2–9
cocktails, recipes
        bitter lemon Collins, 19
        blackberry martini, 233
        Black Velvet, 86
        Blue Hawaiian snow cone, 21
        brandied red sangria, 130
        Chartreuse margarita, 20
        cinnamon apple Collins, 169
        citrus-berry cosmo, 16
        citrus martini, 232
        classic martini, 10
        coconut margarita, 105
        creamsicle martini, 13
        dirty martini, 10
        espresso craic martini, 169
        Flaming Passion, 204
        French kiss martini, 83
        fresh fig martini, 83
        gazpacho sling, 131
        Gibson, 11
        ginseng vodka, 24
        Grasshopper shots in chocolate
                cups, 105
        Lady Godiva, 233
        lemon rum martini, 12
        Lillet martini, 12
        lychee snow martini, 202
        Manhattan, 18
        party pitcher cosmo, 17, *17*
        party pitcher green tea martini,
                14, 14–15
        pear sparkle, 231
        Pink Pearl, 232
        Pink Pussycat, 104
        plum wine sangria, 23
        pomegranate cosmo, 16
        raspberry royale, 231
        rosé sangria, 23
        sake martini, 205
        sake sangria, 23

sangria rubaiyat, 22
sherry sangria, 22
sparkling white sangria, 130
coconut
        cayenne almonds, 115
        cilantro dipping sauce, 197
        cream, 55
        margarita, 105
cookies, chocolate fortune, 200
cosmopolitan, 16
        citrus-berry, 16
        Manhattan, 18
        party pitcher, 17
        pomegranate, 16
crab croissant sandwich, 96
creamsicle martini, 13, *13*
cream topping, for orange and almond
        shortcake, 128–29
creamy chive dip, 222
creamy lemon sauce, for oysters
        gratinées, 80
crisps, tortilla, 58
crispy cheese and pepper straws, 158
crispy triangles of satay chicken with
        peanut sauce, 186–87
croissant quiche Lorraine, *148*, 165
crudités with skinny dip, 99
crust, for banana cream pie, 167
cucumber vodka mix, for oyster
        shooters, 156–57
curry sauce, for Eggs Benedict, 159–61

dark chocolate mousse, 198–99
deconstructed vegetable sushi in a
        take-out box, *190*, 191–92
dijon-BBQ sauce, 127
dip(s). *See also* sauce(s)
        artichoke, asiago and roasted
                hazelnut, 114
        citrus peel, for paprika grilled
                shrimp, 120
        creamy chive, 222

skinny, with crudités, 99
sun-dried tomato and
  garbanzo, 114
dirty martini, 10
dressing, honey-lemon, 166
dressing, pink peppercorn sherry, 85
drizzle, balsamic honey, 84
drizzle, teriyaki, 181
duck quesadillas, 195

edamame, spicy lemon, 117
Eggs Benedict, 159–63
eggs, shrimp-stuffed, 97–98
elements of flavour, 29–32
Emmental, Swiss chard and mushroom
  hand pies, 118–19
empanadas, vegetarian, 118–19
endive citrus salad with honey-lemon
  dressing, 166
endive spears, ratatouille and chèvre–
  topped, 230
espresso craic martini, 169
espresso fudge, 102

fennel and orange spiced olives, 117
feta-olive filling, for cheese gougères,
  214–15
feta-stuffed lamb meatballs with tomato
  olive tapenade, 121–22
fig(s)
  -infused vodka, 83
  martini, 83
  and mascarpone sandwich, 96
  stuffed, with prosciutto, 84
Flaming Passion (passion fruit and
  pineapple cocktail), 204
flavour, elements of, 29–32
fluffy homemade marshmallows, 103
focaccia, gingered, 188–89
fondue, chocolate, 86
fortune cookies, chocolate, 200
French kiss martini, 82, 83

fresh fig martini, 72, 75, 83
fries, taro, 197
fruit platter, 201
fruit topping, for orange and almond
  shortcake, 128–29
fudge, espresso, 102

garbanzo sun-dried tomato dip, 114
gazpacho sling with a Caprese
  skewer, 131
Gibson, 11
gingered focaccia, 188–89
ginger syrup, for green tea martini,
  14–15
ginger tea with honey, 25
ginseng vodka, 24
gougère dough, 214–15
gougères with assorted toppings, 214–15
Grasshopper shots in chocolate cups, 105
gravlax, Asian, 188–89
green pepper, tomato and bocconcini
  skewer, 131
green tea martini, 14–15
grilled lobster and cheese
  sandwiches, 87
grilled red bell peppers and hummus in
  chapatti sandwich, 90, 96
grilled shrimp in smoked paprika with
  citrus peel dip, 120

hanger steaks grilled with dijon-BBQ
  sauce, 126, 127
hangover helper, 25
hazelnut, artichoke and asiago dip, 114
herb-lemon aioli, 124–25
hollandaise sauce, for Eggs Benedict, 159–
  62
home fries with Spanish onions, 164
homemade mayonnaise, 97
honey balsamic drizzle, for stuffed figs, 84
honey-lemon dressing, 166
hot and sour dipping soy, 182

hummus and grilled red bell peppers in
  chapatti sandwich, 96
hummus, sun-dried tomato garbanzo, 114

jack filling, for cheese gougères, 214–15
jerk marinade, for chicken skewers, 54–55

Lady Godiva (chocolate cocktail), 233
lamb meatballs, stuffed, 121–22
lemon. *See also* citrus
  Collins, 19
  edamame, 117
  -herb aioli, 124–25
  -honey dressing, 166
  rum martini, 12
  sauce, for oysters gratinées, 80
  -vermouth olives, 10
lemonade, boiled, 19
Lillet martini, 12
lobster and cheese sandwiches, 87
lobstercide, 88
lobster rolls, 218
lychee snow martini, 202

mango and shrimp salad rolls, 184–85
mango chutney dipping sauce, 51
Manhattan, 18
maple-cinnamon sausage strata with brie,
  89
margarita, Chartreuse, 20
margarita, coconut, 105
marinated scallops, for paella salad, 123–24
marshmallows, fluffy homemade, 103
martini
  blackberry, 233
  citrus, 232
  classic, 10
  creamsicle, 13
  dirty, 10
  espresso craic, 169
  French kiss, 83
  fresh fig, 83

green tea, 14–15
    Lady Godiva, 233
    lemon rum, 12
    Lillet, 12
    lychee snow, 202
    sake, 205
mascarpone and fig sandwich, 96
mayonnaise, homemade, 97
mayonnaise, wasabi, 184
meatballs, stuffed lamb, 121–22
meat toppings, for Eggs Benedict,
    161–62
minced pork and star fruit canapés, 56
mini lobster rolls, *206*, 218
Mojito, Thai, 19
mornay sauce, for Eggs Benedict,
    159–61
mousse, chocolate, 198–99
mushroom
    and asparagus risotto, 146–47
    and pesto, romano and pine nut
        flatbread, 58
    spring rolls, 222–23
    and Swiss chard and Emmental
        hand pies, 118–19

nori rolls, chicken and vegetable, 217
nut and caramel clusters, 101

olive(s)
    bombes, 59
    -feta filling, for cheese gougères, 214–
    15
    lemon-vermouth, 10
    orange and fennel spiced, 117
    tomato tapenade, 121–22
onion-apple curry sauce, for Eggs
    Benedict, 159–61
onions, spiced pearl, 11
orange and almond shortcake with berries
    and cream, 128–29
orange and fennel spiced olives, *116*, 117

oysters, buying and serving, 43–45
oysters gratinées with creamy lemon
    sauce, 80–81
oyster shooters, 156–57

paella *aire libre*, 125
paella salad with lemon-herb aioli, *106*,
    123–25
palmiers, parmesan pesto, 100
pancakes, wild rice and scallion, 225–26
pappadam shrimp with mango chutney
    dipping sauce, *50*, 51
paprika grilled shrimp, 120
paprika, smoked Spanish, 120
parmesan pesto palmiers, 100
parmesan-prosciutto filling, for cheese
    gougères, 214–15
party pitcher cosmo, 17
party pitcher green tea martini, 14–15
party planning, 63–71, 73–79, 91–95, 107–
    13, 133–43, 149–55, 171–79, 207–13
    bar requirements for 40 guests, 65
    bar set-up per 25 guests, 69
    glass requirements per 25 guests, 69
    party supply guidelines, 67
    troubleshooting, 70
pastry dough, wine, 118
peanut sauce, for crispy triangles of satay
    chicken, 186–87
pearl onions, spiced, 11
pear sparkle, 231
Peking duck quesadillas, 195
pepper and cheese straws, 158
peppercorn sherry dressing, 85
pesto parmesan palmiers, *90*, 100
pesto, romano, mushroom and pine nut
    flatbread, 58
pie, Swiss chard, mushroom, and
    Emmental, 118–19
pie, top banana cream, 167–68
pineapple pre-mix, for French kiss
    martini, 83

pine nut, pesto, romano and mushroom
    flatbread, 58
Pink Pearl (strawberry and cranberry
    cocktail), *ii*, 232
pink peppercorn sherry dressing, 85
Pink Pussycat (sparkling passion fruit
    cocktail), 104, *104*
plum wine sangria, 23, *23*
poker mix sandwiches, 96
pomegranate cosmo, 16
pork and star fruit canapés, 56
pork ribs, barbecued, 193–94
potatoes, fried, with Spanish onions, 164
pot stickers, chicken, 182–83
pot stickers, fable of, 183
pot stickers, vegetable, 52–53
potato and shrimp blinis, 229
potatoes with Spanish onions, 164
prosciutto
    and chèvre-stuffed figs with
        walnuts and balsamic honey
        drizzle, *72*, *84*, 84
    -parmesan filling, for cheese
        gougères, 214–15
    rosebuds with baby bocconcini, 219
    and tapenade, chèvre and roasted
        pepper flatbread, 58

quesadillas, Peking duck, 195
quiche Lorraine croissant, 165

radicchio salad, 85
raspberry royale, *206*, 231
ratatouille and chèvre–topped endive
    spears, *206*, 230
red bell peppers and hummus in chapatti
    sandwich, 96
red sangria, brandied, 130
red wine sauce, for beef tenderloin, 144
ribs, barbecued, 193–94
risotto, asparagus and wild mushroom,
    146–47

roasted hazelnut, artichoke and asiago dip, 114
roasted pepper, tapenade, chèvre and prosciutto flatbread, 58
romano, pesto, mushroom and pine nut flatbread, 58
Romeo and julienne radicchio, 85
rosé sangria, 23, *23*

sake martini, 205, *205*
sake sangria, 23, *23*
salad
    endive citrus, 166
    lobster, 218
    paella, 123–25
    rolls, shrimp and mango, 184–85
salmon
    gravlax, Asian, 188–89
    smoked, and caviar club sandwich, 96
    smoked, hearts, 220–221
sandwiches
    brie and asparagus, 96
    chicken Waldorf salad, 96
    crab croissant, 96
    figs and mascarpone, 96
    grilled lobster and cheese, 87
    grilled red bell peppers and hummus in chapatti, 96
    mini lobster rolls, 218
    shrimp and smoked salmon, 220–21
    smoked salmon and caviar club, 96
    tuna muffuletta, 96
sangria, 22
    brandied red, 130
    plum wine, 23
    rosé, 23
    rubaiyat, 22
    sake, 23
    sherry, 22
    sparkling white, 130
satay chicken triangles, 186–87

satay marinade, for chicken skewers, 54–55
sauce(s). *See also* dip(s)
    apple-onion curry, for Eggs Benedict, 159–61
    balsamic honey drizzle, for stuffed figs, 84
    caramel, 167–68
    cheddar mornay, for Eggs Benedict, 159–61
    coconut cilantro, 197
    creamy lemon, for oysters gratinées, 80
    dijon-bbq, 127
    hollandaise, for Eggs Benedict, 159–62
    homemade mayonnaise, 97
    hot and sour dipping soy, 182
    lemon-herb aioli, 124–25
    mango chutney, 51
    peanut, for crispy triangles of satay chicken, 186–87
    red wine, for beef tenderloin, 144
    spicy soy, 52
    tangy tomato-beer mix, for oyster shooters, 156–57
    tequila ceviche mix, for oyster shooters, 156–57
    teriyaki drizzle, for beef and spinach rolls, 180–81
    vodka cucumber mix, for oyster shooters, 156–57
    wasabi mayonnaise, 184
sausage strata, maple-cinnamon, with brie, 89
scallion and wild rice pancakes, 225–26
scallops, marinated, for paella salad, 123–24
Shanghai Lily sling, 203
sherry peppercorn dressing, 85
sherry sangria, 22
shrimp
    and mango salad rolls with wasabi mayonnaise, *170*, 184–85, *185*

pappadam-crusted, 51
    and potato blinis, 229
    in smoked paprika, 120
    and smoked salmon hearts, *206*, 220–21, *221*
    -stuffed eggs, *90*, 97–98
simple syrup, 20
skinny dip with crudités, 99
sling, gazpacho, 131
sling, Shanghai Lily, 203
smoked paprika grilled shrimp, 120
smoked salmon and caviar club sandwich, 96
smoked salmon hearts, 220–21
smoked Spanish paprika, 120
snow cone, Blue Hawaiian, 21
soupçon of chocolate mousse, 198–99
soybean pods (edamame), 117
Spanish onions and home fries, 164
Spanish paprika, smoked, 120
sparkling white sangria, *106*, 130
spiced Asian walnuts, 49
spiced olives, orange and fennel, 117
spiced pearl onions, 11
spicy jack filling, for cheese gougères, 214–15
spicy lemon edamame, *116*, 117
spicy soy dipping sauce, for vegetable pot stickers, 52
spinach and beef rolls, 180–81
spread, basic, for tortilla crisps, 58
spring rolls, wild mushroom, 222–23
star fruit canapés with minced pork and cilantro, 56
steaks grilled with dijon-bbq sauce, 127
stock, chicken, 123–24
strata, brie, with maple-cinnamon sausages, 89
stuffed baguette, 57
stuffed eggs, 97–98
stuffed lamb meatballs with tomato olive tapenade, 121–22
sun-dried tomato garbanzo dip, 114

sushi, deconstructed vegetable, 191–92

Swiss chard, mushroom and Emmental hand pies, 118–19

syrup, ginger, for green tea martini, 14–15

syrup, simple, 20

tandoori marinade, for chicken skewers, 54–55

tangy tomato-beer mix, for oyster shooters, 156–57

tapenade, chèvre, prosciutto and roasted pepper flatbread, 58

tapenade, tomato olive, 121–22

taro frites with coconut cilantro dipping sauce, *196*, 197

tea, ginger, with honey, 23

tea mixture, for green tea martini, 14–15

tequila ceviche mix, for oyster shooters, 156–57

teriyaki drizzle, for beef and spinach rolls, 180–81

Thai Mojito, 19

toasted asparagus rolls, 227

tomato
    beer mix, for oyster shooters, 156–57
    and bocconcini and green pepper skewer, 131
    olive tapenade, 121–22
    sun-dried, and garbanzo dip, 114

top banana cream pie, 167–68

tortilla crisps with savoury toppings, 58

tropical fruit platter, 201

tuna muffuletta sandwich, *90*, 96

vanilla vodka, 83

vegetable and chicken nori rolls, 217

vegetable pot stickers, 52–53

vegetable sushi, deconstructed, 191–92

veggie platter with skinny dip, 99

veggie toppings, for Eggs Benedict, 161–62

Vietnamese-style barbecued ribs, 193–94

vodka
    cucumber mix, for oyster shooters, 156–57
    fig-infused, 83
    ginseng, 24
    vanilla, 83

Waldorf salad sandwich, 96

walnuts, spiced Asian, 49

wasabi mayonnaise, 184

white chocolate mousse, 198–99

white sangria, sparkling, 130

wild mushroom and asparagus risotto, 146–47

wild mushroom spring rolls with creamy chive dip, 222–23

wild rice and scallion pancakes, *224*, 225–26

wine
    alternatives, from John Szabo, 76–77, 94, 110–11, 152, 175–76, 211
    and cheese pairings, 41–42
    and food pairings, 27–35
    order of service, 35
    and oyster pairings, 45
    pastry, for hand pies, 118
    -tasting, 133–47